WORKPLACE BULLYING IN HIGHER EDUCATION

Higher education leaders, managers, human resource professionals, faculty, and staff increasingly face uncivil, bullying behaviors in academe. This can manifest itself as constant public humiliation by a new department chair, exclusion of a contingent faculty member, undermining of work performance by a supervisor, stalking by a staff member, or taunting. As higher education institutions continue to face budget issues and external pressure, the incidences of bullying are on the rise. This edited volume provides guidance on the nature and impact of bullying, legal and ethical issues, and approaches to assist leaders in facing these challenges in their colleges and universities.

Research-based chapters cover the impact of bullying on the workforce, the ways that bullying manifests within different sub-cultures and at different institutions including community colleges, the legal and ethical issues of bullying, and recommendations to address bullying on campus. Exploring bullying policies and innovative programs, this book provides a better understanding of how to rethink current policies and practices to proactively create more civil cultures. *Workplace Bullying in Higher Education* is a valuable resource for all higher education leaders and professionals on understanding, mediating, and preventing bullying.

Jaime Lester is Associate Professor of Higher Education at George Mason University, USA.

WORKPLACE BULLYING IN HIGHER EDUCATION

Edited by Jaime Lester

Routledge
Taylor & Francis Group

NEW YORK AND LONDON

First published 2013
by Routledge
711 Third Avenue, New York, NY 10017

Simultaneously published in the UK
by Routledge
2 Park Square, Milton Park, Abingdon, Oxon OX14 4RN

Routledge is an imprint of the Taylor & Francis Group, an informa business

© 2013 Taylor & Francis

Library of Congress Cataloging in Publication Data

Workplace bullying in higher education / [edited] by Jaime Lester.
    p. cm.
    Includes bibliographical references and index.
    1. Bullying in schools—United States.   2. Universities and colleges—
United States—Professional staff.   3. College teachers—Abuse of—
United States.   I. Lester, Jaime.
LB3013.32.W67   2012
378.1'250973—dc23   2012026906

ISBN: 978-0-415-51964-9 (hbk)
ISBN: 978-0-415-51965-6 (pbk)
ISBN: 978-0-203-12293-8 (ebk)

Typeset in Bembo
by Apex CoVantage, LLC

Printed and bound in the United States of America by Publishers Graphics,
LLC on sustainably sourced paper.

CONTENTS

PREFACE

Jaime Lester

This book began in the public on the front pages of newspapers, as the subject of weblogs, and highlighted on television programs. It began on college campuses in the office, in the campus dormitory, and over email or other online communications. It began for the individual when he or she experienced taunting, marginalization, and constant criticism. It is workplace bullying, a form of interpersonal aggression that is on the rise in organizations, including colleges and universities. Let me give you a few examples: A faculty member who is under internal investigation for unethical behavior toward three female colleagues is denied tenure. He alleges that his tenure case was treated unfairly and the allegations were included as part of the tenure decision. A long-term contingent faculty member is not given a new annual contract. She claims there is no basis for her nonrenewal other than an uncivil new department chair who has "locked her out" of all departmental business since she questioned the chair's decisions on a student matter. A staff member calls human resources to complain about and seek information on her rights when a new supervisor consistently and publicly humiliates her; the supervisor comments on the staff member's clothing and lack of productivity in meetings. A new faculty member is distraught when a student consistently, openly, and aggressively challenges her in the classroom. The department chair is unsure how to handle the situation when the faculty member comes to her office upset. Finally, a staff member complains that another staff member is stalking him, sending inappropriate and aggressive emails. These are just a few examples of uncivil, bullying behaviors in academe that managers, human resources professionals, and higher education leaders face each day with little to no guidance on how to define, address, mediate, and possibly adjudicate these claims.

The prevalence of workplace bullying in organizations has been documented for quite some time. Studies show that over 35% of workers report having been bullied at work, yet little is know about workplace bullying in higher education

(Adams, 1992; Byrne, 1994; Namie, 2007; Randall, 1997; Rayner & Hoel, 1997; Rayner, Hoel, & Cooper, 2002; Rayner & Keashly, 2005; Spurgeon, 1997). We have reports of bullying in academic outlets, similar to those described above, that describe academic bullies who systematically undermine a colleague's credibility by spreading rumors and discounting their opinions in meetings (Fogg, 2008). *The Chronicle of Higher Education* has reported on workplace bullying at the University of Virginia, University of North Florida, and Rutgers University, to name a few. These reports and incidents led to several institutions creating campus-wide campaigns and legislation to address bullying, suggesting that bullying is a widespread and significant occurrence on their campuses. Rutgers University, for example, started the Project Civility[1] campaign to promote niceness on campus. Prince George's Community College has a campus-wide cultural change initiative to promote civility. They created videos, posters, flyers, outreach programs, and introduced a new code of conduct for the entire community. The code of conduct is posted around campus and on all course syllabi. Recent legislation passed in New Jersey sparked by the death of Rutgers student Tyler Clementi, demands that schools, K–12 and higher education, create anti-bullying policies and training for faculty and staff. For a more thorough review of the legal issues, see Kerri Stone's Chapter 6 in this book.

Despite the recent attention to bullying, only a few studies empirically examine the prevalence and nature of bullying in academe. In 2000, a study of all faculty and staff of the University of Manchester Institution of Science and Technology found that women were bullied by both colleagues and supervisors, bullies are often at a higher rank in the university than the victims, and women report bullying more readily than men (Rayner, Hoel, & Cooper, 2002). A more recent national study on bullying in higher education found that over 80% of respondents were bullied at one time in their career (Goodyear, Reynolds, & Both Gragg, 2010), whereas Keashly and Neuman (2008) found bullying rates of 32% and McKay, Arnold, Fratzl, and Thomas (2008) at 52% in higher education. Other studies note that faculty have an uncivil culture (Hume, 2003) and experience bullying in the classroom (Braxton & Bayer, 2005). There is also a high prevalence of mobbing—bullying by a group of people—on college campuses (Westhues, 2006). Yet, as Loraleigh Keashly and Joel H. Neuman argue in Chapter 1 of this book, these studies are limited due to their sample, the particular definition of bullying, and the country where the study was conducted. Comparisons across the studies to glean a more thorough understanding of bullying have been difficult.

The prevalence of bullying found in the higher education media and the lack of empirical work results in much confusion about (a) the nature and definition of bullying; (b) the impact of bullying in individual and organizations; (c) legal and ethical issues; (d) bullying between and among sub-groups (faculty and staff); and (e) ways to address bullying behaviors. Human resources managers, academic managers, and faculty and staff have little to no guidance of how to define, address, and resolve bullying. The purpose of this book is to address this need and educate human resources professionals and academic managers about the nature of, impact, legal and ethical issues, and practices to address bullying in colleges and universities among faculty and staff.

Definition of Workplace Bullying

Workplace bullying is not a simple definition or concept. In fact, campus administrators often question the validity of workplace bullying. They might make remarks or ask questions such as, "How do we know the difference between constructive criticism and bullying," or "Can't a negative evaluation be misconstrued as bullying?" These are critical, if not uninformed, questions since how we define workplace bullying, and how we separate it as behavior from other organizational practices and behaviors, will determine what we consider bullying in our organizations.

Workplace bullying is characterized as a type of interpersonal aggression that is frequent, intense, and occurs over a specific time period. Bullying may be verbal abuse, threatening and intimidating conduct, constant criticism, undermining of work performance, exclusion, marginalization, overloading with work, and taunting (Vega & Comer, 2005). To respond to the administrator's questions above and to separate a single incident from workplace bullying, bullying must be a continuous pattern of unwarranted mistreatment toward a co-worker that causes psychological or emotional harm to the victim. Einarsen, Hoel, Zapf, and Cooper (2003) described workplace bullying as a process:

> Harassing, offending, socially excluding someone or negatively affecting someone's work tasks . . . It has to occur repeatedly and regularly (e.g., weekly) and over a period of time (e.g., at least six months). Bullying is an escalating process in the course of which the person confronted ends up in an inferior position and becomes the target of systematic negative social acts. (p. 15)

Using the examples above, the constant public humiliation by the new department chair, exclusion of the contingent faculty member, public humiliation by the supervisor, stalking by the staff member, and taunting are all examples of bullying that regularly occur in the workplace. These behaviors are constant and continuous and show a pattern of abuse that causes psychological harm to the victim.

This is not to suggest that workplace bullying is always evident. Often, cultural values and context play a role in what is considered a bullying behavior. Many studies in organizational settings find that perpetrators of bullying are often supervisors, indicating a power dimension to workplace bullying (Hoel, Cooper, & Faragher, 2001). Hoel and colleagues (2001) found that three out of four individuals who reported being bullied were targeted by a manager or supervisor. Within academia, however, Keashly and Neuman (2010) found that faculty were more likely to identify colleagues as bullies whereas staff were more likely to identify their superiors as the perpetrators of bullying. Other studies note that students bully faculty in the classroom (McKay et al., 2008) and anecdotal evidence exists that staff may bully faculty. The combinations and power dynamics associated with bullying in academe vary, which illustrates a need to understand bullying in the context of higher education.

Audience and Need to Examine Workplace Bullying in Higher Education

The recent attention to workplace bullying in the media has likely highlighted just a small fraction of the bullying incidences that occur on college campuses each year. Yet, the consequences of workplace bullying are many. Bullying has negative effects on victims, who are more likely to be frequently absent from work, have lower productivity, or leave their jobs altogether (Hoel et al., 2003; Keashly & Harvey, 2005). Bullying increases anxiety and nervousness, which leads to decreased self-esteem and increased difficulty in performing the tasks of one's job. Furthermore, abused employees are found to be at increased risk for depression, have chronic stress, high blood pressure, and have more difficulty in interpersonal relationships (Jennifer, Cowie, & Anaiadou, 2003; Kivimäki et al., 2005; Rayner et al., 2002). The anxiety and stress that is created within the workplace can spill over into one's personal life, creating emotional and interpersonal problems. Those who witness bullying also experience an emotional response that can lead to decreased satisfaction with the unit or department and organization.

One of the main audiences for this book is human resources offices that offer training for staff and administrators and academic managers who are confronted with bullying in their units or departments. Workplace bullying is considered an employee relations issue, as bullying are not illegal.[2] Human resources professionals, as opposed to Offices of Equity that manage illegal forms of harassment, are the unit within colleges and universities that provide employee support in the form of mediation, employee psychological assistance programs, and preventative training to the campus. Without a clear understanding of bullying and the complexity of the legal, ethical, and effective process for remediation, academic managers often have little guidance when confronted with bullying in their unit or department. This book provides a better understanding of the legal issues, practices for addressing bullying, and greater understanding of the complexity of bullying across each constituent group. This book serves as a valuable resource for all human resources departments and academic managers on ways to mediate and prevent bullying.

Another main audience for this book will be higher education leaders who are concerned with bullying on their campus. As higher education institutions continue to face budget issues and external pressure, the incidences of bullying will increase. Bullying is known to be highly correlated with leadership changes and resources shortages (Hoel et al., 2003). Higher education leaders are challenged to rethink current policies and practices to proactively create more-civil cultures and manage those bullies on their campus. This book provides information on the impact of bullying, legal and ethical issues, and practices that are currently being developed to assist leaders in facing these challenges on their individual campuses.

In addition to assisting higher education leaders and human resource professionals and academic managers, this book will also be of interest to those individual faculty, staff, and students who are working to challenge institutional leaders to create more civil campuses. As those who are most impacted by a lack of policy development, faculty, staff, and students are challenged with trying to push forward organizational change and convince leaders of the prevalence of bullying and need for policies and/or practices to address it. This book provides the necessary information to highlight the issues surrounding bullying, such as the impact on organizational dynamics and individual psychological issues resulting from bullying. In addition, these constituents will be interested in the resources provided in the book's appendix. The resources include examples of bullying policies, descriptions of innovative programs, and a list of organizations and reports.

Finally, this book appeals to higher education scholars who work on issues related to workplace dynamics. The research in organizational studies illustrates the correlation between job satisfaction, morale, psychological distress, job retention, and bullying. Unfortunately, there's too much anecdotal evidence and only some empirical evidence on the prevalence of workplace bullying on college campuses. What is needed is a thorough understanding of the literature, issues, and complexity of bullying to help leaders, human resource professionals, and scholars begin to understand bullying in a college environment. This book fills that need.

Outline of Chapters

Chapter 1, written by two established workplace bullying scholars, Loraleigh Keashley and Joel Neuman, provides a thorough review of the literature on workplace bullying in higher education. They explicitly seek to test their confidence that workplace bullying does exist in higher education and review the empirical evidence to test their assumptions about bullying. Their chapter is a thorough introduction to the literature and concludes with several important areas for future research, including a call for more robust theoretical conceptualizations and more qualitative studies needed to fully conceptualize bullying in higher education.

The second chapter of the book focuses on an unusual workplace factor found in higher education institutions that intersects with workplace bullying dynamics—tenure. Using data from an empirical study on the role of tenure in higher education, Susan Taylor provides solid evidence that tenure status does make a difference in faculty members' experience of being bullied and the frequency of exposure to bullying behaviors. Her analysis also addresses the implication for bullying on nontenured faculty. She concludes with specific recommendations of how individual faculty, academic managers, and human resources professionals can address bullying in organizations with the protections of tenure.

Chapter 3, written by Margaret Sallee and Crystal Diaz, focuses on various identity groups, specifically those targeted based on gender, race, or sexuality. Their central argument is that hidden biases within academic culture facilitate the marginalization of particular social identity groups and lead to more incidents of bullying. This chapter offers a thorough review of the literature on bullying and social identities in higher education and organizational settings as well as several theoretical frameworks—organizational culture and theories of the gendered, raced, and heteronormative university.

The fourth chapter in the book, written by Jae Fratzl and Ruth McKay, takes a different view from others in this book to look at the use of aggression in the work environment and the unique role of professional staff—administrators, assistants, information technology technicians, librarians, cleaning and repair staff—who are typically the first people students interact with at a university. The authors argue that professional staff are uniquely sandwiched between students and academics, both of whom may display aggressive behavior in order to deal with threats and meet their needs. Recognizing the differences between these styles of aggression is helpful in dealing with behaviors. The pressures and demands of the position will often drive the way aggression and bullying is expressed.

Chapter 5, authored by Soko Starobin and Warren Blumenfeld, focuses on one sector of higher education—community colleges. They frame workplace bullying in a sociological context using a model of social ecology of bullying to understand how the social environment interacts with the unique functions of community colleges. Their analysis on two functions—gender and geography—concludes that community colleges have several enabling structures that lead to bullying. The authors conclude with a call for more critical discourse on workplace bullying in community colleges.

Kerri Stone, a law professor, focuses the sixth chapter on the legal ramifications of workplace bullying with examples of cases that illustrate the struggle with fitting individual bullying. She details some of the extant federal and state claims related to workplace bullying to provide readers with a greater understanding of individual legal rights in bullying cases, which is essential for individuals who manage bullying incidents. The chapter concludes with examples of cases of the struggle to fit individual bullying claims into viable, existing legal frameworks and contexts.

Tricia Bertram Gallant presents an ethical argument in Chapter 7. She positions bullying as an ethical issue for the organization, one that demands new and expansive responses beyond compliance and the legal ramifications presented in the Stone chapter. She argues that although one person bullying another may be unethical or wrong, the phenomenon of bullying is complex, with conflicting ethical dimensions, and shaped by numerous forces emanating from four levels of the system: individual, organizational, education system, and societal. The chapter concludes with five recommendations of ways to address bullying through an ethical lens.

Chapter 8 is authored by three human resource professionals, Linda H. Harber, Patricia Donini, and Shernita Rochelle Parker, and focuses on identifying resources to help individual victims of bullying and creating a culture that does not tolerate bullying behavior. Their "no blame approach" frames their recommendations, and they provide specific examples of their efforts at George Mason University. Throughout the chapter are detailed vignettes that human resource professionals may use as they develop strategies to address workplace bullying, create individual awareness, and promote organizational change.

Chapter 9, the final chapter of the book, written by Jaime Lester and Carrie Klein, summarizes the strategies and best practices offered throughout the chapters as well as additional recommendations based on their research on workplace bullying. This chapter also includes recommendations for future research, such as the need for large-scale studies and evaluation of intervention strategies.

Notes

1. Many of the civility campaigns on college campuses do not directly address bullying behaviors; rather, they promote an overall sense of personal responsibility and ethical behavior that indirectly speaks to bullying behaviors.
2. Recent legislation was passed in New Jersey that made bullying illegal.

References

Adams, A. (1992). *Bullying at work—How to confront and overcome it.* London: Virago Press.

Braxton, J. & Bayer, A. (Eds). (2005). Addressing faculty and student classroom improprieties. In *New Directions for Teaching and Learning.* San Francisco, CA: Jossey-Bass.

Byrne, B. (1994). *Bullying—A community approach.* Dublin: The Columbia Press.

Einarsen, S., Hoel, H., Zapf, D., & Cooper, C.L. (2003). The concept of bullying at work: The European tradition. In S. Einarsen, H. Hoel, D. Zapf, & C.L. Cooper (Eds), *Bullying and emotional abuse in the workplace: International perspectives in research and practice* (pp. 1–30). London: Taylor & Francis.

Fogg, P. (2008). Academic bullies: The web provides new outlets for combating workplace aggression. *Chronicle of Higher Education,* B10.

Goodyear, R.K., Reynolds, P., & Both Gragg, J. (2010). *University faculty experiences of classroom incivilities: A critical-incident study.* Paper presented at the American Educational Research Association annual conference, Denver, CO.

Hoel, H., Cooper, C.L., & Faragher, B. (2001). The experience of bullying in Great Britain: The impact of organizational status. *European Journal of Work and Organizational Psychology, 10*(4), 443–465.

Hoel, H., Einarsen, S., & Cooper, C. (2003). Organisational effects of bullying. In S. Einarsen, H. Hoel, D. Zapf, & C. Cooper (Eds), *Bullying and emotional abuse in the workplace: International perspectives in research and practice* (pp. 2–30). London: Taylor & Francis.

Hume, K. (2003). Department politics as a foreign language. *Chronicle of Higher Education*, B5.

Jennifer, D., Cowie, H., & Anaiadou, K. (2003). Perceptions and experience of workplace bullying in five different working populations. *Aggressive Behavior, 29*, 489–496.

Keashly, L., & Harvey, S. (2005). Emotional abuse in the workplace. In S. Fox & P. Spector (Eds), *Counterproductive work behaviors* (pp. 201–236). Washington, DC: American Psychological Association.

Keashly, L., & Neuman, J.H. (2008). *Final report: Workplace behavior (bullying) project survey*. Mankato: Minnesota State University.

Keashly, L., & Neuman, J.H. (2010). Faculty experiences with bullying in higher education: Causes, consequences and management. *Administrative Theory & Praxis, 32*(1), 48–70.

Kivimäki, M., Ferrie, J.E., Brunner, E., Head, J., Shipley, M.J., Vahtera, J., & Marmot, M.G. (2005). Justice at work and reduced risk of coronary heart disease among employees. *Archives of Internal Medicine, 165*, 2245–2251.

McKay, R., Arnold, D.H., Fratzl, J., & Thomas, R. (2008). Workplace bullying in academia: A Canadian study. *Employee Responsibilities and Rights Journal, 20*, 77–100.

Namie, G. (2007). *U.S. workplace bullying survey*. Retrieved from http://www.workplace bullying.org/research/WBI-Zogby2007Survey.html

Randall, P. (1997). *Adult bullying: Perpetrators and victims*. London: Routledge.

Rayner, C., & Hoel, H. (1997). A summary of literature relating to workplace bullying. *Journal of Community & Applied Social Psychology, 7*, 181–191.

Rayner, C., Hoel, H., & Cooper, C.L. (2002). *Workplace bullying: What we know, who is to blame, and what can we do?* London: Taylor & Francis.

Rayner, C., & Keashly, L. (2005). Bullying at work: A perspective from Britain and North America. In S. Fox & P. Spector (Eds), *Counterproductive work behaviors* (pp. 271–296). Washington, DC: American Psychological Association.

Spurgeon, A. (1997). Commentary. *Journal of Community and Applied Social Psychology, 7*, 241–244.

Vega, G., & Comer, D. (2005). Sticks and stones may break your bones, but words can break your spirit: Bullying in the workplace. *Journal of Business Ethics, 58*(1–3), 101–109.

Westhues, K. (2006). *The remedy and prevention of mobbing in higher education*. Lewiston, NY: Edwin Mellen Press.

1

BULLYING IN HIGHER EDUCATION

What Current Research, Theorizing, and Practice Tell Us

Loraleigh Keashly and Joel H. Neuman

We begin this chapter with some trepidation. We have both been involved in academia and higher education for close to a quarter century. In Loraleigh Keashly's case, it has always been her working environment, and for Joel Neuman, it has been his second career, after more than a decade managing in the private sector. We are a bit concerned about writing this chapter because we recognize that workplace bullying in academia (and other social settings) is a problem but, at the same time, we sense the presence of a bandwagon effect among the general public and academic researchers—"The tendency for people in social and sometimes political situations to align themselves with the majority opinion and to do or believe things because many other people do or believe the same" (American Psychological Association, 2009, p. 39). This is reflected in the popular perception that universities are hotbeds of conflict and hostility and this, in part, is due to particular contextual variables associated with academic settings. For example, in his discussion of workplace bullying among faculty, Lamont Stallworth (cited in Schmidt, 2010) observes that "big egos, an individualistic ethic, and tolerance for behaviors not accepted elsewhere" are determinants of bullying by faculty. One has only to look at *The Chronicle of Higher Education* over the last several years to detect this line of reasoning, in, for example, Fogg's (2008) "Academic Bullies" and Gravois (2006) piece "Mob Rule." Even in our own conversations as academics, we see these portrayals as common. In short, not only are we on the bandwagon but we have played a significant role in driving it.

In part, our concern arises because we have devoted the better part of two decades to exploring aggression and bullying in work settings and the past three years focusing on bullying in higher education. We have thus played a significant role in informing the public of bullying in academe. Recently, we explored the stereotypes of hostility and egotistical faculty within our own respective departments and concluded that these common perceptions about academia and academics do not fit with our personal experiences. We have certainly seen (and, heaven forbid, may have contributed to) some of this behavior, but is such conduct inherent in the professoriate and academic settings? Are our own experiences in academia unique? Or, are our personal experiences typical and other departments or institutions the oddities? Presently, we do not have sufficient data to answer this question decisively. To avoid contributing to a self-fulfilling prophecy, in which we frame our research questions based on what we expect to find, propose theories to support these assumptions and, as a result, add to the perception that these are common occurrences, we will attempt to take a more value-neutral position. In short, we will attempt to address the issue of bullying in higher education (and, to some degree, other work settings) within a broader typology of knowledge in which we explicitly test our confidence about what we know, what we think we know, and what we do not know, based on an examination of the empirical literature. On the pages that follow, we will explore conceptual, empirical, and practical issues related to workplace aggression and bullying in higher education. This will include suggestions for closing known gaps and being open to unknown gaps in our knowledge (Stewart, 1997).

Definitional and Conceptual Issues

Kleinginna and Kleinginna (1981) noted that a major difficulty in exploring the psychology of motivation was a lack of consensus as to its defining characteristics. At the time, these authors identified 140 different definitions for that construct. Although workplace bullying might not seem to be as elusive a concept as motivation, opinions do vary as to the name of the construct, its nature, and its defining characteristics. To illustrate this variety, we thought it would be useful to highlight the conceptualization of these hostile relationships from well-known researchers in the bullying domain.

Beginning with the seminal work of Carroll Brodsky, the phenomenon was labeled harassment and defined as "repeated and persistent attempts by one person to torment, wear down, frustrate, or get a reaction from another. It is treatment which persistently provokes, pressures, frightens, intimidates or otherwise discomforts another person" (Brodsky, 1976, p. 2). In the 1980s, Heinz Leymann referred to the construct using the terms "psychological terror" or "mobbing" behavior in working life and defined it as:

> hostile and unethical communication, which is directed in a systematic way by one or a few individuals mainly towards one individual who, due to mobbing, is pushed into a helpless and defenseless position, being held there by means of continuing mobbing activities. These actions occur on a very frequent basis (statistical definition: at least once a week) and over a

long period of time (statistical definition: at least six months of duration). (Leymann, 1990, p. 120)

In England, the term "workplace bullying" gained prominence with the pioneering work of Andrea Adams. She defined bullying as "persistent criticism and personal abuse in public or private, which humiliates and demeans the person" (Adams & Crawford, 1992, p. 1).

Following Hadjifotiou's (1983) work on sexual harassment, Ståle Einarsen, a prominent scholar in the area of workplace bullying, defined the construct as "all those repeated actions and practices that are directed to one or more workers, which are unwanted by the victim, which may be done deliberately or unconsciously, but clearly cause humiliation, offence and distress, and that may interfere with job performance and/or cause an unpleasant working environment" (Einarsen, 1999, p. 17).

For many researchers, the distinction between mobbing and bullying is purely semantic. For example, Zapf, Einarsen, Hoel, and Vartia (2003) note that the phenomenon of bullying has been labeled "mobbing at work" in some Scandinavian and German countries and "bullying at work" in many English-speaking countries. Others view the distinction as one of perspective—with bullying focused on the actions of one actor and one or more targets and mobbing involving multiple actors and one target (Zapf & Einarsen, 2005). Still other researchers believe that mobbing is distinct from bullying in that there is a "ganging-up" process (a group dynamic) in which the organization plays a role, as compared with bullying, which involves actions by a lone perpetrator (Sperry, 2009).

To complicate matters further, North American research involving related forms of negative workplace behavior has been conducted under an almost inexhaustible list of constructs that includes, but is not limited to, workplace aggression, emotional abuse, incivility, psychological aggression, petty tyranny, abusive supervision, social undermining, generalized work harassment, scapegoating, workplace trauma, insidious work behavior, counterproductive work behavior, organizational misbehavior, and desk rage (for more detail, refer to Einarsen, 2000; Fox & Spector, 2005; Greenberg, 2010). With respect to the different constructs and definitions that have been employed in empirical workplace bullying research in higher education reviewed in this chapter, please refer to Table 1.1.

While there seems to be agreement on the notion that workplace bullying involves persistent forms of workplace mistreatment that endure for long periods of time, the range of behaviors reported in the workplace bullying literature, and the vast array of ad hoc survey instruments used to capture these data, make it difficult—if not impossible—to engage in comparative research. Furthermore, the timeframe presented to respondents varies across studies. Some questionnaires ask respondents to report instances of mistreatment occurring during the previous 6, 12, or 18 months and some extend this time frame to 5 years or an entire working

TABLE 1.1 Empirical Studies of Workplace Bullying in Academic Settings with Samples, Methods, Constructs, and Definitions

Study	Sample	Method	Timeframe	Prevalence Rates	Actors	Constructs/Definitions
Björkqvist et al. (1994) Finland	Employees at one university; N = 338 (47% response rate)	Mail questionnaire: behavioral checklist	Prior 6 months	Experienced: 20.5%; 24.4% women; 16.9% men Witnessed: 32%	Superior 55.5%; Peer 32.1% Subordinate 12.4%	Work harassment/repeated acts of aggression, aimed at bringing mental (but sometimes also physical) pain, and directed toward one or more individuals who, for one reason or another, are not able to defend themselves.
Price Spratlen (1995) USA	Employees at one university; N = 805 (51% response rate)	Mail questionnaire: single item regarding mistreatment	Prior 18 months	Experienced: 23%; 26% women; 19% men Witnessed: 27%	Superior 48.7% Peer 29.7% Subordinate 9.2%	Interpersonal conflict and improper workplace behavior. Respondents were instructed to describe incidents and experiences that were nonsexual in nature and that represented interpersonal conflict, which included mistreatment.
Lewis (1999) Wales	Further/higher ed union members; 32 institutions; N = 415 (50.3% response rate)	Mail questionnaire: single item regarding bullying	Not reported	Experienced: 18% Witnessed: 22%	Not asked	Workplace bullying/no specific definition provided. Study participants provided their own characterizations.
Richman et al. (1999) USA	Employees at one university; N = 2492 (51.6% response rate)	Mail questionnaire: behavioral checklist	Prior 12 months	Experienced: 54.9%; 56.1% women; 53.5% men	Not asked	Generalized workplace abuse/degrading workplace interactions not explicitly involving gender. These involve psychologically demeaning and physically aggressive modes of aggression.

(Continued)

Study	Sample	Method		Prevalence	Source	Definition
Kinman & Jones (2004) UK	Members of University Teachers Association; 99 institutions N = 1,100 (22% response rate)	Mail questionnaire: single item regarding bullying	Not reported	Experienced: 18%; women report more frequent exposure than men	Not asked	Workplace stressors, including bullying; workplace bullying was simply described as unacceptable behavior.
Simpson & Cohen (2004) UK	Employees at one university; N = 378 (19.8% response rate)	Mail questionnaire: respond to definition and behavioral checklist	Not reported	Experienced: 25%; 28.5% women; 19.8% men Witnessed: 33%; 67.5% women; 29.4% men	Superior: 80% Peer: 20%	Workplace harassment and bullying—both harassment and bullying concern unwanted behavior that causes offence to the targeted individual and that is not justified by the working or professional relationship. Behavior could be considered harassment when directed against someone because of their race, sex, disability, age, sexual orientation, or some other physical group–oriented feature. Yet it might be considered as bullying when based on "individual" factors such as personality traits, work position, or levels of competence in the job.
Boynton (2005) UK	Self-selected sample of higher education employees; N = 843	Online questionnaire: respond to definition and behavioral checklist	Not reported	Experienced: over 40% Witnessed: 75%	Not reported	Workplace bullying/respondents were provided with an opportunity to define bullying at the beginning of the survey.

(Continued)

Study	Sample	Method	Timeframe	Prevalence Rates	Actors	Constructs/Definitions
Raskauskas (2006) New Zealand	Higher ed employees; 7 institutions; N = 1,117	Online questionnaire: respond to definition and behavioral checklist	Previous year	Experienced: 67.7%; of these: 27.4% report 1–2 incidents; 37.8% report 10 or more incidents	Peer: 18.1% 1 bully 38.4% 2 bullies 29% > 5 bullies 9.4%	Workplace bullying is defined as deliberate, repeated, and hurtful acts that take place at work and/or in the course of employment. Bullying may include direct or indirect harassment, professional misconduct, or abuse of power. It is characterized by unfair treatment, rumor spreading, or any repeated action found to be offensive, intimidating, malicious, or insulting. Any actions that could reasonably be regarded as undermining an individual's right or dignity at work are considered workplace bullying.
Keashly & Neuman (2008a) USA	Employees at one university; N = 1,185 (34.3% response rate)	Online questionnaire: respond to definition and behavioral checklist	Prior 12 months	Experienced: 32%; 33% women; 27% men Witnessed: 41%	Superior: 43% Peer: 42.2% Subordinate: 4% Customer/ student: 2% 1 bully 43% 2 bullies 30% ≥ 3 bullies 27% Superior: 44.3% Peer: 40% Subordinate: 6% Customer/ student: 2%	Workplace bullying/all those repeated actions and practices that are directed to one or more workers, which are unwanted by the victim, which may be done deliberately or unconsciously, cause humiliation, offense, and distress, and that may interfere with job performance and/or cause an unpleasant working environment.

(Continued)

Study/Country	Sample	Method	Time period	Prevalence	Perpetrator	Definition
McKay et al. (2008) Canada	Teaching staff and librarians at one university; N = 100 (12% response rate)	Online questionnaire: define bullying in own words and behavioral checklist	Prior 5 years	Experienced: 52% (32% "seriously")	Superior: 34% Peers: 61% Students: 16%	Workplace bullying. The survey began by asking respondents to define workplace bullying in their own words.
Court (2008) UK Stress survey (April–May)	Members of University and College Union; N = 14,270 (9,740 in higher education; 3,190 in further education)	Online questionnaire on stress: single item regarding having been bullied	Not reported	Experienced: 27.3% further education; 23.4% higher education	Not reported	Bullying may be characterized as offensive, intimidating, malicious, or insulting behavior.
Court (2008) UK Negative behaviors survey	Members of University and College Union; N not specified (48% in higher education; 44% in further education)	Online questionnaire: respond to definition and behavioral checklist	Prior 6 months	Experienced: 25.9%; 15.6% now and then; 10.3% at least several times per month	Can indicate more than one category. Superior: 75.4% Peer: 38.7% Subordinate: 9.7% Clients: 1.6% Students: 6.0%	Workplace bullying as a situation where one or several individuals persistently over a period of time perceive themselves to be on the receiving end of negative actions from one or several persons, in a situation where the target of bullying has difficulty in defending him- or herself against these actions. We will not refer to a one-off incident as bullying.
Fox (2010) USA	Faculty; convenience sample; N = 228	Online questionnaire: behavioral checklist	Prior 5 years	Experienced: 36.6%	Superior: 22.1% Peer: 23.9%	Workplace bullying/workplace bullying is behavior that threatens, intimidates, humiliates, or isolates people at work, or undermines their reputation or job performance.

(Continued)

Study	Sample	Method	Timeframe	Prevalence Rates	Actors	Constructs/Definitions
Neuman (2009) USA	Faculty at one university; $N = 241$ (55% response rate)	Online questionnaire: respond to definition and behavioral checklist	Prior 12 months	Experienced: 26% Witnessed: 46%	Superior: 24% Colleague: 66% Senior colleague: 37% Equal status: 21% Junior colleague: 8% 1 bully 43% 2 bullies 21% ≥ 3 bullies 36% Superior: 28% Colleague: 71% Senior colleague: 49% Equal status: 15% Junior colleague: 7%	Workplace bullying/all those repeated actions and practices that are directed to one or more workers, which are unwanted by the victim, which may be done deliberately or unconsciously, cause humiliation, offense, and distress, and that may interfere with job performance and/or cause an unpleasant working environment.
Tigrel & Kokalan (2009) Turkey	Faculty at two universities; $N = 103$ (85.5% response rate)	Mail questionnaire: respond to definition and behavioral checklist	Not reported	Experienced: 11.7%	Not reported	Workplace mobbing/practicing violence by a group and involves psychological terror, emotional attacks, or being against something or someone.

life (refer to Table 1.1 for methodological differences). Also, although perceived power differences (between actors and targets) are seen as central to many definitions of bullying, this is by no means universal across all studies. In the case of vertical aggression, in which there is a hierarchical relationship between a perpetrator (superior) and victim (subordinate), the power relationship is explicit. However, all bullying and mobbing researchers would agree that actors and targets may be coworkers/colleagues, equal in hierarchical terms (Lester, 2009; Rayner & Keashly, 2005). Although perceived power differences may exist, independent of ascribed formal organizational power, sources of power are typically not assessed in bullying studies.

Another issue exists that has conceptual and practical implications. Many researchers require that psychological, emotional, or physiological harm be inflicted on a target before bullying is said to have occurred. This perspective is captured in the definition provided by Einarsen (1999), shown above, in which negative actions must *clearly cause humiliation, offence, and distress.* An interesting question that arises here is, if there are no negative effects of exposure to these actions, then has bullying occurred? Other researchers focus more on the nature of the actions and the underlying intentions of the perpetrator, as opposed to the consequences of these behaviors on a target. Consistent with this perspective, *attempts* at harming a target are sufficient to classify the behavior as aggressive or hostile, regardless of the actual outcome (e.g., a failed attempt to get a target fired by spreading vicious and untrue rumors about this person would be sufficient). This point of view also stresses the fact that actor intent is important in distinguishing between acts of malice and actions resulting from ignorance or accident. Unfortunately, even when intent is included as a defining characteristic, the actual intent of actors is often assumed rather than explicitly examined in the workplace bullying literature. As we will discuss below, all of these factors have very practical consequences when it comes to classifying behavior and taking action to prevent or manage such conduct.

Finally, some researchers employ a labeling approach in which respondents are provided with a definition of bullying and then are asked to respond to specific questions, to assess the nature and prevalence of the problem. This phenomenological technique captures the "experience of victimization." Other surveys employ a behavioral approach, in which respondents are presented with specific examples of "negative behavior" and asked to indicate the extent to which they have experienced or witnessed each of these behaviors. This method is more accurately characterized as assessing "exposure" to behaviors. Empirical evidence suggests that these two approaches impact reported prevalence rates. For example, in research conducted comparing both procedures in a single study, Salin (2001) obtained a reported prevalence rate of 8.8% using the labeling approach and 24.1% using a behavioral checklist. However, in two studies that we conducted in university settings, we obtained prevalence rates of 32% and 26% using the labeling approach, and 23% and 19% using a behavioral checklist, respectively

(Keashly & Neuman, 2008b; Neuman, 2009). In short, some research suggests that the behavioral approach results in higher reported prevalence rates as compared with the labeling approach, but other studies point in the opposite direction. Since somewhat different wordings were employed in the instructions and survey designs, the reasons for these differences are open to question—as are the implications for the nature of the data collected by each approach.

As noted above, these conceptual and methodological issues result in a wide variety of ad hoc measures presently being employed to explore workplace bullying. Consequently, even when a single measure is used, it is difficult to generalize the results across studies. For example, Hubert and van Veldhoven (2001) surveyed 66,764 employees representing 11 business sectors in the Netherlands but used four items to measure what they characterized as "unpleasant" and "aggressive" behaviors between respondents and their supervisors and coworkers. Since no operational definitions were provided to their study participants, we are unable to align their findings with other measures of bullying. In short, their large sample size and comparative sampling across business sectors is not necessarily generalizable beyond the study sample.

With this brief overview of some of the many challenges confronted by workplace bullying scholars, we trust that you can understand the importance of considering (and questioning) the validity and reliability of the available data when summarizing what we know and what we think we know about workplace bullying within and beyond the academy.

Empirical Data: What We Know and What We Think We Know

Even in the face of the many methodological challenges noted above, studies using behavioral checklists do reveal that academics report witnessing and experiencing "negative/problematic" behaviors from others in their workplace. Furthermore, studies employing the labeling approach find that significant percentages of academics identify themselves as the targets of bullying—using explicit definitions of bullying. So it is possible to develop a picture based on data from specific studies regarding the likelihood of exposure to negative behaviors characterized as part of a bullying experience, as well as some idea of the likelihood of what are considered bullying relationships.

The Prevalence of Bullying in Higher Education

Building from our initial review of empirical studies in academic settings (Keashly & Neuman, 2010), we captured the findings from several of these studies in Table 1.1. Review of this table reveals several interesting findings. First, like the broader workplace bullying literature, the estimated prevalence of bullying varies depending on the nature of the sample, the operationalization of the construct, the timeframe for experiences, and the country in which the research was conducted (for an excellent review of prevalence rates across work settings, see Zapf, Escartín, Einarsen, Hoel, & Vartia, 2011). The rates of bullying range from 18% to almost 68%, with several studies in the 25%–35% range. These rates seem relatively high when compared to those noted in the general population, which range from 2%–5% in Scandinavian countries, 10%–20% in the UK, and 10%–14% in the United States (Keashly & Jagatic, 2011; Rayner & Cooper, 2006). The rates of people witnessing bullying range from 22% to 75%. Based on the high prevalence rates reported by targets and witnesses, bullying appears to be an unfortunately familiar aspect of academic settings. In our reading of the literature in this area, there has been an assertion that bullying is on the rise in academe (e.g., Twale & De Luca, 2008). Such a statement requires documentation of rates over time. The cross-sectional nature of these studies and their reliance on an array of measures does not presently permit an examination of this claim. It will be important to discern whether there has been an actual increase in the proportion of academics who have been exposed to bullying, or whether people are reporting it more as a result of becoming sensitized to the phenomenon through the heightened social awareness and sanctioning of bullying in schools or through recent public campaigns regarding workplace hostility (Namie, Namie, & Lutgen-Sandvik, 2011).

The Relationship Between Actors and Targets

The nature of the relationships between actors (perpetrators) and targets (victims) involves both conceptual and practical issues. First, vertical (hierarchical) bullying seems to characterize the UK and European studies, whereas U.S. studies suggest that bullies are equally likely to be superiors or coworkers/colleagues. These findings are consistent with the broader workplace aggression literature (Rayner & Keashly, 2005). The difference in findings is probably due to methodological differences in the way bullying is measured. In the UK and European studies, definitions tend to focus on perceived power differences between actors and targets. Consequently, superior-subordinate relationships may be called to mind. This is not so in the case of North American behavioral checklist measures.

With the exception of Lewis (1999), McKay, Arnold, Fratzl, and Thomas (2008), and Neuman (2009), the study samples involved a number of occupational groups including faculty, administrators, professional and frontline/clerical staff, and in some studies, students. In our own research, we have found that the relevance of the actor–target relationship is strongly influenced by organizational structure. For example, in a recent study that we conducted with 1,185 university employees (Keashly & Neuman, 2008a), colleagues were more likely to be identified as bullies by faculty (63.4%), whereas superiors were more likely to be identified as bullies by frontline staff (52.9%). Looking within the "colleague as bully" category, Neuman's (2009) study found that senior colleagues were more likely to be identified as bullies. These results suggest that an individual's location within the institutional structure, as defined by occupational group and hierarchical and/or professional status, may leave specific targets vulnerable to abuse from particular actors/agents. These findings may also reflect different dynamics within the dyad and potentially different antecedents and consequences (Aquino & Lamertz, 2004). For example, in our 2008 study, we found that faculty were more vulnerable to bullying from colleagues, whereas staff were more vulnerable to bullying from their direct supervisors.

Number of Actors Involved in an Incident

Another observation concerns the number of actors purportedly involved in the incidents. As reported by Raskauskas (2006), and captured in our own research (Keashly & Neuman, 2008b), the majority of situations reported by targets involved two or more actors; that is, these incidents involved acts of mobbing. Westhues (2008), in discussing the mobbing of professors by their colleagues and administrators, has argued that the experience of being mobbed by a number of actors is very different from the experience (however upsetting) of being harassed by a single actor. In our 2008 sample, we found that rates of mobbing differed as a function of occupational group being studied. Faculty members were almost twice as likely as staff to report being the victims of mobbing by three or more actors (14.5% vs 8%, respectively). These figures are higher than previously estimated rates of 2%–5% (Westhues, 2006). Frontline staff members, on the other hand, were 1.5 times more likely to be bullied by a single perpetrator. This differential pattern highlights the need to consider the actor–target relationship as well as the number of actors involved within the broader context of the occupational group, status differentials, and formally (and informally) defined working relationships.

Duration of Exposure to Bullying

Duration of exposure to bullying in academic settings is notable. McKay et al. (2008) found that 21% of their sample reported bullying that had persisted for more than five years. In our 2008 and 2009 projects, we found that 34% and 49%, respectively, reported bullying lasting for more than three years. There are individual cases detailed in the workplace bullying literature that show similar and even longer exposure (Westhues, 2004, 2005), but what is surprising is the number of people who tolerate these enduring situations. It may be that academia is a particularly vulnerable setting for such persistent aggression, as a result of tenure, which has faculty and some staff in very long-term relationships with one another. Both the conflict (Holton, 1995, 1998; Pruitt & Rubin, 1986) and aggression (Jawahar, 2002) research note that the longer and more interactive the relationship, the greater the opportunity for conflict and potential aggression. Further, while ensuring a "job for life," tenure may also restrict mobility so that once a situation goes bad, there are few options for leaving (Berryman-Fink, 1998).

Zapf and Gross (2001) observed that the number of actors was linked to the duration of bullying. They found that the longer a situation continued, the more people would join in, concluding that it may become increasingly difficult for bystanders to remain neutral as bullying proceeds and intensifies. Given that faculty are typically in long-term ongoing relationships suggesting little opportunity for exit, it would seem likely that once bullying begins, the longer it is permitted to continue, the more likely it is that other colleagues will be drawn into the situation. Thus, witnesses run the risk of becoming accomplices to the situation (Namie & Lutgen-Sandvik, 2010). Further, such situations unchecked could potentially spawn spillovers to others, creating the infamous dysfunctional departments that are believed to be the nature of academic institutions (Pearson Andersson, & Porath, 2000). These are the kinds of situations that Westhues (1998, 2004, 2005, 2008) specifically discusses as academic mobbing. Such spiraling and snowballing highlight the importance of addressing these interactions before bullying becomes entrenched; that is, focusing on the not-yet-bullied period (Rayner & Keashly, 2005).

Interventions: What We Know and Think We Know

As tentative as some of the findings are with respect to the nature and prevalence of bullying in academic settings, substantially less is known about remediation. In fact, "what we know" is more theoretical than practical in nature because of the limited number of studies designed to systematically evaluate the efficacy of bullying interventions (e.g., Leiter, Spence Laschinger, Day, & Gillon Oore, 2011; Osatuke, Ward, Dyrenforth, & Belton, 2009). The most frequently offered suggestion for dealing with workplace mistreatment is the development and implementation of "effective" workplace bullying policies and practices. Though we certainly agree that such procedures have potential value, we wonder if this common reaction is somewhat premature, given the limits of the data we have just discussed. In particular, what are "effective" policies and practices? Before we suggest or assume the value of specific strategies and practices, we need to understand how individuals have typically responded to bullying, and evaluate their judgments about the effectiveness of the strategies they have employed. By learning what they are doing and how effective those strategies have been, from their perspectives, we are better positioned to identify approaches that seem to be working, improve those that are not working, and design new practices based on what we have learned. Consistent with a central theme of this chapter, we are suggesting a data-driven/evidence-based approach.

So What Do Targets Do in the Face of Workplace Bullying?

When targets' responses to bullying are examined, the effectiveness of those responses is typically inferred from their correlation to, and moderation of, indicators of the individual's stress and strain (e.g., Richman, Rospenda, Flaherty, & Freels, 2001a). What has not been examined is the individual target's own assessment of how effective the actions undertaken have been. Their perception of effectiveness has implications for the outcomes they experience. If they do not think it worked, or indeed they perceive it worsened the situation, then the impact of bullying will likely be more negative. Further, their perceptions of effectiveness have implications for their sense of efficacy in their ability to address bullying, as well as a sense of organizational responsiveness to, and efficacy in, handling these concerns. In our 2008 study, we drew on the extant workplace bullying literature on responding (Einarsen, Hoel, Zapf, & Cooper, 2003; Hogh & Dofradottir, 2001; Lee & Brotheridge, 2006; Rayner, 1999; Richman et al., 2001a) as well as the workplace stress coping literature (Carver, Scheier, & Weintraub, 1989) to identify a range of possible responses. Employees who self-identified as being bullied were asked to indicate what responses they had tried and whether the response had improved, worsened, or had no discernible impact on the bullying (see Table 1.2).

TABLE 1.2 Target Responses to Bullying and the Perceived Effectiveness of Each Approach

Responses to Bullying	% Using This Approach	Effectiveness	
		Made Situation Worse	Made Situation Better
Talked to coworkers	92.1	15.5	**24.4**
Talked with family and friends	88.5	2.5	**36.0**
Stayed calm	79.8	10.6	**26.1**
Avoided the bully	76.4	11.5	**30.9**
Told supervisor/chair/dean	57.1	**26.7**	23.8
Acted as if I didn't care	54.8	16.5	**18.6**
Asked colleagues for help	52.5	13.7	**31.6**
Ignored it or did nothing	52.3	**17.0**	10.6
Asked bully to stop	40.4	**38.9**	15.3
Behaved extra nice	38.5	**21.7**	14.5
Went along with behavior	36.9	**18.2**	7.6
Lowered productivity	35.6	**29.7**	9.4
Not take behavior seriously	33.3	11.9	**20.3**
Told union	30.8	**23.2**	16.1
Told HR	28.6	**32.7**	15.4
Had someone speak to bully	27.9	**34.0**	16.0
Made formal complaint	16.3	**37.9**	24.1
Asked for transfer	9.5	35.3	**52.9**
Threatened to tell others	7.8	**28.6**	7.1

Note: Percentages are reported for strategies that were viewed as helping or hurting the situation. We do not report data in those instances in which the responses neither helped nor hurt or those instances in which targets were unable to make a judgment. Data are presented in descending order of use. Bold italics indicate the larger of the two effectiveness percentages. Sample sizes varied from 300 to 308.

Consistent with Lutgen-Sandvik's (2006) observations, targets did not simply "lie down and take it;" rather, they utilized, on average, eight different strategies. The top strategies (used by at least 75% of the targets) involved talking with co-workers, talking with family and friends, staying calm, and avoiding the bully, all of which can be considered relatively passive, indirect, and informal strategies, yet deliberate and thoughtful responses. Respondents were least likely to utilize the formally sanctioned mechanisms of the union, HR, formal complaints, and transfers. In terms of effectiveness, strategies that involved buffering the target in the situation, such as seeking social support and managing one's own thoughts and emotions, were more effective, from the target's perspective. Interestingly, reducing contact with the bully whether temporarily, by avoiding the person (harder to do if this is the target's supervisor), or permanently, by transferring to another unit, seemed particularly effective—although the latter was rarely implemented. For faculty, in particular, transferring from one's disciplinary home is rarely possible or even desirable.

Before commenting on the relative effectiveness of different actions, it is important to note that none of the strategies that we will discuss substantively changed the situation for a sizeable proportion of the self-identified victims. This is a point we will revisit later. Attempts to pretend the mistreatment is not bullying by ignoring or going along with behavior or placating the actor were not viewed as particularly effective. Telling the bully to stop was clearly problematic—reflected in the highest percentage of people saying that doing so made the situation worse. Giving voice via more formal strategies of the union, HR, and formal complaints had a greater likelihood of making the situation worse (cf. Cortina & Magley, 2003). This is particularly disturbing given the fact that this is a fairly standard recommendation for addressing bullying and, more generally, any form of harassment or discrimination in the workplace (Cowan, 2011; Lutgen-Sandvik & Tracy, 2012). Thus, targets appear to try a number of different strategies, with the more successful (at least in the immediate term) being more passive and, in some cases, employing avoidant strategies of seeking support, comfort, and help from those immediately around them. Managing these situations by themselves or via more formal mechanisms is particularly risky. Evidence that such action actually does worsen the situation for targets has been documented by Richman and her colleagues (Richman et al., 2001a, 2001b) in their multi-wave longitudinal study of university employees. They found that active problem-focused responses, particularly those that involved engaging members of the organization who have the "power" to alter the situation, had a limited effect on ending bullying and when it failed, the effects on the individual were devastating. Research in other work settings finds similar results (Lutgen-Sandvik, 2006; Zapf & Gross, 2001). An interesting exception in our study is that getting help from colleagues did have a beneficial impact. This speaks to the power of the peer (particularly among faculty) and hence, the value in enhancing witness/bystander engagement (Ashburn-Nardo, Morris, & Goodwin, 2008).

Actions of Witnesses/Bystanders

Given the potential for bullying situations to escalate and involve others in the work unit, as well as the evidence that targets look to coworkers for help, consideration of the presence and responses of witnesses becomes important. First, the prevalence rates for witnessing hostile interactions are an indicator of the climate of an organization; that is, that others in the environment are aware of these experiences. Second, data from other settings finds that witnesses experience negative effects, such as, anxiety, stress, depression, and sleep disorders, similar to those of targets (Hoel, Einarsen, & Cooper, 2003; Vartia, 2001). Finally, witnesses can play a very helpful role in the prevention and management of aggression and bullying (Keashly & Neuman, 2007). Unfortunately, there is little in the workplace bullying literature about what witnesses actually do with respect to responding to what they see. In our 2008 study, those who identified as witnessing bullying indicated what actions they took and their perception of the effectiveness of that action in addressing the situation.

As can be seen in Table 1.3, a large percentage of witnesses seemed uncertain of what to do, but many did indeed take action. Most frequent responses involved talking to others (coworkers, family and friends) about what they had observed and also talking with the targets, possibly in an effort to understand what was happening. For example, Lewis (2001), in his interview study of academics, noted that colleagues can be significant in terms of legitimizing and validating a target's experiences. Some relatively successful actions involved buffering the victim by advising them to avoid the bully or the witness keeping the bully away. The more successful actions appear to be what Bowes-Sperry and O'Leary-Kelly (2005) characterize as low-involvement strategies; that is, the witnesses not putting themselves out publicly and potentially risking retaliation. As can be seen, some witnesses did become more overtly involved by confronting the bully or reporting to management; actions that appeared to worsen the situation. Just as we saw with the targets, the action of reporting is often perceived as worsening the situation, a very disturbing finding given that institutional policies often prescribe formal reporting for mistreatment and harassment. These findings suggest that such approaches may inadvertently intensify the situation; the question is, why that would be the case? To the extent that witnesses worry about possible escalation, this may result in underreporting and, thus, the institution being unaware of the extent of bullying issues. With faculty, underreporting may well be associated with the belief they have that given the autonomous nature of faculty, they do not have the "legitimacy" to comment on another's behavior (see Keashly & Neuman, 2010, for further discussion).

We recognize that these data are all from one institution and may reflect its unique character and climate. We suggest that as a mechanism for determining the "profile" of a work environment, finding out the experience of people "on the ground" provides important feedback regarding available formal approaches and

TABLE 1.3 Witness Responses to Bullying and the Perceived Effectiveness of Each Approach

Responses to Bullying	% Using this Approach	Effectiveness	
		Made Situation Worse	Made Situation Better
Talked to coworkers or other people	87	15.0	**18.2**
Talked to the victim about what I saw happening	77	5.3	**28.7**
Talked to family or friends	74	4.5	**21.0**
Did not know what to do	57	**11.5**	1.5
Advised the victim to report the incident	55	**17.0**	13.2
Did nothing (ignored it)	53	**22.5**	6.9
Reported incident to management or higher-ups	43	**27.5**	15.0
Advised the victim to avoid the bully	39	7.4	**23.6**
Got other people to denounce the conduct	32	14.9	**22.3**
Tried to keep the bully away from the victim	28	16.8	**23.4**
Told the bully to stop the behaviors	25	**35.8**	24.2
Helped the bully and the victim talk to each other	12	25.0	**31.3**
Went with the victim when they reported the incident	11	20.9	**30.2**

Note: Percentages are reported for strategies that were viewed as helping or hurting the situation. We do not report data in those instances in which the responses neither helped nor hurt or those instances in which targets were unable to make a judgment. Data are presented in descending order of use. Bold italics indicate the larger of the two effectiveness percentages. Sample sizes varied from 349 to 392.

potentially more effective informal ones. Similar to the methodological problems in collecting prevalence data, the evaluation of the efficacy of various approaches requires consistency across future studies.

So Where Do We Go From Here?

As evidenced by the studies of aggregated data reviewed here, and supported by a developing qualitative literature of individuals' experiences in academia (e.g., Lester, 2009; Nelson & Lambert, 2001; Westhues, 2004), bullying and mobbing exist in academic environments. The prevalence of bullying and the question of whether or not it is changing (particularly as relates to the assumptions that it is increasing) remain empirical questions to be tested. Further, while there are thoughtful conceptual analyses that suggest that the structures and processes operating in academic institutions may make universities particularly vulnerable to bullying and related phenomena (e.g., Bertram Gallant, 2011; Keashly & Neuman,

2010; Twale & De Luca, 2008; Zabrodska, Linnell, Laws, & Davies, 2011), there is insufficient empirical evidence to adequately test this assumption. In order to do so, we need to have consistent measurement of core constructs collected over time and across various institutional contexts. In this chapter, we have identified the current challenges to accomplishing this much-needed research.

Within the extant empirical literature on bullying in academia, there are numerous intriguing questions to be explored. Given space limitations, we will focus on three questions that we believe to be of immediate import because of their implications for prevention and management of bullying and its impact on individuals. First, what is the connection between exposure to behaviors (as assessed by the behavioral checklist approach) and the experience of victimization (as assessed by self-labeling in response to a definition)? It is unlikely to be a perfect correlation, as people vary in their evaluations of behavior. These evaluations are influenced by the context within which they occur. For example, critique of one's ideas and contributions may be experienced as particularly threatening to employees in a corporate environment, while it is in fact expected in an academic environment and, thus, less likely to be experienced as unfair, hostile, or bullying. We do acknowledge that within academic environments, junior faculty members going for tenure are more likely to experience such critique as threatening than would a tenured faculty member. Detailing and understanding this connection opens up places for helping manage the target's experience and thus mitigating negative impact. The second question concerns the issue of actor motive and intent. In the workplace bullying literature (both within and beyond academic settings), there is very little known about actors—beyond their relationship to the targets. Understanding the motive of the actor opens up possibilities for management of bullying. For example, if the faculty member's behavior reflects limited social skill in managing relationships, their emotions, or lack of awareness of impact of behavior on others, actions such as interpersonal skill training and coaching may alleviate the problem (e.g., Avtgis & Chory, 2010). If the academic's motive is removing a rival for a coveted position, then intervention by an organizational authority, such as a chair or dean, is necessary. The third question concerns the role and effectiveness of formal mechanisms such as HR, unions, and supervisors/department chairs in the response to, and management of, these situations. Given that much appears to be invested in policies and procedures for setting a more productive climate, it is important to understand how and when these will be effective.

We want to be clear that this chapter is not meant to grant a license to those who believe that bullying is not a problem. Rather, we believe that bullying is a significant problem, but we must increase the conceptual and methodological rigor with which we explore and discuss the phenomenon. In short, we have not jumped off the bandwagon nor are we urging others to do so. We simply want to be sure that the wagon is headed in the right direction and the passengers have a legitimate reason for being on board.

References

Adams, A., & Crawford, N. (1992). *Bullying at work: How to confront and overcome it*. London: Virago.

American Psychological Association. (2009). *APA college dictionary of psychology*. Washington, DC: Author.

Aquino, K., & Lamertz, K. (2004). Relational model of workplace victimization: Social roles and patterns of victimization in dyadic relationships. *Journal of Applied Psychology, 89*, 1023–1034.

Ashburn-Nardo, L., Morris, K.A., & Goodwin, S.A. (2008). The Confronting Prejudiced Responses (CPR) Model: Applying CPR in organizations. *Academy of Management Learning & Education, 7*, 332–342.

Avtgis, T.A., & Chory, R.M. (2010). The dark side of organizational life: Aggressive expression in the workplace. In T. A. Avtgis, & A. S. Rancer (Eds), *Arguments, aggression, and conflict: New directions in theory* (pp. 285–304). Hoboken, NJ: Routledge.

Berryman-Fink, C. (1998). Can we agree to disagree? Faculty-faculty conflict. In S. A. Holton (Ed.), *Mending the cracks in the ivory tower: Strategies for conflict management in higher education* (pp. 141–163). Bolton, MA: Anker Publishing.

Bertram Gallant, T. (2011). *Creating the ethical academy: A systems approach to understanding misconduct and empowering change*. New York: Routledge.

Björkqvist, K., Österman, K., & Hjelt-Back, M. (1994). Aggression among university employees. *Aggressive Behavior, 20*, 173–184.

Bowes-Sperry, L., & O'Leary-Kelly, A.M. (2005). To act or not to act: The dilemma faced by sexual harassment observers. *Academy of Management Review, 30*, 288–306.

Boynton, P. (2005). Higher Education Supplement Bullying Survey. Preliminary findings from the Boynton-THES Bullying Survey. Retrieved from http://www.unitetheunion.org/pdf/Preliminary%20Findings%20from%20Bullying%20survey.pdf

Brodsky, C.M. (1976). *The harassed worker*. Lexington, MA: Lexington Books.

Carver, C.S., Scheier, M.F., & Weintraub, J.K. (1989). Assessing coping strategies: A theoretically based approach. *Journal of Personality and Social Psychology, 56*, 267–283.

Cortina, L.M., & Magley, V.J. (2003). Raising voice, risking retaliation: Events following interpersonal mistreatment in the workplace. *Journal of Occupational Health Psychology, 8*, 247–265.

Court, S. (2008). *The extent of bullying and harassment in post-16 education*. Paper presented at the meeting of the Union of Colleges and Universities Tackling Bullying conference, London.

Cowan, R.L. (2011). "Yes, we have an anti-bullying policy, but. . .": HR professionals' understandings and experiences with workplace bullying policy. *Communication Studies, 62*, 307–327.

Einarsen, S. (1999). The nature and causes of bullying at work. *International Journal of Manpower, 20*, 16–27.

Einarsen, S. (2000). Harassment and bullying at work: A review of the Scandinavian approach. *Aggression and Violent Behavior, 5*, 379–401.

Einarsen, S., Hoel, H., Zapf, D., & Cooper, C.L. (Eds). (2003). *Bullying and emotional abuse in the workplace: International perspectives in research and practice*. London: Taylor & Francis.

Fogg, P. (2008). Academic bullies. *Chronicle of Higher Education, 55*(3), B10.

Fox, S. (2010, April). *Bullying in academia: Distinctive relations of power and control*. Paper presented at the meeting of the Society for Industrial/Organizational Psychology Conference, Atlanta, GA.

Fox, S., & Spector, P.E. (Eds). (2005). *Counterproductive work behavior: Investigations of actors and targets.* Washington, DC: American Psychological Association.

Gravois, J. (2006). Mob rule: In departmental disputes, professors can act just like animals. *The Chronicle of Higher Education, 52*(32), A32.

Greenberg, J. (Ed.). (2010). *Insidious workplace behavior.* Hillsdale, NJ: Routledge Academic.

Hadjifotiou, N. (1983). *Women and harassment at work.* London: Pluto Press.

Hoel, H., Einarsen, S., & Cooper, C.L. (2003). Organisational effects of bullying. In S. Einarsen, H. Hoel, D. Zapf, & C. L. Cooper (Eds), *Bullying and emotional abuse in the workplace: International perspectives in research and practice* (pp. 145–161). London: Taylor & Francis.

Hogh, A., & Dofradottir, A. (2001). Coping with bullying in the workplace. *European Journal of Work and Organizational Psychology, 10,* 485–496.

Holton, S.A. (1995). And now . . . the answers! How to deal with conflict in higher education. *New Directions for Higher Education, 92,* 79–90.

Holton, S.A. (Ed.). (1998). *Mending the cracks in the ivory tower: Strategies for conflict management in higher education.* Bolton, MA: Anker Publishing.

Hubert, A.B., & van Veldhoven, M. (2001). Risk sectors for undesirable behaviour and mobbing. *European Journal of Work and Organizational Psychology, 10,* 415–424.

Jawahar, I.M. (2002). A model of organizational justice and workplace aggression. *Journal of Management, 28,* 811–834.

Keashly, L., & Jagatic, K. (2011). North American perspectives on hostile behaviors and bullying at work. In S. Einarsen, H. Hoel, D. Zapf, & C. L. Cooper (Eds), *Bullying and harassment in the workplace: Developments in theory, research, and practice* (2nd ed., pp. 41–71). London: CRC Press.

Keashly, L., & Neuman, J.H. (2007, November). Stepping up: Developing peer strategies for managing bullying at work. In S. Dickmeyer (Chair), *Building workplace bullying seminars: Grounding training and development in strong communication scholarship.* Symposium conducted at the meeting of the National Communications Association, Chicago, IL.

Keashly, L., & Neuman, J.H. (2008a). *Final report: Workplace behavior (bullying) project survey.* Mankato: Minnesota State University.

Keashly, L., & Neuman, J.H. (2008b). [Workplace Behavior Project Survey]. Unpublished raw data.

Keashly, L., & Neuman, J.H. (2010). Faculty experiences with bullying in higher education: Causes, consequences, and management. *Administrative Theory and Praxis, 32,* 48–70.

Kinman, G., & Jones, F. (2004). Working to the limit: Stress and work-life balance in academic and academic related employees. Retrieved from http://www.atn.edu.au/docs/workingtothelimit.pdf

Kleinginna, P.R., Jr., & Kleinginna, A.M. (1981). A categorized list of motivation definitions with a suggestion for a consensual definition. *Motivation and Emotion, 5,* 263–292.

Lee, R.T., & Brotheridge, C.M. (2006). When prey turns predatory: Workplace bullying as a predictor of counteraggression/bullying, coping, and well-being. *European Journal of Work and Organizational Psychology, 15,* 352–377.

Leiter, M.P., Spence Laschinger, H.K., Day, A., & Gillon Oore, D. (2011). The impact of civility interventions on employee social behavior, distress, and attitudes. *Journal of Applied Psychology, 96,* 1258–1274.

Lester, J. (2009). Not your child's playground: Workplace bullying among community college faculty. *Community College Journal of Research and Practice, 33,* 444–464.

Lewis, D. (1999). Workplace bullying—Interim findings of a study in further and higher education in Wales. *International Journal of Manpower, 20,* 106–118.

Lewis, D. (2001). Perceptions of bullying in organizations. *International Journal of Management, 2*, 48–64.

Leymann, H. (1990). Mobbing and psychological terror at workplaces. *Violence and Victims, 5*, 119–126.

Lutgen-Sandvik, P. (2006). Take this job and. . . : Quitting and other forms of resistance to workplace bullying. *Communication Monographs, 73*, 406–433.

Lutgen-Sandvik, P., & Tracy, S.J. (2012). Answering five key questions about workplace bullying: How communication scholarship provides thought leadership for transforming abuse at work. *Management Communication Quarterly, 26*(1), 3–47.

McKay, R., Arnold, D.H., Fratzl, J., & Thomas, R. (2008). Workplace bullying in academia: A Canadian study. *Employee Responsibilities and Rights Journal, 20*, 77–100.

Namie, G., & Lutgen-Sandvik, P. (2010). Active and passive accomplices: The communal character of workplace bullying. *International Journal of Communication, 4*, 343–373.

Namie, G., Namie, R., & Lutgen-Sandvik, P. (2011). Challenging workplace bullying in the USA: A communication and activist perspective. In S. Einarsen, H. Hoel, D. Zapf, & C. L. Cooper (Eds), *Bullying and harassment in the workplace: Developments in theory, research, and practice* (2nd ed., pp. 447–468). London: CRC Press

Nelson, E.D., & Lambert, R.D. (2001). Sticks, stones, and semantics: The ivory tower bully's vocabulary of motives. *Qualitative Sociology, 24*, 83–106.

Neuman, J.H. (2009). [Workplace Behavior Project Survey]. Unpublished raw data.

Osatuke, K., Ward, C., Dyrenforth, S.R., & Belton, L.W. (2009). Civility, respect, engagement in the workforce (CREW): Nationwide organization development intervention at Veterans Health Administration. *The Journal of Applied Behavioral Science, 45*, 384–410.

Pearson, C.M., Andersson, L.M., & Porath, C.L. (2000). Assessing and attacking workplace incivility. *Organizational Dynamics, 29*, 123–137.

Price Spratlen, L. (1995). Interpersonal conflict which includes mistreatment in a university workplace. *Violence and Victims, 10*, 285–297.

Pruitt, D.G., & Rubin, J.Z. (1986). *Social conflict: Escalation, stalemate, and settlement.* New York: Random House.

Raskauskas, J. (2006). *Workplace bullying in academia.* San Francisco, CA: American Educational Research Association.

Rayner, C. (1999). From research to implementation: Finding leverage for prevention. *International Journal of Manpower, 20*, 28–38.

Rayner, C., & Cooper, C.L. (2006). Workplace bullying. In E. K. Kelloway, J. Barling, J. Hurrell, & J. Joseph (Eds), *Handbook of workplace violence* (pp. 121-146). Thousand Oaks, CA: Sage.

Rayner, C., & Keashly, L. (2005). Bullying at work: A perspective from Britain and North America. In S. Fox & P. E. Spector (Eds), *Counterproductive work behavior: Investigations of actors and targets* (pp. 271–296). Washington, DC: American Psychological Association.

Richman, J.A., Rospenda, K., Flaherty, J.A., & Freels, S. (2001a). Workplace harassment, active coping and alcohol-related outcomes. *Journal of Substance Abuse, 13*, 347–366.

Richman, J.A., Rospenda, K.M., Nawyn, S.J., Flaherty, J.A., Fendrich, M., Drum, M.L., & Johnson, T.P. (2001b). Sexual harassment and generalized workplace abuse among university employees: Prevalence and mental health correlates. *American Journal of Public Health, 89*, 358–363.

Salin, D. (2001). Prevalence and forms of bullying among business professionals: A comparison of two different strategies for measuring bullying. *European Journal of Work and Organizational Psychology, 10*, 425–442.

Schmidt, P. (2010). Workplace mediators seek a role in taming faculty bullies. Retrieved from http://chronicle.com/article/Workplace-Mediators-Seek-a/65815/

Simpson, R., & Cohen, C. (2004). Dangerous work: the gendered nature of bullying in the context of higher education. *Gender, Work & Organization, 11*, 163–186.

Sperry, L. (2009). Mobbing and bullying: The influence of individual, work group, and organizational dynamics on abusive workplace behavior. *Consulting Psychology Journal: Practice and Research, 61*, 190–201.

Stewart, T.A. (1997). *Intellectual capital: The new wealth of organizations.* New York: Doubleday.

Tigrel, E.Y., & Kokalan, O. (2009). Academic mobbing in Turkey. *International Journal of Behavioral, Cognitive, Educational and Psychological Sciences, 1*, 91–99.

Twale, D.J., & De Luca, B.M. (2008). *Faculty incivility: The rise of the academic bully culture and what to do about it.* San Francisco, CA: Jossey-Bass.

Vartia, M. (2001). Consequences of workplace bullying with respect to the well-being of its targets and the observers of bullying. *Scandinavian Journal of Work, Environment and Health, 27*, 63–69.

Westhues, K. (1998). *Eliminating professors: A guide to the dismissal process.* Lewiston, NY: The Edwin Mellen Press.

Westhues, K. (2004). *Workplace mobbing in academe: Reports from twenty universities.* Lewiston, NY: The Edwin Mellen Press.

Westhues, K. (2005). *Winning, losing and moving on: How professionals deal with workplace harassment and mobbing.* Lewiston, NY: The Edwin Mellen Press.

Westhues, K. (2006, Fall). The unkindly art of mobbing. *Academic Matters: The Journal of Higher Education,* 18–19. Retrieved from http://www.ocufa.on.ca/Academic%20Mat ters%20Fall2006/Unkindly_art_of_mobbing.pdf

Westhues, K. (2008). *Critiques of the anti-bullying movement and responses to them.* Paper presented at the meeting of the 6th International Conference on Workplace Bullying, Montreal.

Zabrodska, K., Linnell, S., Laws, C., & Davies, B. (2011). Bullying as intra-active process in neoliberals universities. *Qualitative Inquiry, 17*, 709–719.

Zapf, D., & Einarsen, S. (2005). Mobbing at work: Escalated conflicts in organizations. In S. Fox, & P. E. Spector (Eds), *Counterproductive work behavior: Investigations of actors and targets* (pp. 237–270). Washington, DC: American Psychological Association.

Zapf, D., Einarsen, S., Hoel, H., & Vartia, M. (2003). Empirical findings on bullying in the workplace. In S. Einarsen, H. Hoel, D. Zapf, & C. L. Cooper (Eds), *Bullying and emotional abuse in the workplace: International perspectives in research and practice* (pp. 104–126). London: Taylor & Francis.

Zapf, D., Escartín, J., Einarsen, S., Hoel, H., & Vartia, M. (2011). Empirical findings on prevalence and risk groups of bullying in the workplace. In S. Einarsen, H. Hoel, D. Zapf, & C. L. Cooper (Eds), *Bullying and harassment in the workplace: Developments in theory, research, and practice* (2nd ed., pp. 75–105). London: CRC Press.

Zapf, D., & Gross, C. (2001). Conflict escalation and coping with workplace bullying: A replication and extension. *European Journal of Work and Organizational Psychology, 10*, 497.

2

WORKPLACE BULLYING: DOES TENURE CHANGE ANYTHING?

The Example of a Midwestern Research University

Susan Taylor

> Academe is the perfect petri dish for the culture of mobbing.
> (Westhues, 2006b)

The issue of workplace bullying seems to be gaining momentum in the public discourse. Self-help books (Kohut, 2008; Namie & Namie, 2000; Spindel, 2008), news stories (Price, 2009; Field, 2010), and articles in trade publications (Gravois, 2006; Fogg, 2008) are becoming more common as people begin to recognize the phenomenon and are able to label and discuss their experiences. Higher education workplaces are no exception in this regard (Schmidt, 2010; Twale & DeLuca, 2008; Wilson, 2011). While news article abound with reports of faculty, staff, and students experiencing bullying, a few researchers have begun to examine how and why bullying is occurring in the academy. Westhues (2004) synthesizes multiple case studies from faculty members' self-described experiences with workplace bullying. Twale and DeLuca (2008) discuss how higher education's organizational factors have led to a culture of incivility, and Cipriano's (2011) book offers strategies for facilitating faculty collegiality.

Several unusual workplace features in higher education institutions make recognizing and addressing workplace bullying more complicated than it is in other workplaces. A major unique feature is tenure, a structural form of job security that provides protection for certain groups of faculty. The job security enjoyed by those with tenure may actually make them workplace bullying targets (Westhues, 1998). If an organization wishes to terminate a tenured faculty member, it may be easier to convince the person to leave through bullying tactics than to end employment through official processes (Westhues, 1998). Conversely, the job security enjoyed by those with tenure may serve as a factor enabling tenured faculty to bully others. If faculty members believe tenure protects them from disciplinary action, they may engage in bullying behaviors, because there are no perceived negative consequences (Salin, 2003).

Another complicating factor related to tenure is the relationship between tenure, academic freedom, and an often-used term—civil discourse. Faculty members who engage in civil but opposing discourse may be accused of bullying, or faculty members who engage in personal attacks may claim protection under academic freedom. As the American Association of University Professors (AAUP) points out, it is not always easy to distinguish a lack of collegiality from controversial academic debate. The AAUP suggests weaving expectations of collegiality throughout the performance measures for teaching, research, and service (American Association of University Professors, 2006). This practice may help with feedback to faculty members regarding the civility of their behavior, but it does not provide a mechanism for a bullied employee to seek redress. Richards and Daley (2003) discuss the importance of institutional workplace bullying policies and best-practice components of such policies.

There is not a single standard definition for workplace bullying, but most definitions have some consistent features. Part of the difficulty in development of a standard definition and standard terms is the emergence of bullying research in many different academic disciplines. For the purpose of this chapter, I used a definition similar to that described in Chapter 1 of this book, and conceptualized workplace bullying as characterized by actions. Keashly and Jagatic (2003) report that "most hostile behavior in the workplace is verbal, indirect and passive" (p. 35), and they provide a chart of example behaviors cited in other literature. These behaviors include, but are not limited to, name calling, belittling, false accusations, rumor spreading, ignoring memos or messages, deliberate exclusion, assigning work overload or taking away meaningful work, turning others against the target, public criticism, interrupting, silent treatment, withholding information or resources, and imposing unreasonable deadlines (Davenport, Schwartz, & Elliott, 1999; Keashly & Jagatic, 2003).

Research indicates that higher education organizations are at risk for fostering workplace bullying (Björkqvist, Österman, & Hjelt-Bäck, 1994; Price Spratlen, 1995; Westhues, 2002, 2004, 2005b, 2006a, 2006b), but lacks adequate exploration of this workplace's differentiating factors. Understanding how academic freedom and tenure intersect with workplace bullying experiences will help explain and address the issue in these unusual workplace environments. The purpose of this chapter is to explore how tenure in higher education institutions intersects with workplace bullying dynamics. The intersection of these factors is examined through discussion of higher education institutions as workplaces and a study of a Midwestern research university. In the study, the faculty's workplace bullying experiences and responses are analyzed through the lens of tenure, a focus that is new to the workplace bullying literature. Moreover, this chapter serves as a guide for higher education stakeholders seeking a greater understanding of how tenure plays a role in workplace bullying. First, the chapter explores tenure and academic freedom concepts, followed by a review of workplace bullying risk factors in higher education organizations. The second section of this chapter is a case study overview focusing on tenure status and its relationship to faculty workplace bullying experiences and responses. The chapter ends with recommendations for faculty, administrators, and human resources professionals.

Tenure and Academic Freedom

Tenure and academic freedom are concepts that are often misunderstood. Some believe tenure provides rule-free guaranteed lifetime jobs for faculty members, regardless of competence, performance, or behavior. Academic freedom is often viewed as the freedom to engage in trivial, nonsensical, or even abusive behavior for pay. However, the concept of tenure developed as a way to protect academic freedom. Tenure is a means to an end (Thilen, 2011) and gives faculty members the academic freedom to explore the truth and report new knowledge, with the financial security necessary for institutions to attract competent scholars.

The concept of tenure began in the early 1900s, when university presidents customarily fired faculty for having opposing social or political views or for engaging in behavior the president deemed radical (Altbach, Berdahl, & Gumport, 1999). During these years, well-respected institutions began following some common best practices, including the development of a professional professoriate (Thelin, 2011). The development of higher education teaching as a professional career included the creation of standard ranks (instructor, assistant professor, associate professor, professor), a process for promotion, and the foundations of tenure (Thelin, 2011).

In 1915, the newly formed American Association of University Professors (AAUP) drafted a statement of principles covering several issues, including academic freedom and tenure (Altbach et al., 1999). This document provided the first formal structure for tenure by outlining the steps one must take to remove a professor. The AAUP scholars recognized that knowledge expansion depended on colleges and universities tolerating a wide range of controversial views expressed by faculty members (Altbach et al., 1999). By instituting a standard process to follow for the removal of professors, the AAUP helped thwart the arbitrary removal of faculty for political or personal reasons (which would stunt the expansion of knowledge) and laid the foundations of tenure.

Work on defining tenure continued in 1925 when the American Council on Education (ACE) issued a shorter statement on academic freedom, endorsed by the Association of American Colleges (AAC). A resulting collaboration between AAC and AAUP produced the 1940 Statement of Principles on Academic Freedom and Tenure (American Association of University Professors, 2006). The 1940 Statement of Principles on Academic Freedom and Tenure describes the right of academic freedom as well as the responsibility to show respect for others' opinions and to only introduce controversial material that is relevant to the subject matter at hand.

The statement on tenure is brief: "After the expiration of a probationary period, teachers or investigators should have permanent or continuous tenure, and their service should be terminated only for adequate cause" (American Association of University Professors, 2006). The 1940 Statement (with interpretive comments added in 1970 and gendered language removed in 1990) is the one that is still used as the standard for nearly all institutions and organizations of higher education (Altbach et al., 1999).

One of the AAUP statements that is directly related to bullying and the notion of civil discourse is titled "On Collegiality as a Criterion for Faculty Evaluation" (American Association of University Professors, 2006). The statement indicates that a growing number of institutions are using collegiality as an evaluative measure distinct from teaching, scholarship, and service. The AAUP posits that a separate evaluation of collegiality threatens academic freedom, diversity, and healthy debate because it could easily be confused with an expectation of deference, harmony, or dedication, which contradicts the principles of academic freedom. The statement acknowledges that it is very difficult to distinguish "constructive engagement" from "obstructionism" (American Association of University Professors, 2006, p. 40). Though the statement acknowledges the inappropriateness of professional and ethical misconduct or personal attacks, it argues that collegiality should only be evaluated within the parameters of teaching, scholarship, and service—not as a separate construct. The charge is to incorporate collegiality as a relevant aspect of each of the three measures. The statement ends with a declaration that a "lack of collegiality" (American Association of University Professors, 2006, p. 40) should never be considered a basis for personnel decisions.

The AAUP's statement on collegiality reflects the pervasiveness of the issue in higher education, and the complexity of workplace bullying. In recent years, the tensions between collegiality and academic freedom have risen with the rise of faculty incivility (Twale & DeLuca, 2008). The concept of collegiality will almost certainly spur debate in any higher education institution. Civil debate and constructive criticism are hallmarks of higher education, but where criticism crosses the line and becomes uncivil is often left up to personal interpretation or exists in professional identities defined by critique. Faculty members whose primary work is to critique the work of their peers in the peer review process, their students in their role as instructors, and oftentimes social or political issues as public intellectuals can create a culture accepting of multiple forms of critique, which may exceed the standards of collegiality. Some would argue that academic pursuits and collegiality cannot coexist, while others would argue that a lack of collegiality hinders any pursuit. This tension is present in the structure of tenure that protects those faculty who engage in critique, and the definition of collegiality versus constructive critique may lead to forms of workplace bullying that are unique to the academy.

Organizational Factors in Higher Education

The literature indicates some workplace bullying risk factors that are features of higher education institutions, and helps to frame the relationship between tenure and bullying. The first set of factors concerns the role of organizational structure and change. Leymann's (1990) investigation of organizational risk factors for workplace bullying identifies frequently changing leadership and strict hierarchical structure as predisposing factors. When organizational and unit leadership turns over, bullying rates increase, suggesting that instability in hierarchy may lead to more overt political behaviors and less attention to collegiality. Einarsen and Skogstad (1996) also found that large and hierarchical organizations are at greater risk of workplace bullying. Large and hierarchical organizations are more fragmented and rely on chain of command.

Higher education institutions in the United States often meet the criteria described as risk factors in the literature. Some universities, particularly research institutions, are large organizations with multiple campuses, expanding missions, and diverse student populations. In addition, college and university leaders in recent years have higher turnover rates. The average tenure of college presidents has decreased and retirements are on the rise, leaving more instability in leadership and making changes in leadership ranks more frequent. In addition, hierarchical structure is often a feature of higher education administration, and it exists within the faculty through rank and tenure status, among leadership through supervisory capacity, and among multiple employment contracts across a college or university. Leymann (1996) also cites "poor organizational conditions" (p. 177) as a factor contributing to the bullying rate in universities and other overrepresented sectors in his study. Some of the poor conditions Leymann notes are helpless management, poorly organized work, and role conflict.

In the context of large, hierarchical organizations, tenure plays a distinct role that may increase the rates of bullying. Westhues (2004), who has spent a considerable amount of time on workplace mobbing, describes the world of higher education as having the perfect climate for bullying. Although Westhues acknowledges the role that individual qualities play in bullying situations, he contends that higher education's organizational factors of high job security, subjective performance measures, and conflicting goals are reasons bullying is so prominent in this sector. Each of these areas is represented in the literature and relates to tenure.

High job security is a factor connected to tenure; faculty members with tenure are difficult to dismiss, so those who wish to see them leave may resort to bullying tactics until the faculty member decides to leave on his or her own. Or, those tenured faculty bullies are often difficult to fire, since bullying is not illegal and does not fall under the federal protected categories (see Chapter 6 in this book). Human resources departments are often left with mediation and other techniques to try and manage a tenured faculty bully (see Chapter 8 in this book).

Subjective performance measures pose a bullying risk for higher education institutions and are also related to tenure. Such measures are inherent in faculty evaluations used to make tenure decisions, particularly in the areas of teaching and service. Faculty tenure dossiers, for example, may rely on student evaluations that are subjective measures of the quality of a faculty member's teaching. The AAUP's suggestion to measure collegiality within the parameters of teaching, research, and service adds another subjective layer. Conflicting goals are related to the tenure process in higher education. Faculty members on a tenure-track must balance teaching, scholarship, and service in ways that will prove favorable as they pursue tenure. Several of the higher education organizational risk factors are related to tenure. The existence of tenure may actually contribute to management's helplessness, as it can be difficult for supervisors to deal with tenured faculty members' performance issues (Raelin, 2003; Tornyay, 1985).

Another relationship between bullying and tenure is found in the increasingly competitive nature of faculty work. In a Finnish study (Björkqvist et al., 1994) of university employees, respondents cited their perceived reasons for being targeted by bullies. The top four (of nine) reasons were envy, competition for positions, the aggressor being uncertain about themselves, and competition for status. One could argue that all of these reasons easily relate to tenure status. Faculty members may see themselves as competing for increasingly rare tenured positions and the status of rank and tenure, and they may feel threatened by colleagues' superiority. In fact, Vartia (1996) and Zapf (1999) cite envy and competition as commonly perceived reasons for bullying, as does Westhues (2004, 2005a) in his collection of university bullying stories. The previous studies cite factors related to tenure, but do not examine tenure itself as a variable affecting the experience of being bullied and a faculty member's responses to such experiences. The following study examined tenure and its role in faculty members' experiences and responses as bullied targets.

The Case of a Midwestern Research University

In 2010, faculty members at a Midwestern research university responded to a survey about their experiences and perceptions as bullied targets and bullying witnesses (Taylor, 2012a). The survey was part of a dissertation study described in this chapter as the case of a Midwestern research university. Unpublished quotes from some of the respondents are included in this chapter (Taylor, 2012b).

In the survey, respondents indicated their exposure to bullying behaviors, their target status (bullied or not bullied), and the likelihood they would exhibit specific behaviors in response to dissatisfaction with the workplace environment. The survey ended with an optional, open-ended comments section. The results revealed relationships between faculty members' tenure status, their workplace bullying experiences, and behavioral responses to dissatisfaction. Open-ended comments such as "I have been publicly humiliated in my workplace, something I never thought possible, especially at an academic institution" (Taylor, 2012b) provide rich detail on the respondents' perceptions.

The study participants were 1,034 full-time faculty members who responded to an invitation to complete an online survey about their workplace experiences. More than half of the respondents were tenured, about 18% were on a tenure track, and about 19% were not on a tenure-track. The percentage of faculty respondents in each tenure status group mirrored the percentage of faculty in each respective group university-wide.

Respondents answered questions about exposure to 22 specific behaviors from the Negative Acts Questionnaire—Revised (NAQ-R) by indicating the frequency with which they were targeted with each behavior (Einarsen & Hoel, 2001). The behaviors were not labeled as bullying behaviors and included items that were work-related, person-related, or constituted intimidation or abuse. Some examples of the behaviors listed in the survey are "excessive monitoring of your work," "someone withholding information which affects your performance," "spreading of gossip and rumors about you," "being shouted at," and "intimidating behaviors such as finger-pointing, invasion of personal space, shoving or blocking your way" (Einarsen & Hoel, 2001). Response options ranged from "never" to "daily" (Einarsen & Hoel, 2001). After indicating the frequency of being targeted by the specific behaviors, respondents answered a single question asking whether they are bullied at work, given a definition of workplace bullying (Einarsen & Hoel, 2001).

Respondents answered questions about workplace dissatisfaction by indicating the likelihood they would exhibit behaviors from five scales representing five different types of dissatisfaction responses. The Exit, Voice, Loyalty, Neglect, and Cynicism scales include behaviors such as the Exit item "intend to change employers," the Voice item "in work meetings express your point of view to suggest improvements," the Loyalty item "trust the decision making process of the organization without your interference," the Neglect item "report sick because you do not feel like working," and the Cynicism item "talk to your colleagues about management's incompetence" (Hirschman, 1970; Naus, van Iterson, & Roe, 2007; Rusbult, Farrell, Rogers, & Mainous, 1998). Response options ranged from "definitely not" to "definitely" (Naus et al., 2007) on a seven-point scale.

Results

In data analysis, respondents were categorized as bullied or not bullied based on their answers to the single-item question asking whether they were bullied, according to a provided definition. Approximately 12% (n = 123) of the faculty indicated they were targets of bullying behaviors during the six months prior to the survey. Data analysis of the frequency with which respondents were targeted with the 22 specific behaviors revealed there was a significant difference in the exposure to the behaviors between those who labeled themselves as bullied and those who did not. Those who labeled themselves as bullied reported a significantly greater frequency of being targeted by the behaviors, although the behaviors were not identified on the survey as bullying behaviors.

Three of the survey items pertained to physical intimidation or aggression. A disturbing result of the survey is that 269 faculty members reported having been targeted by at least one of the three physically intimidating or aggressive behaviors. Of these 269 respondents, 13 of them indicated experiencing the item "threats of violence or physical abuse or actual abuse" (Einarsen & Hoel, 2001). One survey respondent noted, "[I] observed an individual threaten the lives of some of my colleagues" (Taylor, 2012b).

The Relationship of Tenure Status and Being Bullied

Analysis of the variables revealed that tenure status made a significant difference in the faculty members' experience of being bullied. While tenure status was not significantly related to whether a faculty member was targeted, it was significantly related to the frequency of exposure to the specific bullying behaviors, which is expressed as the NAQ-R score.

The overall mean NAQ-R score was 6.45. Comparing the tenure status groups, the non-tenure-track faculty had the highest mean NAQ-R score (7.33), significantly higher than the tenure-track faculty. Non-tenure-track faculty members may feel they have no power to address the situation. One non-tenure-track respondent added the comment, "I feel trapped and powerless" (Taylor, 2012b).

The tenured faculty had the second-highest mean NAQ-R score (6.63), also significantly higher than the tenure-track faculty. This finding supports Westhues's contention that "even tenured professors are ganged up on, humiliated" (2002, p. 30). One might assume that tenured faculty members are untouchable, but Westhues argues this is the very reason they are targeted. If others want to see a tenured faculty leave the institution, the most effective way may be to bully the person until he or she decides to leave. In addition, research described earlier in this chapter cites envy as a key motivator for bullying. It is not hard to imagine that others might envy the job security and status enjoyed by tenured faculty.

Tenure-track faculty had the lowest NAQ-R mean score (4.71). One might rationalize that these faculty members are not as powerless as the non-tenure-track faculty, making others less likely to bully them than the non-tenure-track colleagues. In comparison to tenured faculty, tenure-track faculty can be eliminated through official processes more easily, making others more likely to remove them through official means rather than by bullying them until they leave on their own.

The Relationship of Tenure Status and Responses to Dissatisfaction

Respondents indicated the likelihood they would engage in behaviors from five scales representing different types of workplace dissatisfaction response behaviors. The Exit, Voice, Loyalty, Neglect, and Cynicism (EVLNC) scales include behaviors representing the types of behaviors described by the name of each scale (Hirschman, 1970; Naus et al., 2007; Rusbult et al., 1998).

A high percentage of the faculty members who were bullied indicated that the experience bothered them, with over half of the bullied faculty indicating it bothered them a great deal. This study found that there is a significant difference between the bullied and not bullied faculty members' workplace dissatisfaction responses on all five scales. The study also found that tenure status is related to the expression of Exit behaviors. Tenure status was not significantly related to the other four types of response behaviors.

Those who exhibit Exit behaviors express dissatisfaction by leaving or planning to leave the organization. Intent to leave an organization is considered a psychological exit, though the actual separation has not yet occurred (Naus et al., 2007). One respondent's open-ended comment illustrates the Exit dissatisfaction response. "I am an associate professor. I have to deal with a full professor on a regular basis who is rude, unprofessional, and a bully. It is appalling to me that he can get away with this behavior. I would gladly take another job if I could find one. I am looking" (Taylor, 2012b). A faculty member's target status (bullied or not bullied) made a significant difference in whether or not the respondent exhibited Exit behaviors. The overall mean Exit score was 13.40 for all respondents. The bullied faculty's mean Exit score was 17.15, significantly higher than the faculty who were not bullied, whose mean score was 12.90.

After controlling for the faculty's NAQ-R score, a faculty member's tenure status significantly improved the prediction of Exit behaviors. In other words, the experience of having been bullied predicts whether a faculty member will leave, and tenure status significantly adds to the predictive power for the Exit response. Not surprisingly, the lower the tenure status, the more likely the faculty member will leave the organization.

The tenured faculty members are the most likely to stay, and the non-tenure-track faculty members are the most likely to leave. It is interesting that tenured faculty members are bullied to a greater degree than tenure-track faculty, but the tenured are significantly more likely to stay with the institution, even if they are bullied. One tenured respondent described the situation with the comment, "After 37 years, I am nearing retirement and therefore it would be silly of me to seek to change employers, change jobs, etc. However, I often felt like trying to change jobs" (Taylor, 2012b).

Although the other four types of response behavior were not significantly related to tenure status, the results are interesting as they relate to the bullied and not-bullied faculty. Faculty members who are bullied are significantly less likely to exhibit Voice and Loyalty behaviors, and they are significantly more likely to exhibit Exit, Neglect, and Cynicism behaviors.

Through Voice behaviors, the individual voices discontent by suggesting solutions for positive change (Hirschman, 1970). Voice behaviors represent active attempts to improve the situation, such as this respondent's self-reported behavior: "I am senior faculty and have learned enough lessons over time to make me want to actively intervene if someone is treated unfairly, but also to find a kind way to accomplish that goal" (Taylor, 2012b).

Target status (bullied or not bullied) made a difference in whether faculty exhibited Voice behaviors. The overall mean Voice scale score was 24.78. The bullied faculty had a mean score of 23.47, significantly lower than the 24.99 mean score for those who were not bullied. In other words, the bullied faculty is significantly less likely to make positive suggestions for change.

When individuals exhibit Loyalty behaviors, they respond to dissatisfaction by staying with and contributing to the organization while optimistically and passively waiting for change from leaders they believe in (Hirschman, 1970). One respondent indicated loyalty behaviors with the comment, "My boss has done a good job of managing the financial crisis in a way that maintains as much as possible the dignity of everyone. I like working here" (Taylor, 2012b).

The mean Loyalty score was 13.53 for all faculty members. Bullied faculty had a 10.92 mean score, significantly lower than the not-bullied faculty's mean score of 13.94. In other words, those who are bullied are less likely to have faith in the organizational leaders' ability to make positive change.

Those who exhibit Neglect behaviors tend to stay with the organization, but they become disengaged, no longer actively contributing to the welfare of the organization (Rusbult et al., 1988). The individual ceases to perform as expected; may have high rates of tardiness, absenteeism, and errors; and no longer cares about the organization (Naus et al., 2007).

One respondent illustrated Neglect behaviors with the comment, "[I have a] lack of confidence in my immediate administration . . . [I am] apathetic about [the] future of [my] department/college" and another respondent commented, "Faculty meetings are indescribably unpleasant. Fortunately, in my department you can just skip them" (Taylor, 2012b). The mean Neglect score was 9.41 for all of the study's respondents. The bullied faculty had a Neglect score (10.30) significantly higher than the not-bullied faculty (9.29). This result indicates that bullied faculty members are significantly more likely to neglect professional duties than are those who are not bullied.

The Cynicism response involves an actively negative attitude toward the organization, but the cynical employee also cares about the organization. The individual no longer believes in the integrity of the organization and may withhold suggestions (believing they will not be heard) or talk negatively about the organization or management. A non-tenure-track respondent illustrated this type of response with the following comment: "I believe that chairs at the [institution] have way too much power to determine the well being of individual faculty members, whether it is salaries, honors, etc. They are distant, unapproachable, incompetent and overpaid for the little they are doing" (Taylor, 2012b). Target status was significantly related to whether a faculty member exhibited Cynicism behaviors. The bullied faculty had a mean Cynicism score of 18.47, significantly higher than the 15.58 mean score for those who were not bullied. The mean was 15.97 for all respondents.

Discussion of Findings

Workplace bullying in higher education settings is a longstanding problem with a short history of research. Failure to address this problem results in serious negative effects for individuals and their employers (Arehart-Treichel, 2006; Brodsky, 1976; Kivimäki et al., 2003; Leymann & Gustafsson, 1996). There is a compelling need for higher education leaders and employees to recognize, address, and prevent this problem. Measures to address the problem are best informed by knowledge gained from research tailored to the higher education work environment.

The research study described in this chapter provides some insight on how tenure status is related to workplace bullying experiences and targets' responses. Previous literature and other chapters in this book are clear about the negative individual and organizational effects of workplace bullying. Bullied employees are more likely to suffer negative health effects, which impact the individual and the organization (Glendinning, 2001; MacIntosh, 2005; Niedl, 1996; Zapf & Einarsen, 2001). An organization that allows workplace bullying does so at its own risk, including negative financial impacts and decreased productivity (Johnson & Indvik, 2001; Rayner & Cooper, 1997). One survey respondent recognized its impact on the study institution with the comment, "Nothing is being done about it and it impacts productivity greatly" (Taylor, 2012b).

The study described in this chapter reveals that a tenured faculty member is not as likely as other faculty to leave the employer, even if they are bullied targets. This finding has implications for higher education institutions as employers. Bullied faculty members are more likely to stay, meaning the organization may employ an unhealthy workforce and be at greater risk for negative health effects, absenteeism, and decreased productivity. Another concern is the potential escalation of bullying to violence. If bullied faculty members stay with an institution because of tenure status, and the bullying continues, escalation into workplace violence, though rare, is an understandable concern. In the study described in this chapter, over one-fourth of the respondents indicated they were on the receiving end of physical intimidation, verbal threats, and abuse.

In this study, tenure status was significantly related to the faculty's Exit behaviors, but tenure status was not significantly related to the other four types of response behaviors. Bullied faculty members were found to be more likely to Exit (leave) the institution than those who were not bullied. Glendinnig (2001) asserts that organizations allowing workplace bullying effectively lose the best faculty and keep the most uncivil. If faculty members are targeted out of envy (Westhues, 2005a), this outcome seems likely. Bullied faculty members also reported a greater tendency to exhibit Neglect and Cynicism behaviors than do those who are not bullied. One could assume that higher education institutions would not want 12% of the faculty neglecting professional duties and actively criticizing leadership. If workplace bullying is tolerated, some bullied faculty members, particularly those with tenure, will stay with the organization and exhibit such behaviors.

Some faculty members respond to organizational issues with Voice behaviors, such as making positive problem-solving suggestions. Bullied faculty members in this study were less likely to exhibit Voice behaviors than were the faculty who were not bullied. The bullied faculty was also less likely to exhibit Loyalty behaviors, such as believing in leadership's ability to make positive change. If the bullied faculty does not offer ideas and does not believe that others can provide competent leadership, they will fail to contribute their talents toward institutional improvement and positive change. The omission of these positive behaviors, coupled with the exhibition of the negative behaviors described above, creates a stagnant and unpleasant work environment.

Another significant finding of this study concerns non-tenure-track faculty. This study shows that non-tenure-track faculty members are the most-targeted group. The non-tenure-track faculty members were also the most likely to leave the organization. Institutions relying on non-tenure-track faculty and allowing workplace bullying may develop an unhealthy and revolving workforce. The practice of hiring the lowest-paid employees in order to balance the budget may negatively affect the budget in terms of absenteeism, lowered efficiency, and increased hiring costs from turnover.

There have been very few workplace bullying studies of colleges and universities. The few studies on higher education workplace bullying lack focus on employment factors such as tenure. Other studies have documented the negative individual and organizational effects of workplace bullying and the increased likelihood that bullied employees leave their workplaces. The study results described in this chapter indicate that tenured faculty members tend to remain even if they are bullied. In addition, bullied faculty members (of any tenure status) tend to exhibit undesirable response behaviors and not to exhibit desirable ones. Higher education institutions failing to address workplace bullying do so at their own peril.

Recommendations

Recommendations on how to address workplace bullying in a higher education setting include both formal and informal processes. Informal collective action by faculty peers helps shape the culture of the unit or institution. Formal processes provide structure for addressing and preventing workplace bullying and, if enforced, will also help shape the culture. The following recommendations may be helpful for the specified stakeholder groups.

Recommendations for Faculty

It would serve faculty members well to educate themselves about workplace bullying. Understanding the difference between congenial debate, conflict, and bullying is crucial as faculty members sort out how to respond to situations at work. For example, debate may involve passionate differences in opinion, but the expression of these differences remains civil. Properly labeling and recognizing the behavior is a first step toward resolution. Faculty may consider reading the AAUP statements on "On Collegiality as a Criterion for Faculty Evaluation" and other definitions of workplace bullying in order to identify and possibly modify behaviors in the workplace.

Moreover, Twale and DeLuca (2008) point out that in preparation for academic careers, future faculty members are not educated about civility. In order to understand higher education culture, they recommend that new faculty become students of higher education. Many faculty members believe that the time they have spent as students of their discipline equates with being students of higher education. Observing and reading about how higher education functions as a system and on an organizational level goes a long way toward avoiding frustration from unexpected circumstances and processes. Having such an understanding may help individual faculty members moderate their own behavior in situations they might not have otherwise understood. In addition to monitoring their own behavior, informally pointing out the unacceptable behavior of others helps define the cultural rules (Tierney, 1997). Allowing any faculty member to exhibit bullying behavior trains new faculty and graduate students to perpetuate the bully culture (Twale & DeLuca, 2008).

Recommendations for Administrators (Chairs, Deans, and Top-Level Leaders)

The faculty recommendations apply to administrators as well, but administrators have additional responsibilities. Administrators have the formal responsibility to respond to performance issues and the informal responsibility to model professional conduct. Responses to faculty bullying situations must be based on a clear understanding of workplace bullying, academic freedom, and tenure, as well as institutional policies and procedures. Administrators may not have received any training on these concepts or processes before assuming their leadership roles. For example, they may not realize that the AAUP's guidelines on collegiality as an evaluation factor state that a lack of collegiality should never be used as a separate basis for personnel decisions. However, the statement also asserts that "malfeasance," "professional misconduct," or "efforts to obstruct the ability of colleagues to carry out their normal functions, to engage in personal attacks, or to violate ethical standards" (American Association of University Professors, 2006, p. 40) are legitimate personnel issues worthy of investigation and evaluation.

Supervisors could increase their own and their faculty's awareness of applicable policies and procedures by inviting a human resources administrator to discuss them at a faculty meeting. Several of the narrative comments in the study described in this chapter revealed that the respondents had no awareness of relevant institutional policies or resources, though the institution studied has several in place (Taylor, 2012b).

Top-level administrators, such as presidents, provosts, and vice presidents, have responsibility for employees and the institution. These leaders can show leadership through policy development, education and training, communication, and having the courage to take action in bullying situations. Leaders help shape the social and cultural structure of the institution (Twale & DeLuca, 2008). If the institution does not have a policy addressing workplace bullying, or if the existing policy is ineffective, a top-level decision to develop or improve the policy gives credence to the issue. Higher education institutions likely have a student code of conduct, but an employee code of conduct is equally important. If expectations are clearly communicated at the onset of employment, it is much easier to prevent problems and to address issues as they arise.

Another way administrators may increase awareness and prevent problems is through a civility campaign. Such a campaign may serve to make all university community members more aware of their own behavior, and may encourage self-monitoring by individuals and groups. Leaders can also shape opportunities available for faculty members. Sheehan and Jordan (2003) suggest that leadership-training opportunities incorporate education about workplace bullying and options for addressing problems.

From a logistical perspective, campus administrators can affect the infrastructure relevant to workplace bullying complaints and resolution. Faculty may take bullying complaints to human resources, the affirmative action/equal employment opportunity office, or the faculty union. Multiple reporting sites may cause confusion and hinder data collection for monitoring policy effectiveness. Dziech and Weiner (1990) recommend a confidential hotline as a central contact point for workplace bullying complaints. Campus administrators can create such an infrastructure, perhaps with an outside vendor to ensure confidentiality. Although this model likely requires resources, it gives the message that top-level leaders take the issue seriously.

Recommendations for Human Resources

Faculty who are bullied, who witness bullying, or who supervise perpetrators or targets will likely turn to human resources at some point in the process for help. While human resources leaders likely have a basic understanding of employment law, those in higher education workplaces also need to be students of tenure and academic freedom concepts and how they relate to employment law (see Chapter 6 in this book). Access to legal counsel from an attorney with special expertise in these issues will help provide credible options.

Every human resources professional should have access to the AAUP's Redbook. In addition to the aforementioned statements, the Redbook and/or the AAUP website also include helpful summaries on topics such as "Ensuring Academic Freedom in Politically Controversial Academic Personnel Decisions" (American Association of University Professors, 2011). Understanding the AAUP's position on such issues will help human resources professionals move forward with personnel decisions. For example, the AAUP does not recommend evaluating collegiality or civility as a separate measure because of the dangers to academic freedom, but it acknowledges the role that behavior may play in evaluating effective teaching, research, and scholarship.

Higher education institutions today are likely to have sexual harassment policies, but few have general harassment or bullying policies (Twale & DeLuca, 2008). It is difficult to address bullying behavior without a policy in place. Higher education institutions should not only have policies, they should be effective, enforced, and shared with all employees. The development, implementation, and monitoring of effective workplace bullying policies are addressed by Richards and Daly (2003). In addition to policy development, the human resources office should be involved in data collection regarding the number and type of bullying complaints and periodic assessment of the policy's effectiveness. This may be done with or without access to identifying information. For example, if the institution elects to channel all reports to an outside vendor for the sake of confidentiality and anonymity, the vendor may provide data to the human resources office without identifying the personnel involved in the complaints.

Human resources professionals may also assume responsibility for increasing awareness of policies and procedures related to workplace bullying and for training employees at all levels. Training for all employees ideally includes information needed to identify and respond to workplace bullying, as well as the consequences of failing to address the issue. Administrators would benefit from additional training regarding institutional policies, legal issues, and options for addressing personnel issues within the parameters of academic freedom and tenure. Training may also be offered for faculty members involved in bullying situations. Twale and

DeLuca (2008) suggest sensitivity training for faculty perpetrators, and Hannabus (1998) suggests conflict management training for perpetrators and assertiveness training for bullied targets.

A survey respondent commented, "I find the University Human Resources dealings with harassment to be very weak and more concerned with covering up the problem than finding long-term solutions in departments with chronic problems" (Taylor, 2012b). Complaints of workplace bullying should be taken seriously and responded to quickly (Ferris, 2004). An early and appropriate response is critical to the healing of the target and a positive outcome for the individual and the organization (Ferris, 2004; Twale & DeLuca, 2008). The human resources office should have a formal process in place for investigating complaints (Merchant & Hoel, 2003), including referrals for the target to seek immediate assistance. Referrals may be to other university offices (such as counseling) or to outside resources, such as providers in an employee assistance program.

References

Altbach, P., Berdahl, R., & Gumport, P. (1999). *American higher education in the twenty-first century*. Baltimore: The Johns Hopkins University Press.

American Association of University Professors. (2006). *Policy documents and reports*. Baltimore: Johns Hopkins University Press.

American Association of University Professors. (2011). Ensuring academic freedom in politically controversial academic personnel decisions. Retrieved from http://www. aaup.org/AAUP/comm/rep/A/ensuring.htm

Arehart-Treichel, O. (2006). Workplace bullying overlooked as cause of severe stress. *Psychiatric News, 41*(14), 20.

Björkqvist, K., Österman, K., & Hjelt-Bäck. (1994). Aggression among university employees. *Aggressive Behavior, 20*(3), 173–184.

Brodsky, C. (1976). *The harassed worker*. Lexington, MA: D.C. Heath and Company.

Cipriano, R., (2011). *Facilitating a collegial department in higher education*. San Francisco, CA: Jossey-Bass.

Davenport, N., Schwartz, R.D., & Elliott, G.P. (1999). *Mobbing: emotional abuse in the American workplace*. Ames, IA: Civil Society Publishing.

Dziech, B., & Weiner, L. (1990). *The lecherous professor* (2nd ed.). Urbana: University of Illinois Press.

Einarsen, S., & Hoel, H. (2001). Negative Acts Questionnaire—Revised. Obtained with permission from the Bergen Bullying Group, November 7, 2006.

Einarsen, S., & Skogstad, A. (1996). Bullying at work: Epidemiological findings in public and private organizations. *European Journal of Work & Organizational Psychology, 5*(2), 185–202.

Ferris, P. (2004). A preliminary typology of organisational responses to allegations of workplace bullying: See no evil, hear no evil, speak no evil. *British Journal of Guidance & Counseling, 32*(3), 389–395.

Field, E. (2010, February 12). Employers have failed to help victims of workplace bullying. *Sydney Morning Herald*. Retrieved from www.smh.com.au/opinion/society-and-culture/employers-have-failed-to-help-victims-of-workplace-bullying-20100211-nuzt.html

Fogg, P. (2008, September 12). Academic bullies. *The Chronicle of Higher Education*. Retrieved from www.chronicle.com/article/Academic-Bullies/2321

Glendinning, P. (2001). Workplace bullying: Curing the cancer of the American workplace. *Public Personnel Management, 30*(3), 269–286.

Gravois, J. (2006, April 14). Mob rule. *The Chronicle of Higher Education*. Retrieved from www.chronicle.com/article/Mob-Rule/36004

Hannabus, S. (1998). Bullying at work. *Library Management, 19*, 304–310.

Hirschman, A.O. (1970). *Exit, voice and loyalty: responses to decline in firms, organizations, and states.* Cambridge, MA: Harvard University Press.

Johnson, P., & Indvik, J. (2001). Slings and arrows of rudeness: incivility in the workplace. *Journal of Management Development, 20*(8), 705–713.

Keashly, L., & Jagatic, K. (2003). By any other name: American perspectives on workplace bullying. In S. Einarsen, H. Hoel, D. Zapf, & C. Cooper (Eds), *Bullying and emotional abuse in the workplace: International perspectives in research and practice*. London: Taylor & Francis.

Kivimäki, M., Virtanen, M., Vartia, M., Elovainio, M., Vahtera, J., & Keltikangas-Järvinen, L. (2003). Workplace bullying and the risk of cardiovascular disease and depression. *Occupational Environmental Medicine, 60*, 779–783.

Kohut, M. (2008). *The complete guide to understanding, controlling and stopping bullies and bullying at work: A complete guide for managers, supervisors and co-workers.* Ocala, FL: Atlantic Publishing Group.

Leymann, H. (1990). Mobbing and psychological terror at workplaces. *Violence and Victims, 5*, 119–126.

Leymann, H. (1996). The content and development of mobbing at work. *European Journal of Work & Organizational Psychology, 5*(2), 165–184.

Leymann, H., & Gustafsson, A. (1996). Mobbing at work and the development of post-traumatic stress disorders. *European Journal of Work & Organizational Psychology, 5*, 251–275.

MacIntosh, J. (2005). Experiences of workplace bullying in a rural area. *Issues in Mental Health Nursing, 26*(9), 893–910.

Merchant, V., & Hoel, H. (2003). Investigating complaints of bullying. In S. Einarsen, H. Hoel, D. Zapf, & C. Cooper (Eds), *Bullying and emotional abuse in the workplace: international perspectives in research and practice*. London: Taylor & Francis.

Namie, G., & Namie, R. (2000). *The bully at work: What you can do to stop the hurt and reclaim your dignity on the job*. Naperville, IL: Sourcebooks.

Naus, F., van Iterson, A., & Roe, R. (2007). Organizational cynicism: Extending the exit, voice, loyalty, and neglect model of employees' responses to adverse conditions in the workplace. *Human Relations, 60*(5), 683–718.

Niedl, K. (1996). Mobbing and well-being: Economic and personnel development implications. *European Journal of Work & Organizational Psychology, 5*(2), 239–249.

Price, D. (2009, August 10). Trial by FBI investigation. *Counterpunch*. Retrieved from www.counterpunch.org/price8102009.html

Price Spratlen, L. (1995). Interpersonal conflict which includes mistreatment in a university workplace. *Violence and Victims, 10*(4), 285–296.

Raelin, J. (2003). Should faculty be managed? *Academe, 89*(3), 40–44.

Rayner, C., & Cooper, C. (1997). Workplace bullying: Myth or reality—can we afford to ignore it? *Leadership & Organisational Development Journal, 18*(4), 211–214.

Richards, J., & Daley, H. (2003). Bullying policy: development, implementation and monitoring. In S. Einarsen, H. Hoel, D. Zapf, & C. Cooper (Eds), *Bullying and emotional abuse in the workplace: international perspectives in research and practice* (pp. 247–258). London: Taylor & Francis.

Rusbult, C., Farrell, D., Rogers, G., & Mainous III, A. (1988). Impact of change variables on exit, voice, loyalty and neglect: An integrative model of responses to declining job satisfaction. *Academy of Management Journal, 31*(3), 599–627.

Salin, D. (2003). Ways of explaining workplace bullying: A review of enabling, motivating and precipitating structures and processes in the work environment. *Human Relations, 56*(10), 1213–1232.

Schmidt, P. (2010, June 8). Workplace mediators seek a role in taming faculty bullies. *The Chronicle of Higher Education.* Retrieved from http://chronicle.com/article/Workplace-Mediators-Seek-a/65815

Sheehan, M., & Jordan, P. (2003). Bullying, emotions, and the learning organization. In S. Einarsen, H. Hoel, D. Zapf, & C. Cooper (Eds), *Bullying and emotional abuse in the workplace: International perspectives in research and practice.* London: Taylor & Francis.

Spindel, P. (2008). *Psychological warfare at work: How harassers and bullies injure individuals and organizations.* Toronto: Spindel & Associates.

Taylor, S. (2012a). *Workplace bullying in higher education: Faculty experiences and responses.* Available from ProQuest Dissertations and Theses database. (UMI No. pending.)

Taylor, S. (2012b). [Citations from doctoral dissertation]. Unpublished raw data.

Thilen, J. (2011). *A history of American higher education.* Baltimore: The Johns Hopkins University Press.

Tierney, W. (1997). Organizational socialization in higher education. *Journal of Higher Education, 68,* 1–16.

Tornyay, R. (1985). Dealing with tenured faculty. *Journal of Professional Nursing, 1*(1), 9–13.

Twale, D., & DeLuca, B. (2008). *Faculty incivility: The rise of the academic bully culture and what to do about it.* San Francisco: Jossey-Bass.

Vartia, M. (1996). The sources of bullying—Psychological work environment and organizational climate. *European Journal of Work & Organizational Psychology, 5*(2), 203–214.

Westhues, K. (1998). *Eliminating professors: a guide to the dismissal process.* Queenston, Ontario: Kempner Collegium Publications.

Westhues, K. (2002). At the mercy of the mob: a summary of research on workplace bullying. *Occupational Health and Safety Canada, 18*(8), 30–36.

Westhues, K. (2004). *Workplace mobbing in academe: reports from twenty universities.* Lewiston, Queenston, Lampeter: The Edwin Mellen Press.

Westhues, K. (2005a). *The envy of excellence.* Lewiston, NY: Mellen Press.

Westhues, K (2005b). *Winning, losing and moving on.* Lewiston, NY: Mellen Press.

Westhues, K. (2006a). *Remedy and prevention of mobbing in higher education* Lewiston, NY: Mellen Press.

Westhues, K. (2006b). The mobs of academe, colloquy. *The Chronicle of Higher Education.* Retrieved from http://chronicle.com/colloquy/2006/04/mobbing/

Wilson, R. (2011, August 8). Documentary delves into a suicide and allegations of workplace bullying. *The Chronicle of Higher Education.* Retrieved from http://chronicle.com/article/Documentary-Delves-Into-a/128555

Zapf, D. (1999). Organisational, work group related and personal causes of mobbing/bullying at work. *International Journal of Manpower, 20*(1/2), 70–85.

Zapf, D., & Einarsen, S. (2001). Bullying in the workplace: recent trends in research and practice. *European Journal of Work & Organizational Psychology, 10,* 369–374.

3

SEXUAL HARASSMENT, RACIST JOKES, AND HOMOPHOBIC SLURS

When Bullies Target Identity Groups

Margaret W. Sallee and Crystal R. Diaz

Bullying is a trending headline that streams across media tickers and receives frequent attention in the national news. There are countless tragic stories linked to youth being singled out, such as the brutal murder of Matthew Shepard in October 1998 near Laramie, Wyoming. More recently, a Rutgers University student committed suicide in September 2010 after his roommate posted a video on the internet of him having sex with another man. Even more recently, in November 2011, 10-year-old Ashlynn Conner was found hanging in her closet, reportedly having committed suicide after she was teased by other girls for having a boy's haircut. As these examples suggest, bullying has become a significant social problem, but much of this attention has been focused on the experiences of youth (Roscigno, Lopez, & Hodson, 2009). Though there has been significant attention to the harassment and bullying experiences of youth, only recently has bullying among adults in the workplace received attention in the academic literature and national press. Even further, while there has been increasing attention on workplace bullying, there has been limited attention to workplace bullying among different identity groups.

This lack of attention is somewhat surprising given that some identity characteristics are protected under federal law. Characteristics protected against discrimination include "race, color, religion, sex, national origin, age, physical or mental handicap" (Solis, 2010, para. 7). In other words, it is illegal to target someone based upon his or her race or gender. Even the elderly are protected under federal law. However, sexual identity is excluded from this list of federally protected classes, leaving the LGBTQ (Lesbian, Gay, Bisexual, Transgender, Queer, or Questioning) community without legal protection from workplace bullying based upon sexual or gender identity. The illegal behaviors cited in Title VII, federal legislation pertaining to the workplace, include harassment based on any of the previously listed characteristics, retaliation against any employee filing a discrimination complaint, employment decisions based on any assumptions or stereotypes of abilities, and denying employment to anyone married to someone of a particular race, religion, national origin, or disability (Solis, 2010). We draw attention to these disparities to underscore the fact that some bullying behaviors are not protected under the law, which has implications for the frequency and tolerance of discrimination for the LGBTQ community. (For a more detailed discussion of the legal issues linked to bullying behaviors, see Chapter 6.)

In this chapter, we consider the bullying experiences of various identity groups, focusing specifically on gender, race, and ethnicity, and sexuality. In particular, we argue that academic culture facilitates the marginalization of particular social identity groups and that this marginalization is a reason for higher rates of bullying among gender, racial and ethnic, and sexual identity minorities in academe. We begin this chapter by discussing the literature on the types of bullying directed toward minority social identity groups. Given that organizational context plays a significant role in shaping the degree to which bullying is tolerated, we next discuss how academia creates an organizational culture that might facilitate some types of bullying over others. We conclude the chapter by offering a set of suggestions for faculty, administrators, and other practitioners interested in creating and fostering a nonhostile work environment for all.

Bullying Across Identity Groups

Though a single definition of workplace bullying does not exist, scholars tend to agree that workplace bullying is defined by a continuous pattern of unwarranted mistreatment toward a co-worker that causes psychological or emotional harm to the victim (Einarsen, Hoel, Zapf, & Cooper, 2003; Leymann, 1990; Roscigno, Lopez, & Hodson, 2009). For a more comprehensive discussion of the definition of bullying, (please see Chapter 1). Bullying occurs in different forms and can be enacted by a number of different individuals. Supervisors can bully subordinates; coworkers can bully co-workers; in some cases, subordinates can even bully their superiors (Hoel, Cooper, & Faragher, 2001; Keashly & Neuman, 2010; Lewis & Gunn, 2007; McKay, Arnold, Fratzl, & Thomas, 2008). But how do these behaviors vary, based on an individual's social identity? How do women and men experience bullying differently? How does racial and ethnic identity shape bullying experiences? How do the experiences of sexual minorities differ from those of their straight peers? In this section, we consider how bullying varies based on gender, race, and ethnicity, and sexuality. In particular, we discuss different rates of bullying experienced by various groups, the types of bullying, and those who are most likely to perpetrate bullying. We focus our discussion on the literature that considers bullying by social identity in settings typically outside of higher education. There are limited studies that consider bullying by social identity in business settings and virtually none that focus on higher education. As such, we use the literature from other settings to consider some of the issues faced by gender, racial, and sexual minorities. Although we treat our discussions of various identities as mutually exclusive groups (women, African Americans, lesbians, and so forth), every individual is composed of multiple identities. An African American lesbian could be bullied due to her race, her gender, her sexuality, or some intersection of those identities. We try to engage with these intersections throughout our discussion, but we encourage the reader to keep these intersections in mind as we discuss the experiences of these perhaps artificially discrete groups.

Gender

A number of studies have concluded that women are more likely than men to be bullied (Hoel & Cooper, 2001; Hoel et al., 2001; Lewis & Gunn, 2007; Salin, 2003). For example, in their study of 247 individuals in the UK, Lewis and Gunn (2007) found that 24% of women had been bullied, compared with 17% of men. Their numbers were somewhat higher than some other studies, such as Salin's (2003) study of 385 individuals in Sweden, in which 11.6% of female respondents reported being bullied, compared with just 5% of men. In a somewhat larger study of 5,288 individuals in the UK, Hoel and Cooper (2001) found that 11.4% of women compared with 9.9% men reported being bullied in the previous six months. When the time period was extended to include bullying experienced in the previous five years, 27% of women versus 22% of men reported being bullied. Though there is a wide variation in the percentages of individuals who report being bullied, the studies tend to underscore the fact that women are more likely to experience bullying than are their male counterparts.

It should also be noted that gender is not a discrete identity of simply man or woman, or those born as a boy or a girl. A small proportion of the population identifies as transgender and may have transitioned—or be in the process of transitioning—from their gender assigned at birth to a more comfortable identity. As Rankin, Weber, Blumenfeld, and Frazer (2010) found in their survey of over 5,000 students, faculty, and staff who identify as LGBTQ, those who are transgender are more likely to report bullying than men or women. Whereas 20% of men and 19% of women reported experiencing harassment, 39% of transmasculine respondents, 38% of transfeminine respondents, and 31% of gender nonconforming respondents reported the same. In short, across a number of studies, certain genders are more at risk for experiencing bullying than others.

In addition to different rates of bullying, the types of bullying experienced by men and women also vary slightly. Generally, women tend to experience more gender-focused harassment than do men. For example, Hoel and Cooper (2001) queried respondents about 29 possible types of bullying behaviors and found that women reported a higher frequency of only two forms: receiving unwanted sexual attention and receiving insulting messages. There was no difference in the percentages of women and men reporting other behaviors, such as having their opinions ignored, being the subject of gossip, or being humiliated or ridiculed. The differences reported were solely focused on gender-based harassment. Salin's (2003) study echoes these findings. She found that 9.3% of women, but only 3.1% of men, reported being subjected to sexual harassment or unwanted sexual attention in the workplace in the previous twelve months. When considered in light of the studies on different rates of harassment, these studies suggest that women experience more bullying behaviors because they are targeted based on their gender.

Men and women also differ not only in the degree to which they are bullied, but in the gender and job status of the bully-bullied pairing. Hoel et al. (2001) reported that, in their survey of 5,288 employees in 70 organizations in the UK, men were more likely to be bullied by other men; 62.2% of men were bullied by other men. In contrast, only 37.3% of women were bullied by other women. This study suggests that men are the primary perpetrators of bullying. Another study both corroborates and challenges these findings. In a survey of 4,000 adults, the Workplace Bullying Institute (WBI) found that men bully other men 55% of the time and women 45% of the time (Namie, 2010). Of particularly startling note and in contrast to the UK study, the WBI further found that women bullies target other women 80% of the time, thus pointing to the fact that women shoulder significant blame for creating a hostile work environment for their female colleagues.

In addition to different patterns of bullying by gender, men and women also report different types of bullying based on job status. Recall from our earlier review that employees might be bullied by their superiors, coworkers, or subordinates. Women in a variety of organizational roles are more likely to be bullied than are men. Salin (2003) found that men were most likely to be bullied by their superiors, whereas women reported bullying from superiors, coworkers, and subordinates. The author found that while women reported being bullied by superiors and coworkers in equal numbers, one-fourth of women reported being bullied by subordinates. Data from Hoel et al.'s (2001) study underscores the tendency of women in more-senior positions to be bullied. They found that 54.5% of female supervisors reported being bullied, compared with just 17.1% of male supervisors. The authors also noted that 15.5% of female senior managers reported being bullied, versus 6.4% of male managers. It should be noted that these data do not disaggregate who was perpetuating the bullying, merely that women in senior-level positions report experiencing bullying on a regular basis.

To review, women are much more likely to report being bullied than are men. The majority of this additional bullying takes the form of sexual harassment or other behaviors that revolve around gender. Of concern, some studies have noted that women are more likely to be bullied by other women. In addition, women tend to be bullied by a variety of employees throughout the organizational structure—from supervisors to coworkers to subordinates—whereas men report primarily being bullied by their superiors. Just as rates and patterns of bullying differ by gender, so too do they vary by race and ethnicity.

Race and Ethnicity

Patterns of bullying among racial and ethnic groups echo the bullying behaviors and differences between women and men. In particular, people of color are more likely to report being bullied than are their White counterparts (Fox & Stallworth, 2005; Hoel & Cooper, 2001; Lewis & Gunn, 2007; Namie, 2010). For example, Lewis and Gunn (2007) found that 9% of all White respondents, but 35% of all respondents of color reported being bullied in the workplace. Studies differ, however, as to which racial or ethnic group experiences the highest prevalence of bullying. For example, the Workplace Bullying Institute (Namie, 2010) reported that 40% of all Latinos, 38.6% of all African Americans, but 13.5% of all Asian Americans were currently being bullied or had been bullied in the past. In contrast, Hoel and Cooper (2001) found that Asian respondents to their survey were more likely than any other racial or ethnic group to report being bullied; nearly 20% of Asian respondents reported being bullied versus 10% of White respondents and 5% of Afro-Caribbean respondents who reported similar behaviors. These discrepancies point to the importance of organizational and national context in shaping conditions for bullying. Hoel and Cooper's (2001) study comes out of the UK, an environment characterized by higher tensions with those of Asian descent, whereas the United States's racial legacy penalizes African Americans and Latinos to a greater degree than their Asian American counterparts. Though rates of bullying among different groups might vary, the studies certainly agree that people of color are bullied more than Whites.

People of color experience different types of bullying than their White counterparts. Much as with women who experienced bullying targeted specifically at their gender, people of color report being subjected to bullying targeted at their racial or ethnic backgrounds. There is some disagreement among scholars as to whether people of color are subjected to general bullying as opposed to racially targeted bullying more than their White counterparts. In their survey of 262 full-time employees, Fox and Stallworth (2005) found that some respondents of color reported similar rates of general bullying behaviors as Whites. In particular, the authors' analyses revealed no difference in rates of bullying for African Americans, Asian Americans, and White respondents. However, the authors found that Latinos experienced more general bullying behaviors than all other racial and ethnic groups.

In contrast, Lewis and Gunn (2007) found that racial and ethnic minorities were more likely to experience bullying than their White counterparts. As we discuss shortly, though the types of bullying inflicted by superiors and colleagues differed, racial and ethnic minorities reported more frequent occasions of being singled out or undermined than White employees. A small percentage of respondents even reported that colleagues and supervisors had written racist graffiti on their workspaces. Hoel and Cooper (2001) also found that Asian and Afro-Caribbean respondents were more likely to be the target of offensive remarks or practical jokes than their White counterparts. These instances of racist graffiti and offensive remarks are examples of micro-aggressions, which Solórzano, Allen, and Carroll (2002) defined as:

> subtle verbal and non-verbal insults directed toward non-Whites, often done automatically and unconsciously. They are layered insults based on one's race, gender, class, sexuality, language, immigration status, phenotype, accent, or surname. (p. 17)

These non-overt discriminatory actions can occur on a daily basis since they are done unconsciously, potentially creating a hostile work environment for the victim. Clearly, multiple studies have established that people of color are more likely to be the target of bullying than Whites.

But who is doing the bullying? As we suggested above, studies point to the fact that supervisors and coworkers are likely to engage in different types of bullying with different racial and ethnic groups. Multiple studies suggest that supervisors are much more likely to bully based on race or ethnicity than coworkers (Fox & Stallworth, 2005; Lewis & Gunn, 2007). Fox and Stallworth (2005) found that among those reporting racial or ethnic bullying, 19% reported being bullied by supervisors and 12% reported being bullied by their coworkers. Although both groups might engage in bullying, the types of bullying performed differ. For example, Lewis and Gunn (2007) found that supervisors were more often noted for behaviors such as assigning demeaning work tasks, belittling their subordinates, offering unnecessary and continued criticism, and spreading rumors. In contrast, coworkers' bullying behaviors most often included jokes, racist remarks, humiliation, and hostility. The results of their study suggest that supervisors often use their position of authority to create unwelcome working conditions for their subordinates whereas coworkers create a hostile and racist work environment.

In sum, research suggests that racial and ethnic minorities are more likely to experience bullying in the workplace than Whites. Some studies suggest that general bullying rates do not differ by racial or ethnic group; rather, people of color are more likely to experience bullying based on their racial or ethnic backgrounds. Both supervisors and colleagues are frequent instigators of bullying, though each group is reported to bully in different ways: supervisors most frequently assign demeaning work tasks whereas coworkers are more noted for engaging in explicitly racist behaviors. There is a significant, though limited, body of literature on bullying by gender and race, but there has been much less research conducted on the bullying experiences of LGBQ individuals in the workplace. We now consider the limited body of literature on this population.

Sexuality

Although the bullying experiences of LGBQ (lesbian, gay, bisexual, and queer or questioning) youth have received much attention in the press in the past decade, there has not been as much attention on the bullying experiences of LGBQ adults. And yet, as the limited literature suggests, LGBQ adults are significantly more likely to be bullied and harassed than their heterosexual peers. Unlike our discussion of bullying by gender and race, in this section we are able to draw on a comprehensive study of bullying based on sexuality at colleges and universities. As the literature confirms, bullying is alive and well inside the academy.

In their study of faculty, staff, and students on American college campuses, Rankin and colleagues (2010) found that 23% of LGBQ respondents had been harassed, compared with just 12% of their heterosexual counterparts. Of more importance, LGBQ respondents were seven times more likely to be harassed based on their sexual identity. These differences parallel the research on bullying among racial and ethnic minorities. While racial and ethnic minorities might experience rates of general bullying similar to their White peers, they are more likely to be the targets of racial or ethnic bullying. In addition to facing greater rates of harassment based on sexual identity, Rankin et al.'s (2010) research also suggests that members of the LGBQ community are more likely to be bullied in general. It should be noted that Rankin et al.'s (2010) survey does not seek to identify bullying behaviors (or those sustained over long periods of time), but rather notes incidents of harassment. However, we draw upon this study for two reasons. First, this comprehensive study stands out in a very limited body of literature and second, their data suggest that LGBQ individuals experience negative climates on campus; regardless of duration of harassment, this population faces sustained negative experiences.

Rates of harassment are not uniform across the LGBQ community. For example, those who identify as queer are more likely to be bullied than those who identify as gay or lesbian. Whereas 21% of gay men and 23% of lesbians experienced general bullying behaviors, 33% of those who identified as queer experienced the same. Of interest, however, gay men were more likely to report being harassed based on their sexual identities than any other identity group; 89% of gay men, 86% of lesbians, 74% of bisexuals, and 81% of those who identified as queer reported harassment based on their sexuality (Rankin et al., 2010). In addition, respondents of color were more likely to experience harassment based on racial identity than were their White counterparts. Only 2% of White respondents and 31% of all respondents of color had been harassed based on their racial identity. However, the majority of respondents of color indicated that they were more likely to experience harassment based on their sexual identity than on their racial identity. The sole exception to this were African Americans; 63% reported being harassed based on racial identity whereas 57% were harassed based on sexuality

(Rankin et al., 2010). Such a finding points to the degree to which racism is still engrained in American society, and underscores the fact that identities intersect in different ways for different populations.

Rates of harassment also differed by faculty and staff status. Of faculty, 81% reported experiencing or observing harassment based on sexual identity, whereas 74% of staff reported similar experiences. LGBQ individuals endure many types of harassment on American college campuses. Rankin et al. (2010) found that LGBQ individuals were twice as likely to be the targets of derogatory remarks and to be stared at as their heterosexual counterparts. Of particular interest, 74% of faculty and 73% of staff reported experiencing derogatory remarks, 27% of faculty and 32% of staff reported being stared at, and 29% of faculty and staff reported intimidation or bullying. Staff were more likely than faculty to report receiving derogatory phone calls (6.2% of staff versus 4.5% of faculty) whereas faculty were more likely to observe individuals receiving a poor performance evaluation; 13.6% of faculty versus 9.5% of staff reported such consequences for LGBQ individuals (Rankin et al., 2010).

LGBQ faculty and staff experience bullying from a variety of individuals, including supervisors, colleagues, and students. Faculty and staff are most likely to be harassed by colleagues or superiors. Sixty-seven percent of faculty and 62% of staff reported being harassed by a peer, whereas 34% of faculty and 26% of staff reported being harassed by a superior. Stated in a different manner, nearly two out of three faculty and staff LGBQ respondents reported being harassed by a colleague in the workplace while one of three faculty and one of four staff members reported being bullied by their superiors (department chairs, deans, or other administrators for faculty and supervisors and other administrators for staff). These statistics underscore that discrimination is a frequent experience for LGBQ individuals. However, LGBQ individuals also report being harassed by subordinates, or in this context, students (Misawa, 2011; Rankin et al., 2010). In his study of the experiences of gay male faculty of color, Misawa (2011) found that some faculty were bullied by their students through incidents such as discounting faculty authority in the classroom. Rankin et al. (2010) found that 54% of faculty and 43% of staff were harassed by students. Such statistics suggest that discrimination based on sexuality still runs rampant and is enacted upon many levels and by many individuals.

Though the literature is limited, existing studies suggest that the workplace can be a particularly hostile environment for sexual minorities. Studies point out that gay and lesbian faculty and staff are likely to be harassed in the workplace and may experience discrimination from coworkers, supervisors, and students. Like their racial and ethnic minority counterparts, LGBQ employees are likely to experience general bullying as well as bullying based on their sexual identities, thus creating a hostile workplace. Across identity groups, there is a trend for individuals to be singled out and bullied for differing from the norm. Given the rates of bullying across these identity groups, the types of bullying behaviors experienced, and the perpetrators of these acts, we now consider why colleges and universities create environments that encourage bullying. We suggest that academic culture shoulders significant responsibility.

Role of Organizational Culture

Organizational culture plays a vital part in shaping the behavior of those within an organization. As Schein (2004) argued, "just as our personality and character guide and constrain our behavior, so does culture guide and constrain the behavior of members of a group through the shared norms that are held in that group" (p. 8). It is within the culture of an organization that behaviors are learned and ultimately accepted. For example, a workplace that facilitates nonconstructive criticism might be one in which bullying takes place. As many have suggested (Keashly & Neuman, 2010; Lester, 2009; Lewis & Orford, 2005; McKay et al., 2008), organizational culture plays a critical role in determining the degree to which bullying is tolerated and, in some cases, fostered. Following Twale and DeLuca (2008), we suggest that the organizational structures and culture in higher education create environments ripe for bullying in general and based on social identities in particular. Why are those who differ from the norm more likely to experience bullying? As many before us have suggested (Acker, 1990; Gillborn, 2005; Winant, 2001), societal structures were built with the needs of the White, heterosexual male in mind. In other words, societal structures are gendered, raced, and heteronormative. Structures within colleges and universities similarly privilege one group over others. In this section, we discuss how university culture privileges men over women (and cisgender over transgender), Whites over people of color, and heterosexuals over the LGBQ community. Such privilege and accompanying discrimination creates an environment that is ripe for bullying.

The Gendered University

The structure of higher education lends itself to gendered practices, creating an atmosphere that can discriminate against women as well as those who fall outside the gender binary (Acker, 1990; Ely & Meyerson, 2000). Some of these systematic gendered practices that disadvantage women include pay structures, the typical workload for female faculty, and the tenure and promotion process. As Misawa (2010) explained, higher education is "still structured around the deeply embedded patriarchic systems that sustain traditional higher education" (p. 9), despite the fact that there are more female students than male students on the typical college campus, and there are more women earning degrees. According to the National Center for Education Statistics ([NCES], 2011), women now account for 57% of all undergraduate students. Although women are overrepresented as undergraduates and have achieved parity with men in the receipt of doctoral degrees, they are still underrepresented in the ranks of faculty. Clearly some processes inhibit women from achieving the same outcomes as men.

Women who persist within the academy still do not achieve equality with men in rank or salary. This is true at all institutional types. West and Curtis (2006) found that while the pay discrepancy is greatest between male and female faculty at doctoral universities, female faculty working at associate degree-granting institutions also earn lower salaries than do men. This is striking, given that female faculty represent 47% of all faculty at community colleges (West & Curtis, 2006). The authors also found that women are less likely to hold a position with senior rank and more likely to hold positions earning a lower salary. In short, female faculty hold positions that are subordinate in both rank and salary to their male counterparts. If female faculty have lower status than male faculty, this puts women at risk for being bullied, due to this unbalanced power differential.

The tendency of female faculty to earn lower salaries is amplified within specific departments. Controlling for characteristics on an individual and structural level, Umbach (2007) found that female faculty earn less than do men, particularly in fields that are traditionally female-dominated. The findings in this same study indicate that women working in traditionally male-dominated fields earn more than do their peers in other departments, but their salaries are still lower than those of male faculty. Women are also less likely to enter these fields in the first place (Umbach, 2007). These findings point to an academic culture in which female faculty are not offered equal opportunities, regardless of their chosen field.

The triad upon which the tenure and promotion process is based—research, teaching, and service—contributes to the gendered nature of higher education because the three are not equally respected. Park (1996) argued that research is generally considered a masculine activity, whereas teaching and service are categorically more feminine activities. Research drives the promotion process, as minimal service rarely causes a faculty member to be denied tenure (Park, 1996). Bird, Litt, and Wang (2004) argued that women are often asked to create the status of women reports that are frequently used in higher education. Ultimately, these reports are not highly regarded within higher education (Bird et al., 2004). Women are often asked to volunteer for different tasks and committees in the name of service, but there is no guarantee that this service will lead to promotion or tenure. Since women are more likely to engage in teaching and service, the organizational structure has set them up as less likely to gain promotion.

Though women face a number of challenges at the university, transgender individuals are also marginalized within higher education, due to the assumptions of the gender binary, not only within the physical structure of the university but also in its paperwork and policies. Beemyn (2001) examined issues for transgender students that can also affect transgender faculty and staff. These issues include structural facilities such as bathrooms, which are frequently designated as "Men" or "Women." For those individuals who may identify as one gender but whose anatomy conforms to another gender, picking which bathroom to use can be a very complicated proposition. Other issues include applications or other paperwork, which ask students and prospective employees to indicate their gender, giving them the choice of "M" or "F" (Beemyn, 2001). State legislation also plays a role in how supportive institutions are of women and transgender faculty. Mann and Hornsby (2008) found that in states that do not support the LGBT community, colleges and universities were less likely to receive funding for supportive programs or facilities advancements. This suggests that transgender faculty and staff living in more conservative states are less likely to find support.

Overall, higher education is not structured to give female or transgender faculty and staff equal opportunity with regard to salary, positions, or job duties. Gendered organizations can lead to bullying among these identity groups because there is a lack of support for them in the first place. How can an institution that does not offer these populations equal opportunities put into place policies that discourage bullying? If no precedent is set at the institutional level that sanctions bullying, individuals will be able to continue to bully without consequence. Higher education's structures serve not just to privilege men over women, but to privilege Whites over people of color.

The Raced University

Faculty and staff of color face some of the same issues as women with regard to the raced structure of organizations such as underrepresentation within departments and inequitable division of teaching, research, and service responsibilities. In Fall 2009, 79% of all faculty at colleges and universities were White (NCES, 2011). These numbers also carried into staff positions, with Black, Hispanic, Asian/Pacific Islander, or American Indian/Alaska Native composing 19% of executive, administrative, and managerial staff and about 33% of non-professional staff during the same time period (NCES, 2011). As these numbers suggest, people of color were underrepresented in the faculty ranks, and overrepresented among clerical staff. Such disparities create an environment in which people of color are depended on to perform the majority of support services for a college or university, but have fewer opportunities to engage in shaping the direction of the organization. And, as our earlier review of the literature suggested, those in subordinate positions are frequently at risk for being bullied.

In addition, faculty and staff of color encounter higher teaching and service loads. Park (1996) argued that, like women, faculty of color are asked to serve on committees more than are their White male counterparts. In addition, they are given a higher teaching load, which can lead to a greater demand for undergraduate advising, especially to students of color (Park, 1996). Though these demands are applied externally from the university, many faculty and staff of color also face the internal desire to serve people, and a sense of obligation to strive for racial justice.

Along with the university expectations for service, faculty of color may feel a sense of responsibility to their ethnicity or race. Tierney and Bensimon (1996) suggested that this connection to culture, along with the expectations from the institution, lead to a "cultural taxation" (p. 115). Most faculty of color see the value in the service and teaching of students of color, but this sentiment can be manipulated and used to portray a commitment to diversity on a campus level (Baez, 2000). The organizational culture of higher education marginalizes faculty and staff of color by demanding extra service. Additionally, faculty are often placed in roles and responsibilities that intensify the raced culture that characterizes universities.

Faculty of color are burdened with responsibilities and expectations above and beyond those of their White peers. Although extra service responsibilities can be burdensome, Bird and colleagues (2004) suggested that both women and faculty of color use these extra service requirements to create a community on campus, by connecting with others from marginalized groups. Park (1996) also argued that faculty of color seek to serve as role models and promote diversity issues because service and teaching likely influenced their decision to enter higher education. Despite the positive nature of these commitments, higher education is a raced organization in which faculty often are pressured into volunteering for service tasks, yet are not rewarded for the service through promotion and tenure. This pressure to serve can come from all levels of the university and may present opportunities for workplace bullying to occur, since these service tasks are not valued for promotion and tenure. Just as faculty and staff of color work in an environment that is ripe for bullying, LGBQ employees also experience an unwelcoming climate.

The Heteronormative University

In addition to being gendered and raced, the university also operates to privilege heterosexuals over their LGBQ peers. And, as we have discussed, unlike gender and race, sexual identity is not a category that is federally protected from discrimination. As such, LGBQ individuals face a climate of discrimination that, in some cases, is sanctioned by federal law. In this section, we focus in particular on discrimination based on marital status.

Some of the issues facing LGBQ individuals stem from their lack of right to marry. Although six states recognize same-sex marriages and nine states recognize civil unions and domestic partnerships, the remaining 35 states prohibit two same-sex individuals from entering into a legally recognized partnership (Human Rights Campaign, 2011). In addition, with few exceptions, if a married same-sex couple from one state moves to another that prohibits same-sex marriage, their union is no longer recognized as valid. And though couples in the few states that allow same-sex marriage might benefit at the state level, they are still denied many benefits at the federal level, including the tax benefits that accrue to opposite-sex married couples.

This inability to marry has a number of consequences for LGBQ individuals at colleges and universities. Campuses are frequently recognized for providing superior health insurance and other benefits for faculty and staff. However, some universities only provide benefits to legally married couples. In states where same-sex individuals are unable to marry, this leaves their partners unable to access benefits. Some campuses have found ways around the law by offering benefits to domestic partners, regardless of marital status. However, state legislatures have subsequently passed laws forbidding the provision of benefits to domestic partners. Colleges and universities in some states, such as Michigan, have found ways to circumvent these laws by offering employees the right to insure an "Other Qualified Adult" in the household. Such machinations have only been necessary due to actions that seek to legislate marriage.

This focus on the institution of marriage has other consequences for LGBQ individuals. Many campuses offer spousal hiring programs to assist faculty and senior-level administrative hires in finding jobs for their husbands and wives. However, this benefit does not always extend to unmarried partners, either same-sex or opposite-sex. Though campuses might go to great lengths to find a position for a male professor's wife, they might not be as willing to do so for his husband. Some more conservative campuses also forbid same-sex or unmarried couples from living together in campus housing. This is particularly an issue for residence life staff, who are required to live on campus as part of their jobs. In a survey of 543 colleges and universities, Horowitz (2010) found that only 303 (or 56%) allowed employees to live with unmarried partners in their residence hall apartments. Clearly, this has significant consequences for LGBQ individuals who are denied the right to marry and subsequently have to choose between professional and personal life. Even first contact with campuses underscores divisions between straight and LGBQ individuals. Most job applications ask about marital status. Although some applications offer an option for "Partnered," others limit choices to Single, Married, Divorced, or Widowed. The LGBQ individual in a committed same-sex relationship is left to decipher where she or he falls among those categories. Clearly, the right to marry has a number of consequences for the lives of LGBQ faculty and staff. Being denied this right suggests that LGBQ individuals are second-class citizens and, as a result, creates a culture that encourages bullying and marginalization for this population. Having described how higher education cultivates an environment for workplace bullying to occur, we now offer a set of suggestions for those interested in creating conditions in which no individual is bullied based on his or her identity.

Suggestions for Practice

Finding ways to combat workplace bullying in higher education can be difficult, given that the behaviors are subtle and often occur behind the closed doors of departments. However, there are ways in which bullying behaviors and climates can be addressed. Change should be implemented at all levels of an organization and should not be the responsibility of one individual. In this section, we offer suggestions for practice for human resource professionals, department chairs, and administrators, but suggest that the most effective change will come through collaboration between all members of the campus community.

Human Resources Professionals

People working within human resources departments play a pivotal role in shaping organizational climate and the degree to which bullying is tolerated. Given higher education's emphasis on inclusivity, human resources professionals should foster an environment in which all identity groups are protected, including those not legally specified.

Gauge the Campus Climate

Organizational culture plays a critical role in shaping the degree to which bullying is tolerated. Climates that are hostile are likely to be those in which bullying is tolerated. Campuses might conduct periodic audits of the campus climate to gauge the experiences of women, people of color, and LGBT faculty and staff. Such audits might include gathering data through both anonymous means, such as surveys, and more public ways, such as campus forums. By having data about the ways in which particular groups feel marginalized, HR professionals will be better able to target interventions for their specific needs.

Create a Campus-Wide Anti-Bullying Campaign

To send the message that bullying is not tolerated in any organization, HR professionals might help create an anti-bullying campaign that includes faculty, staff, and students. The campaign might include specific reference to how bullying affects identity groups. Such a campaign might use promotional materials, such as websites, videos, and other documents, that all send the same message that all individuals on a campus are welcome and that bullying behaviors are not tolerated. The campaign might also incorporate a series of guest speakers who discuss the research on bullying or offer personal testimonials on the impact of being bullied based on race, gender, or sexuality.

Collaborate With Other Campus Departments

Campus culture cannot be changed by the actions of a few dedicated HR professionals. Instead, cultural change must involve a variety of campus constituencies and offices. Given that we have suggested that universities are gendered, raced, and heteronormative, HR professionals might particularly reach out to identity-based groups for both employees and students, such as women's centers, multicultural centers and student associations, and LGBTQ centers. In collaboration, these groups might offer year-long programming, both to support members of marginalized populations as well as the anti-bullying campaign suggested above.

Offer Workshops for the Campus Community

Human resources professionals might also offer continuing education through a series of workshops for staff, faculty, and students to help them understand how to handle instances of workplace bullying, particularly those that revolve around social identities. Workshops might also point out how subtle behaviors and structures can lead to conditions that create bullying, such as how being denied the right to marry has many consequences for LGBQ employees. HR professionals might collaborate with other campus offices, such as those that serve various social identity groups, to develop, implement, and advertise these workshops. Workshops can also provide social identity groups with tools and guidelines on how to identify, report, or stand up to workplace bullying. Such a workshop series allows HR professionals to proactively address workplace bullying rather than create initiatives in response to bullying incidents. While it is vital that there is a proactive stance against workplace bullying across campus, it becomes even more imperative that steps are in place to identify and manage workplace bullying at the department level.

Department Chairs and Administrators

As with HR professionals, department chairs and administrators also play a critical role in creating an inclusive and safe workspace where workplace bullying is not tolerated. Some ways of doing this include offering various training sessions and courses as well as creating an environment supportive of all faculty and staff.

Partner With Campus Offices to Offer
Training Sessions on Identity Groups

Partnering with various organizations on campuses can help departments create and maintain a collegial climate, and these partnerships may also help prevent bullying of specific identity groups. Many institutions have initiatives like the "Safe Zone" training, multicultural and women's centers, and other organizations with missions to educate people on the specific challenges and needs of individual identity groups. By partnering with these organizations to offer workshops or other department-level training, department chairs and administrators can create a culture in which bullying as well as other issues of harassment are addressed regularly. Continuous discussion of these issues fosters an environment in which faculty and staff understand that diversity and other identity groups are valued within the department.

Encourage Participation of All Faculty on Diversity Committees

In order to alleviate the pressure felt by women and faculty of color to serve on committees, departments can encourage White faculty to serve on diversity committees. They can similarly encourage men to serve on committees focused on gender issues. These kinds of opportunities can help raise awareness of not only diversity issues, but also allow White or male faculty to appreciate various identities throughout the university. Though this is not a structured training, faculty who are in the majority population can better understand the struggles of various identity groups, perhaps reducing the instances of workplace bullying within that department.

Engage in Cluster Hires

As we discussed earlier, marginalized groups may feel isolated in their departments, for a variety of reasons. Although universities are frequently interested in increasing the numbers of women and faculty of color, department cultures may not always be welcoming, and these individuals from sought-after groups may leave. To increase retention and help change organizational culture to one that discourages hostile environments, departments might engage in cluster hires by bringing in small groups of faculty (such as women in male-dominated departments or faculty of color in nearly any field) to support one another. Doing so will take steps toward ensuring that groups are not isolated and that faculty are not unduly burdened with extra service or mentoring responsibilities. For example, if students are able to seek out one of several faculty of color for mentoring, instead of just the only faculty of color, this may lead to a more equitable workload. While increasing the numbers of faculty from marginalized groups will not lead to a certain change of campus culture or reduce bullying, it does create pockets of support for individuals, as well as send a message to all in the campus community that diversity is valued.

Create Courses That Focus on Societal Inequities

Academic departments, such as Gender Studies and Ethnic Studies, might be encouraged to offer courses that call attention to the ways in which university structures and practices privilege some groups over others. Such interventions ultimately target students more than employees. However, as the literature suggests, students perpetuate a significant proportion of bullying directed at faculty and staff. Such courses may help to create more understanding for various social groups and reduce incidents of harassment.

In conclusion, as Lewis and Orford (2005) argued, the prevention of bullying may challenge the structures of an organization. Bullying behaviors can be so deeply engrained in daily practices that they inform much of an organization's culture. Given this, it is vital that there are policies in place and people in positions of authority at all levels of an institution who actively fight against workplace bullying. It is only by striving for organizational change and creating climates where bullying is no longer tolerated that higher education can move closer to being an environment where all identities are welcome.

References

Acker, J. (1990). Hierarchies, jobs, bodies: A theory of gendered organizations. *Gender & Society, 4*(2), 139–158.

Baez, B. (2000). Race-related service and faculty of color: Conceptualizing critical agency in academe. *Higher Education, 39,* 363–391.

Beemyn, B.G. (2005). Making campuses more inclusive of transgender students. *Journal of Gay & Lesbian Issues in Education, 3*(1), 77–87.

Bird, S., Litt, J., & Wang, Y. (2004). Creating status of women reports: Institutional housekeeping as "women's work." *NWSA Journal, 16*(1), 194–206.

Cooper, K.J. (2009). A disturbing trend. *Diverse Issues in Higher Education, 29*(9), 20–21.

Einarsen, S., Hoel, H., Zapf, D., & Cooper, C.L. (2003). The concept of bullying at work: The European tradition. In S. Einarsen, H. Hoel, D. Zapf, & C.L. Cooper (Eds), *Bullying and emotional abuse in the workplace: International perspectives in research and practice* (pp. 1–30). London: Taylor & Francis.

Ely, R.J., & Meyerson, D.E. (2000). Theories of gender in organizations: A new approach to organizational analysis and change. *Research in Organizational Behaviour, 22,* 103–151.

Fox, S., & Stallworth, L.E. (2005). Racial/ethnic bullying: Exploring links between bullying and racism in the U.S. workplace. *Journal of Vocational Behavior, 66,* 438–456.

Gillborn, D. (2005). Education policy as an act of white supremacy: Whiteness, critical race theory, and education reform. *Journal of Education Policy, 20*(4), 485–505.

Hoel, H., & Cooper, C. (2001). *Destructive conflict and bullying at work.* Manchester: Manchester School of Management.

Hoel, H., Cooper, C.L., & Faragher, B. (2001). The experience of bullying in Great Britain: The impact of organizational status. *European Journal of Work and Organizational Psychology, 10*(4), 443–465.

Horowitz, R. (2010). *The 2010 live-in/on report.* Retrieved from http://www.residentas sistant.com

Human Rights Campaign. (2011). *Marriage equality and other relationship recognition laws.* Washington, DC: Author. Retrieved from http://www.hrc.org/files/assets/resources/Relationship_Recognition_Laws_Map(1).pdf

Keashly, L., & Neuman, J.H. (2010). Faculty experiences with bullying in higher education: Causes, consequences, and management. *Administrative Theory & Praxis, 32*(1), 48–70.

Lester, J. (2009). Not your child's playground: Workplace bullying among community college faculty. *Community College Journal of Research and Practice, 33,* 446–464.

Lewis, D., & Gunn, R. (2007). Workplace bullying in the public sector: Understanding the racial dimension. *Public Administration, 85*(1), 641–665.

Lewis, S.E., & Orford, J. (2005). Women's experiences of workplace bullying: Changes in social relationships. *Journal of Community & Applied Social Psychology, 15,* 29–47.

Leymann, H. (1990). Mobbing and psychological terror at workplace. *Violence and Victims, 5*(2), 251–275.

Mann, S.L., & Hornsby, E.E. (2008). Work-life: Policy and practice implicating LG faculty and staff in higher education. Paper presented at the Academy of Human Resource Development International Research Conference in the Americas, Panama City, FL.

McKay, R., Arnold, D.H., Fratzl, J., & Thomas, R. (2008). Workplace bullying in academia: A Canadian study. *Employee Responsibilities and Rights Journal, 20,* 77–100.

Misawa, M. (2010). Racist and homophobic bullying in adulthood: Narratives from gay men of color in higher education. *New Horizons in Adult Education and Human Resource Development, 24*(10), 7–23.

Misawa, M. (2011). The intersection of racist and homophobic bullying in adult and higher education. Paper presented at the Midwest Research-to Practice Conference in Adult, Continuing, Community, and Extension, St. Charles, MO.

Namie, G. (2010). The WBI U.S. Bullying Workplace Survey. *Workplace Bullying Institute Research Studies.* Retrieved from http://workplacebullying.org/multi/pdf/WBI_2010_Natl_Survey.pdf

National Center for Education Statistics (NCES). (2011). *Digest of education statistics, 2010* (NCES 2011–015), Table 213, Table 214, and Table 256.

Park, S.M. (1996). Research, teaching, and service: Why shouldn't women's work count? *The Journal of Higher Education, 67*(1), 46–84.

Rankin, S., Weber, G., Blumenfeld, W., & Frazer, S. (2010). *2010 State of higher education for lesbian, gay, bisexual and transgender people.* Charlotte, NC: Campus Pride.

Roscigno, V.J., Lopez, S.H., & Hodson, R. (2009). Supervisory bullying, status inequalities, and organizational context. *Social Forces, 87*(3), 1561–1589.

Salin, D. (2003). The significance of gender in the prevalence, forms and perceptions of workplace bullying. *Nordiske Organisasjonsstudier, 5*(3), 30–50.

Schein, E.H. (2004). *Organizational culture and leadership.* San Francisco, CA: Jossey-Bass.

Solis, H. L. (2010). U. S. Department of Labor website. Retrieved from http://www.dol.gov/dol/topic/discrimination/ethnicdisc.htm

Solórzano, D., Allen, W., & Carroll, G. (2002). Keeping race in place: Racial microaggressions and campus racial climate at the University of California, Berkeley. *Chicano-Latino Law Review, 23*(15), 15–112.

Tierney, W.G., & Bensimon, E.M. (1996). *Promotion and tenure: Community and socialization in academe.* Albany: State University of New York Press.

Twale, D.J., & De Luca, B.M. (2008). *Faculty incivility: The rise of the academic bully culture and what to do about it.* San Francisco, CA: Jossey-Bass.

Umbach, P.D. (2007). Gender equity in the academic labor market: An analysis of academic disciplines. *Research in Higher Education, 48*(2), 169–192.

West, M.S., & Curtis, J.W. (2006). *AAUP faculty gender equity indicators 2006*. Washington, DC: American Association of University Professors. Retrieved from www.aaup.org/AAUP/pubsres/research/geneq2006.htm

Winant, H. (2001). *The world is a ghetto: Race and democracy since World War II*. New York: Basic Books.

4

PROFESSIONAL STAFF IN ACADEMIA

Academic Culture and the Role of Aggression

Jae Fratzl and Ruth McKay

Professional staff are vital to the operation of universities. Their roles are different than those of academics who assume administrative jobs while maintaining their academic privileges and responsibilities. The term "professional staff" refers to administrators, assistants, information technology technicians, librarians, cleaning and repair staff.[1] They are typically the first people students interact with at a university. A study of community college students found that new students, those in their first three weeks of courses, were more likely to have a meaningful encounter with staff than with instructors (Center for Community College Student Engagement [CCSSE], 2010). In many universities, faculty function as independent contractors, setting their own hours and often working from home. As a result, universities need professional staff to create a day-to-day organizational environment and maintain the operations of the organization.

University organizational culture has been described as elitist, hierarchical, slow to change (Twale & De Luca, 2008; Thomas, 2004), masculine (Todd & Bird, 2000), sexist (Thomas, 2004; Ambrose, Huston, & Norman, 2005), and secret (Ambrose et al., 2005). The culture is built on a sense of entitlement (Keashly & Neuman, 2010) and academic freedom (Twale & De Luca, 2008). In some universities, there are schisms and factions within and across departments that lead to isolation, suspicion, resentment, and limited collegiality among employees (Ambrose et al., 2005). Higher education is also known to have bullying and mobbing (Boyton, 2005; Lewis, 2004; McKay, Arnold, Fratzl, & Thomas, 2008; Raskauskas, 2006; Westhues, 2004) and may have higher incidents of bullying than does the average work environment (Keashly & Neuman, 2010), because bullying paradoxically is found to be higher in helping professions such as education (Boyton, 2005). Overt and covert aggression, expressed by employees as bullying, is predominantly the result of envy, job competition, and status (Björkqvist, Österman & Hjelt-Back, 1994).

Workplace bullying in higher education is challenging to address because of the power enshrined in its formal ranking systems (tenured, non-tenured, professors, associate professors, etc.) and academic degrees (B.A., Honors B.A., M.A., Ph.D.) (Twale & De Luca, 2008). As well, tenured faculty have a unique autonomy within university hierarchies, which disrupts the otherwise command-and-control nature of academic organizations and the work and authority of the professional staff. This autonomy, created by academic freedom and tenure, leads to a decentralized organizational structure, which contributes to the prevalence of workplace bullying in higher education (Gunsalus, 2006) (See Chapter 2 in this book for additional discussion of the role of tenure.) Academic professional staff fit into the loosely defined hierarchy, as their power and level of authority is formally and informally linked to the departments and programs for which they work.

Administrative activities, by either academics or professional staff, are in many cases viewed as secondary to the core activities of research and teaching. As Gunsalus (2006, p. 1) explains, an academic who takes on an administrative role at the expense of research is thought to "lose twenty I.Q. points." Such an undertaking can be viewed as a career-limiting move. A study by Björkqvist et al. (1994) about university employee aggression confirmed this bias. The study found that the highest rate of bullying was experienced by those whose work focused on administration, economy, and service, while the lowest level of bullying was experienced by those whose work activities included just teaching or a combination of research, teaching, and administration. The findings indicated a greater vulnerability in academia for people working in administrative roles.

This chapter will start by looking at research on bullying in the area of professional staff. Second, the behavior of key players in academia (professional staff, academics, and students) will be examined. This is critical because professional staff play a support role and therefore cannot be viewed in isolation when considering interpersonal dynamics. In addition, workplace bullying is an interpersonal issue that cannot be examined on only an individual basis (Pepler & Rubin, 2012). Next, levels of conflict and the group goal of survival for professional staff, academics, and students will be discussed. Fourth, a sample of literature on workplace bullying will be applied to the professional staff work situation. Finally, recommendations for addressing bullying by and toward professional staff will be presented.

Bullying of Professional Staff

Workplace bullying involving professional staff is an understudied area. Professional staff may be bullied by their colleagues, by students, or by faculty. A study by Thomas (2004) about professional staff (called support staff) in a UK higher education institution found the majority of them were women. According to Simpson and Cohen (2004), in response to being bullied, women in higher educational settings are more likely than men to perceive some behaviors as threatening or unwelcome. Also, females in academic settings preferred, when bullied, to use self-defensive strategies designed to outwit the bully. The relationship between gender and professional staff experiencing bullying is significant, given the high numbers of women who serve in support roles in college and universities.

Thomas (2004) found the most frequent forms of bullying of professional staff were undermining confidence/self-esteem, abusing power/position/seniority, intimidating/threatening behavior, excluding/ignoring/isolating, and unreasonable/inappropriate pressuring to complete tasks. A second study by Boyton (2005), which included a cross section of employees (academics and professional staff) from British higher education institutions, identified the most common forms of bullying as overriding decisions, removing areas of responsibility, setting one up to fail, not listening to problems, ignoring or overlooking one, and alienation from colleagues. Both studies found that the majority of aggressors were those in positions of authority over the target. These studies may indicate the impact of hierarchy as well as power on interpersonal dynamics. Raskauskas (2006), in a study of support (professional) staff and academics in New Zealand, found that 60.7% of bullied staff experienced top-down bullying, whereas 18.1% were bullied by a coworker at a higher level. Few were bullied by coworkers at the same level. McKay et al. (2008) identified different findings in a Canadian study. They found that peers, more powerful staff, and students bullied the most. Many peers who bullied were viewed as being self-serving and power hungry. Also, respondents noted the high and often unrealistic expectations of students relative to the respondent's time limits and work load. These studies illustrate the need to understand all the players involved in workplace bullying and how the issue cannot be limited to an examination of the players in isolation.

The Other Players

University professional staffers are sandwiched between faculty and students. The majority of students currently in universities are referred to as generation Y, millennials, or the baby boom echo. Generation Ys were born between 1980 and 2000 and most were raised in small families. Some of these were raised as privileged children by parents who tried to grant their offspring's every desire, while insulating them from disappointments and limitations. In this generation, the child became the most important person in a family (Andert, 2011). This has resulted in a generation of young people who have difficulty understanding others' perspectives or circumstances (Twenge, 2006). This does not mean all students are narcissistic, but there is an increasing tendency toward narcissistic behaviors in younger generations. Twenge (2006) concluded that the average American college student in 2006 was 30% more narcissistic than were their counterparts in 1982. They are accustomed to being active in family decisions and to assuming authority or contributing to decisions within the organizations with which they are affiliated (Johns, 2003). These expectations may account for an increase in incidents of aggression by students. In the study by McKay et al. (2008), generation Y students became hostile and, at times, abusive if they were denied individual attention, such as regular and prompt feedback on their performance. According to faculty, students expected that expressing a desire for a better grade would result in faculty complying. Research looking at incidents and media coverage of student incivility indicates inappropriate expressions of aggression by students in higher education are on the rise because of increased class size, more competition for entrance to programs and pressure to complete programs, and for employment purposes (Morrissette, 2001).

Professional staff also interact with academics. Academics have strong group identification and a sense of entitlement that can increase with rank (Keashly & Neuman, 2010). Entitlement, likely evolving out of tenure and academic freedom, gives academics the opportunity to voice disagreement with each other (Keashly & Neuman, 2010; Gunsalus, 2006). This may account for why many higher learning institutions have limited policies on disciplining faculty except in the most extreme case of termination (Euben & Lee, 2006). According to Ambrose et al. (2005), when academics identify reasons for dissatisfaction in their work environment, they identify a lack of collegiality for which three reasons stand out: lack of time and interest on the part of colleagues—particularly senior faculty's interest in junior faculty endeavors—intradepartmental tensions, and incivility. The department tensions were described as "warring sub-groups," "cliques," and "infighting," and the incivility "ranged from thoughtlessness to outright hostility" (Ambrose et al., 2005, p. 815).

Academics can manage much of their work, research, and teaching independently, so they may be able to survive longer in an unpleasant environment than can professional staff, but as a result underlying issues may persist longer in universities. (See Chapter 2 for additional discussion of the role of tenure.) This ability to distance oneself may also lead to other difficult behaviors. As Caton (2005, p. 364), a professor who has studied academics, explains, "Who is not, now and then, vain, arrogant, exploitative, envious, or ambitious? Do not the criteria fit virtually all celebrities and many academics?" Even if there is a common understanding that some faculty members are acting out of line, research has shown there is also a lack of management skills among faculty to deal with these problems (Boyton, 2005).

Professional staff are therefore providing support for two very demanding but different groups—students who have an increasing sense of entitlement, and faculty who have extensive freedom and job independence. Also, magnifying the challenge of the job and interpersonal dynamics for the professional staff member is a dearth of management oversight. According to Boyton's (2005) study of academia in Britain, reasons for bullying behaviors included that the bully was "not trained," "not managed," and "they can do it." Within the sample of over 800 respondents, only 37% said they had management training. This may lead to greater tension among the professional staff, academics, and students.

Systems and Subsystems

It is helpful and arguably necessary to look at the issue of workplace bullying in academia and solutions or interventions from a systems or holistic approach (Senge, 1990), as well as a reductionist approach that examines the subsystems (Kuhn, 1974) or groups within academia—those of professional staff, academics, and students. These groups have different levels of effective conflict (Amason, 1996) and a common group and organizational goal of survival. In the work environment, individuals assume their task, functions, and motivation from the group with which they are associated (Bion, 1970) as well as from the organization as a whole. Members of the group can control, reward, and punish other members through the assignment of tasks. For example, many of the tasks a professional staffer completes are those assigned or requested by other professional staffers. As Raskauskas (2006) found, professional staff noted that being overloaded with work was a common form of bullying they experienced. This is an example of how some in-group aggression is expressed or perceived.

The group approach is important in examining workplace bullying, as individuals cannot be understood or guided to make changes to their behavior without understanding the group in which they exist and the nature of other groups within their environment (Rice, 1969). By looking at the subsystems, one can better understand the differences in norms of behavior within and across subsystems. The challenge in academia is that the motivators of individuals, the goals and factors of success, are very different for students, academics, and professional staff. These differences translated into differences in how aggression, such as workplace bullying, is expressed, understood, and managed.

For example, professional staff, acting in a support role, are expected to assist academics and students as customers within the organization (internal customers) (Ishikawa, 1985). Such a role requires professional staff to manage relations and confrontations. Outright individualized expressions of aggression are discouraged in a professional staffer because of the nature of the support role. An overly aggressive person in a professional staff position may be a poor fit, because professional staff are required to work together for the good of the organization, not their own accomplishments. As a result, covert acts of aggression and bullying may be more common among professional staff. A high level of aggression and self-importance does not fit well with most expectations of service roles, except in a higher-level position where an employee has to defend territory, such as dealing with resource allocation.

Professional staff provide a service role. They are the glue that holds the organization together in a "helping profession." In this line of reasoning, professional staff can be viewed as caretakers. They work together to assist the rest of the members of the organization in a nurturing maternal or matriarchal way. The role of caretaker can be equated with the role of primary caregiver (parent). Professional staff may, therefore, receive infantile projections from those they support—be it students or academics—even if they do not consider themselves in the role of parent. Professional staff can be aggressive as a group in order to protect an aspect of the organization or individuals within. In hierarchical systems, professional staff as caretakers are vulnerable to feelings of powerlessness, because they feed information upward and report up through levels of authority. This process creates dependency and, at times, powerlessness (Stewart, 2010). Given this constraint, working as a group to deal with a threat is a way to overcome the reduced power of the caretaker.

Academics, however, given their independence, individualized pursuits of research and teaching, and academic freedom, are likely more direct and confrontational than professional staff. They still must consider the internal customer but their subculture, which encourages critique and debate, can lead to a higher frequency of accepted confrontation, and at times individualized aggression. The process of defending a doctoral thesis is an early introduction into an academic subculture. The confrontational atmosphere continues once in an academic position, when an academic is challenged by students in the classroom, other academics in the journal submission process, and at conference presentations. In some cases, the conflict, such as student behavior in the classroom, can be abusive (McKay et al., 2008) but the academic is expected, often with little or no training, to manage and adapt to these behaviors. Academics assume they are fundamental to the organization's purpose, which feeds their sense of importance and the demands they make of professional staff. In the "academic star" category, the highly accomplished academics, the stakes and self-importance are even greater. Academic stars "put the university on the map, bringing in significant funding" and attract media coverage (Gunsalus, 2006, p. 53). They see themselves as important and deserving of admiration. Academics, whether a star or not, can be territorial, strongly defending their research methodology, theories, funding, and teaching load with vigor. In universities with more of a teaching emphasis, academics may be less aggressive in terms of research but may still need to defend departmental resource allocation. For academics, regularly and publicly dealing with conflict is critical to survival and, as a result, overt expressions of aggression are more likely.

The nature and extent to which university students become aggressive depends, in part, on the organizational culture (university, department, and course) and the expectations placed on them. If there are very few A grades awarded and the classroom environment is highly competitive and individualized, more conflict and aggression will emerge. Alternatively, if students are encouraged to assist each other, have group assignments, and high grades are more freely assigned, then a more supportive environment will emerge, with less conflict and aggression. In an academic setting, more highly sought-after degrees with high entrance requirements leads to more aggressive behaviors. For example, in an MBA program with high tuition, high GPA and GMAT admission requirements, and emphasis on personal success, one is likely to find more aggressive-type behaviors, whereas in a program where the tuition is lower, entrance requirements less, and more group success emphasized, less aggressive behavior may emerge. Professional staff must adapt to the environment in which they work and the program and students they assist.

When academics, professional staff, and students work together and encounter conflict, the differences in behavior of the groups (as in the level of acceptable conflict in the groups) can lead to misunderstanding. For example, if a professional staffer applies a policy requesting all final exams for a semester be submitted four weeks before a course is finished, an academic may want to debate the necessity to submit so far in advance. The professor may debate the issue, expecting conflict and a spirited exchange of ideas, whereas the professional staffer may view such an exchange as challenging their authority, which leads to an uncomfortable level of conflict. The academic's perspective is individual, a deadline for their exam, whereas the professional staffer is focused on the group task of organizing a semester of exams across many courses. The academic's individualized perspective and higher tolerance for conflict may grate with the professional staffer's group perspective and lower acceptance of conflict.

It is also helpful for professional staff to recognize differences in organizational culture that exists across a university from department to department. Departments operate as subsystems. In some departments there may be a higher level of competition for jobs and resources, creating a more aggressive environment. Those in the department may feel their livelihood is threatened and, therefore, may fight in an effort to defend their accomplishments or their job. In other departments, resources (Meyer & Scott, 1983) may be more plentiful and, therefore, a less aggressive organizational culture emerges. Clashes in organizational subculture may arise when departments interact. Given that professional staff need to interact across departments, it is valuable to be prepared for such differences and to understand the task, functions, and motivation (Kuhn, 1974) of other groups and what conditions will lead to fight or flight behavior.

A group as a system or subsystem should be greater than the sum of its parts. Its primary task is the survival of the group as the group provides synergy, guidance, and identity (Banet & Hayden, 1977). Although the task of survival may be disguised or masked, group survival is the primary preoccupation and motivating force for group members. The emphasis on survival, and the overt and covert expressions of the pursuit of survival, provides the framework for the exploration of group behavior (Banet & Hayden, 1977). If academics or students threaten professional staff, it is likely that the professional staffer will be supported by other professional staff in dealing with the threat, as such actions are seen as a threat to the survival of the group. This can create a sense of "us versus them," where the group sees other groups as different and at times threatening. If a professional staffer is threatened by another professional staffer, it may also be linked to group survival. For example, if a professional staffer makes an error, then this can threaten the organizational view of all professional staff, particularly if the error has major resource consequences or is repeated many times, making professional staff appear negligent.

Group members also have their own personal agendas, such as job advancement or acquiring skills. The subsystem's leadership or internal and external controls should prevent personal agendas from interfering with the group tasks (Bion, 1970), but avoiding such individualized goals is not always possible. Personal agendas are evident in workplace bullying. In the Thomas's (2004) and Raskauskas's (2006) studies, professional staff complained about being set up to fail when others made them appear ineffective or incompetent. This type of bullying could reflect intent, as it stems from an employee not being provided with the required knowledge or authority to complete a task (Peyton, 2003). Putting another employee in this position can discourage unwanted competition among fellow employees. If such destructive agendas are allowed to continue unchecked, this may be a result of weak internal controls or a culture that normalizes bullying (Ferris, 2004).

Despite differences in the subcultures that likely contribute to tension and conflict, academia does not "spend much time communicating the standard operating procedures for successful conduct. While [the] terms of employment and employee handbook [are provided] these are rarely examined except when a problem arises" (Gunsalus, 2006, p. 18). In many cases, a professional staffer has to find solutions on his or her own, and not entirely depend on the rules to solve these problems. They must also understand the unwritten rules on how to interact with other professional staff as well as academics and students. The lack of attention given to standard operating procedures can result in opportunities for workplace bullying behavior. As a result, employees need to consider how to deal with bullying, and which techniques work best for a work situation. The following section outlines a number of self-help books available for guidance for professional staff that help tailor a response to the situation and nature of participants.

Responding to Bullying

The field of inquiry into bullying and effective responses is still in its infancy. Researchers take a variety of approaches, from the idealistic "Can't we just all get along" approach of Coloroso (2002) to the staunch positions of "zero tolerance" of bullying advocated by Westhues (2004) and Abdennur (2000). Abdennur, despite his strong stance, is not in favor of using bully tactics against bullies. At the far end of the range of books are those who advocate bullying tactics to deal with bullies—the "If you can't beat 'em join 'em" approach, such as in the book *The Way of the Rat* (Schrijvers, 2004).

Coloroso's (2002) work to address bullying in elementary schools takes an empathic group dynamic approach, and has contributed such strategies as educating the school community, understanding the reasons for bullying (problems such as abuse, learning difficulties, jealousy, etc.), and addressing those problems with empathy. She uses the term "bystander" to emphasize the importance of empowering witnesses to speak out against bullying and to report bullying to authorities. Coloroso also argues for a model of restoration, and reconciliation to ensure authentic healing. Coloroso's book, even though it is focused on elementary school bullying, is well suited for dealing with the group dynamics in academia.

Abdennur (2000) takes a strong stance on the need for direct communication and constant vigilance against pathological/indirect communication. A healthy organization would be composed of verbally direct communicators in a culture where confrontation has a positive connotation and is the norm. Abdennur's research was likely informed by his experience working in academia and a government bureaucracy. It has propelled him to argue for strong policies and procedures to combat bullying. He viewed his research participants through the lens of psychopathology. Abdennur faults indirect communication and non-confrontational management styles for bullying problems. He outlines a work environment in which all employees are encouraged to "call" other employees on any indirect communication. His view of a healthy workplace is one full of conflict, but not aggression. Abdennur (2000, p. 149) further asserts that there are three dimensions to a successful approach to bullying. He suggests one needs a theoretical framework for understanding the behavior, a consistent approach to issues as they arise, and clear policies. Abdennur's book would assist a professional staffer in understanding how to deal with academics and/or a work environment with a high level of conflict.

Robert Sutton gained recognition for his book *The No Asshole Rule* (2007). A portion of his book is devoted to addressing how to rid an organization of problem employees and how to avoid hiring them in the first place. Sutton also argues that organizations may need at least one problem employee to promote good behavior in others. Employees will make an extra effort to act appropriately if they see one employee act poorly. However, if there is more than one such employee other employees will join in such behaviors (Sutton, 2007). Sutton's approach can help those in academia distinguish between one bad apple or bad individual and a whole barrel of apples or an organization that is bad, where bullying has been normalized.

Sam Horn (2002) focuses on strategies to help the nonconfrontational individual speak up assertively. Her strategies focus on speaking up as a tool to empower the individual and enhance self-esteem, rather than confrontation for confrontation's sake. She, along with Graves (2002) and Tehrani (2001), also asserts that mediation and win-win conflict resolution styles (such as using "I statements") are ineffective for dealing with true bullies—people who engage in behaviors with *intention* to demean as a way to maintain power. Given the professional staffer's focus on cooperation in the support role, these books could assist in empowering the professional staffer.

Authors such as Keith and Bassi (2010) and Rubin and Thomlinson (2006) respond to the question of what to do about bullying from a legal perspective. It speaks to lawyers and a firm's legal responsibilities. Legal advice is most useful at either end of the continuum. Advice is helpful in developing policies and vision statements for a university's initial attempts to address a problem with a code of conduct. A legal perspective is also vital for a formal complaint process, ridding the organization of a severe problem employee or protecting the organization from lawsuits. This may be seen as an approach of the macrocosm, society/culture at large. This culture may not be the culture of the work-environment, however, as there are many examples of workplaces continuing to condone or even encourage inappropriate behavior. For professional staffers, these books can alert them to the legal nature of workplace bullying.

Despite their different approaches about how to deal with bullying, all authors agree that doing nothing is not an option. At the very least, one must engage in self-care (Namie & Namie, 2011) and move on. Making and maintaining change away from a bullying environment requires unflinching self-examination and vigilance of self, situation, and system (Adams & Balfour, 2009; Zimbardo, 2008).

When faced with aggression, the first thing to do is ascertain that there are no immediate safety risks. Having determined the level of risk, the best approach to help resolve the issue is to determine the nature of those one is dealing with and how one classifies themselves and the group or area they work in. Despite best efforts, bullying is still a problem. The above-listed books address some issues facing professional staff (group dynamics, organizational conflict, assertiveness, and legal issues) but each has its own emphasis/bias. It illustrates that there is no one-size-fits-all solution. In tailoring an approach, one must understand (a) the complaint/defense; (b) the psychological issues driving complainant and defendant; (c) their roles as they understand them in the workplace; (d) workplace culture, subculture, and any pressures that may be contributing; (e) policies of the given workplace; and (f) the microcosm in the macrocosm.

Recommendations for Professional Staff

First, any position an employee holds in an academic setting can lead to expressions of aggression. Abdennur (2000, p. 154) refers to the concept of the "psycho-structural marriage" in which the inherent personality characteristics of an employee are related to the needs of the position. As Adams and Balfour (2009) and Zimbardo (2008) clearly identify, one has to consider how an individual is treated by others, impacted by their work situation and job requirements, and how the system (e.g., organizational culture and structure) impacts the individual as well as their individual characteristics. For example, a professional staffer being more aggressive in an effort to solve bullying issues may not receive the same support that an academic taking the same stance might. Or such expressions of aggression by professional staffers may signal ineffective management by administration and that the professional staffer feels she has run out of options. It may also be a genuinely inappropriate response based on personality. Awareness of the natures of the groups in academia can help prepare a response and select a relevant strategy to address the situation. Aggression by a professional staffer may require someone of greater authority to defuse the conflict. If the conflict is peer to peer, there may be a greater need to involve the group as helpful bystanders and definers of norms.

Awareness of the nature of these groups and tactics can help the organization run more smoothly. It can also help in hiring for academic and professional staff positions and in selecting students for a program. In hiring an academic one will look for someone who is more comfortable with independence. They may however need coaching to be more empathetic and to "pull out" the concern of the personnel they are dealing with. Professional staff are typically called on to work in an interactive and cooperative manner. The role requires that they respond to the requests of others, students and academics. If they perceive themselves to have less self-efficacy or power, they will likely engage in more covert communication/aggression, and may need encouragement and clear support to express concerns more directly. Within each group will be a range of behaviors and job requirements. The complexity of the interface of personality and position supports the need for clear expectations to be established at the start of employment and reinforced by the organizational environment.

Third, we all can display aggressive behavior when we feel threatened. Depending on the university, the department, and the program students, academics and other professional staffers will feel threatened by different events. When anyone feels threatened, they will respond with actions intended to defend themselves and reduce or eliminate the threat. These strategies may be affiliative and group-based, ostracizing and group-based, or individual actions of either a covert or overt nature. Depending on the personalities of those involved, those who dislike direct or high-conflict strategies will feel threatened when highly intensified behaviors occur. Those employees who are more confrontational by nature can see the above-mentioned as avoidant, underhanded, or weak. The different personal styles of expressing and dealing with conflict can magnify differences and make situations worse in the workplace. Professional staff should, therefore, consider requesting a code of conduct be developed and posted, in order to set a standard of acceptable behavior that encompasses the nature of their work.

Conclusion

Workplace bullying occurs across and within groups in academia. Professional staff are uniquely sandwiched between students and academics who may display aggressive behavior in order to deal with threats and meet their needs. Recognizing the differences between the styles of aggression used by these groups and professional staff is helpful in dealing with behaviors. The pressures and demands of the position and subculture within the organization will often drive the way aggression and bullying is expressed. Understanding these differences helps one select the most appropriate response to interpersonal conflict and inappropriate behavior.

Note

1. We recognize that employee contracts and titles differ across institutions. For the purposes of this chapter, professional staff are those who do not serve in teaching, leadership, or managerial roles.

References

Abdennur, A. (2000). *Camouflaged aggression: The hidden threat to individuals and organizations.* Calgary, Alberta: Detselog Enterprises.

Adams, G.B., & Balfour, D. L. (2009). *Unmasking administrative evil.* New York: M.E. Sharpe.

Amason, A.C. (1996). Distinguishing the effective of functional and dysfunctional conflict and strategic decision making: Resolving a paradox for top management teams. *Academy of Management Review, 29,* 123–148.

Ambrose, S., Huston, T., & Norman, M. (2005). A qualitative method for assessing faculty satisfaction. *Research in Higher Education, 46*(7), 803–830.

Andert, D. (2011). Alternating leadership as a proactive organizational intervention: Addressing the needs of the Baby Boomers, Generation Xers and Millennials, *Journal of Leadership, Accountability and Ethics, 8*(4), 67–83.

Banet, A. G. & Hayden, C. (1977). A Tavistock primer. In J. E. Jones & J. W. Pfeiffer (Eds), *The 1977 annual handbook for group facilitators* (pp. 155–167). La Jolla, CA: University Associates.

Bion, W.R. (1970). *Attention and interpretation: Scientific approach to insight in psychoanalysis and groups.* New York: Basic Books.

Björkqvist, K., Österman, K., & Hjelt-Back, M. (1994). Aggression among university employees. *Aggressive Behavior, 20,* 173–184.

Boyton, P. (2005). Preliminary findings from Petra Boynton/THES bullying survey August 2005. Retrieved from http://www.unitetheunion.org/pdf/Preliminary%20Findings%20from%20Bullying%20survey.pdf

Caton, H. (2005). The exalted self: Derek Freeman's quest for the perfect identity. *An International Journal of Theory and Research, 5*(4), 359–384.

Center for Community College Student Engagement (CCCSE). (2010). *The heart of student success: Teaching, learning and college completion* (2010 CCCSE Findings). Austin: The University of Texas at Austin, Community College Leadership Program.

Coloroso, B. (2002). *The bully, the bullied, and the bystander.* Toronto: Harper Collins Publishers.

Euben, D. R., & Lee, B. A. (2006). Faculty discipline: Legal and policy issues in dealing with faculty misconduct. *Journal of College and University Law, 32,* 241–308.

Ferris, P. (2004). A preliminary typology of organisational response to allegations of workplace bullying: See no evil, hear no evil, speak no evil. *British Journal of Guidance & Counselling, 32*(3), 389–395.

Graves, D. (2002). *Fighting back—Overcoming bullying in the workplace.* Berkshire: McGraw-Hill International.

Gunsalus, C.K. (2006). *The college administrator's survival guide.* Cambridge, MA: Harvard University Press.

Horn, S. (2002). *Take the bully by the horns—Stop unethical, uncooperative, or unpleasant people from running and ruining your life.* New York: St. Martin's Press.

Ishikawa, K. (1985) *What is Total Quality Control? The Japanese way.* New Jersey: Prentice Hall.

Johns, K. (2003, 11 April). Managing generational diversity in the workforce. *Trends & Tidbits,* Retrieved from www.workindex.com

Keashly, L., & Neuman, J.H. (2010). Faculty experiences with bullying in higher education: Causes, consequences, and management, *Administrative Theory & Praxis, 32*(1), 48–70.

Keith, N., & Bassi, G. (2010). *Human resources guide to preventing workplace violence* (2nd ed.). Aurora, Ontario: Canada Law Book.

Kuhn, A. (1974). *The logic of social systems.* San Francisco: Jossey-Bass.

Lewis, D. (2004). Bullying at work: The impact of shame among university and college lecturers. *British Journal of Guidance & Counselling, 32*(3), 281–299.

McKay, R., Arnold, D., Fratzl, J., & Thomas, R. (2008). Workplace bullying in academia: A Canadian study. *Employee Responsibilities and Rights Journal, 20*(2), 77–100.

Meyer, J., & Scott, W. (1983). *Organizational environments: Ritual and rationality.* Beverly Hills, CA: Sage.

Morrissette, P.J. (2001). Reducing incivility in the university/college classroom. *International Electronic Journal for Leadership in Learning, 5*(4) 2001. Retrieved from http://www.ucalgary.ca/iejll/morrissette

Namie, G., & Namie, R. (2011). *The bully-free workplace: Stop jerks, weasels, and snakes from killing your organization.* New Jersey: Wiley Hoboken.

Pepler, D., & Rubin, K. (2012). *The development and treatment of childhood aggression.* New Jersey: Lawrence Erlbaum Publishers, London.

Peyton, P.R. (2003). *Dignity at work: Eliminate bullying and create a positive working environment.* New York: Brunner-Routledge.

Raskauskas, J. (2006). *Bullying in academia: An examination of workplace bullying in New Zealand universities.* Paper presented at the annual meeting of the American Educational Research Association, San Francisco.

Rice, A.K. (1969). Individual, group and intergroup processes. *Human Relations, 22,* 565–584.

Rubin, J., & Thomlinson, C.M. (2006). *Human resources guide to workplace investigations.* Aurora: Canada Law Book.

Schrijvers, J.P.M. (2004). *The way of the rat—A survival guide to office politics.* Great Britain: Cyan Books London.

Senge, P. M. (1990). *The fifth discipline: The art and practice of the learning organization.* New York: Doubleday Currency.

Simpson, R., & Cohen, C. (2004). Dangerous work; the gendered nature of bullying in the context of higher education. *Gender, Work and Organisation, 11*(2), 163–186.

Sutton, R.I. (2007). *The no asshole rule—Building a civilized workplace and surviving one that isn't.* New York: Warner Business Books.

Tehrani, N. (Ed.). (2001). *Building a culture of respect—Managing bullying at work*. London: Taylor and Francis.

Thomas, M. (2004). Bullying among support staff in a higher education institution. *Health Education, 106*(4), 273–288.

Todd, P., & Bird, D. (2000). Gender and promotion in academia. *Equal Opportunities International, 19*(8), 1–16.

Twale, D.J., & De Luca, B.M. (2008). *Faculty incivility: The rise of the academic bully culture and what to do about it*. San Francisco, CA: John Wiley and Sons.

Twenge, J. M. (2006). *Generation Me: Why today's young Americans are more confident, assertive, entitled—and more miserable than ever before*. New York: Free Press.

Westhues, K. (2004). *Administrative mobbing at the University of Toronto*. Queenston: Edwin Mellen Press.

Zimbardo, P. (2008). *The Lucifer Effect—understanding how good people turn evil*. New York: Random House.

5

A MODEL OF SOCIAL ECOLOGY OF BULLYING IN COMMUNITY COLLEGES

Soko S. Starobin and Warren J. Blumenfeld

In the past few years, issues related to workplace bullying at higher education have received attention through popular media (Twale & De Luca, 2008). Recent articles illustrating misconduct among faculty in colleges and universities particularly highlight a lack of institutional policy on workplace bullying and civility (Schmidt, 2010, 2011). For instance, a false bullying allegation against a faculty member at the time of his tenure review revealed the lack of clarity and fairness in their due process and institutional readiness to handle bullying or harassment allegations with equity and justice, under difficult circumstances (Schmidt, 2011). Additionally, the *Chronicle of Higher Education* (Schmidt, 2010) describes the growing concerns and issues of workplace bullying in colleges and universities, and notes the recent involvement of pharmaceutical companies and other third parties in developing alternative resolution methods within the institutions.

Despite the increase in public interest in workplace bullying, there is evidence of a dearth of literature to encourage constructive discourse among practitioners and scholars regarding workplace bullying in higher education. In fact, the article in the *Chronicle of Higher Education* points out that because of the lack of research and framework to understand the effects and outcomes of institutional policy and alternative resolution methods, the third party involvement (as indicated above) could result in more damage to the victims of workplace bullying (Schmidt, 2010). Lester (2009) further argues that there is a scarcity of literature that provides empirical evidence or a conceptual framework to better understand workplace bullying, specifically at two-year institutions of higher education. Keashly and Neumann present a similar argument in Chapter 1 of this book. Many aspects of institutional characteristics among those institutions (we will refer to them as community colleges) are unique. These unique characteristics are distinctively different from four-year, professional (post-baccalaureate), and proprietary institutions. We hypothesize that the emergence and perpetuation of bullying and uncivilized behaviors at the workplace in community colleges can be explained by such institutional differences, which are themselves explained by two distinct frameworks. The first framework is Cohen and Brawer's (2008) curricular functions of community colleges: (a) academic transfer and general education, (b) vocational-technical, (c) continuing education and community service, and (d) developmental (remedial) education. This framework describes and categorizes the main function of the community college—teaching and learning. Additionally, we will use the Carnegie Classifications™ to help define institutional identity. Carnegie Classifications™ further describe institutional characteristics beyond curricular functions, such as geographic location and size, a focus of our analysis. We believe that such institutional identity, which accounts for internal observations of curricular functions, as well as external assessment of the institutional characteristics measured by the Carnegie Classifications™, will guide us in examining the plausible causes of workplace bullying in community colleges.

Before we present more details of the curricular functions and Carnegie Classifications™, and how those two elements relate to one another, we introduce the notion of social ecology of bullying (Blumenfeld, 2010) and social reproduction framework. More specifically, through the lens of a sociological perspective, we discuss ways in which institutional identity that is articulated and defined by both curricular functions and the Carnegie Classifications™ can influence the plausible causes of workplace bullying in community colleges. To guide our discussion, we identify some evidence from the literature to see how these two proposed measures of institutional identity relate to each other within the contexts of social ecology of bullying and social reproduction framework. We then use the institutional identity of geography and gender to guide our discussion of how our proposed model of social ecology of bullying in community college can be used to examine the plausible causes of workplace bullying. This analysis demonstrates how institutional characteristics, specifically size and gender, reproduce social inequities, as theorized by the social reproduction framework. We conclude this chapter with recommendations for future directions for research on workplace bullying in community colleges.

Social Ecology of Bullying and Social Reproduction Theory

To further discuss ways in which factors can affect the emergence and perpetuation of bullying and uncivilized behaviors among students, faculty, and staff in community colleges, we use the notion of social ecology of bullying and social reproduction framework. We begin with Jonathan Cohen's quote:

> From ancient times to Iraq [, Iran, and Afghanistan] today, people have tried to solve differences with physical force. Instead of talking about needs and working to collaboratively solve problems nonviolently, America today is tragically caught in a cycle of misunderstanding, violence, and despair. (Cohen, 2006)

His quote brings into clear view the fact that institutional bullying and harassment perhaps do not exist within a vacuum, but rather reflect and actually reproduce the messages and actions stemming from the larger social realm. Blumenfeld (2010) refers to this as "the social ecology of bullying and harassment," and interprets *ecology* as the relationships between organisms and their environment (Merriam-Webster, 2003, p. 394). In this regard, social ecology of bullying is strongly related to social reproduction theory (Bowles & Gintis, 1976), which proposes that educational institutions do not, in fact, promote equality of opportunity, but rather, perpetuate or *reproduce* the social inequalities stemming from the larger society, especially in terms of socioeconomic class and race. Researchers have extended Bowles and Gintis's (1976) initial focus to argue that, in addition to socioeconomic class and racial inequity, educational institutions also reproduce the gender (e.g., Gilligan, 1977; Miller, 1976), sexual identity (e.g., Blumenfeld, 1995; McNaron, 1997; Rankin, Weber, Blumenfeld, & Frazer, 2010; Sears, 2002), ability/disability (e.g., Davis, 2006), religious (e.g., Blumenfeld, 2006; Schlosser, 2003), and other inequities emanating from the surrounding culture and larger society.

Put into a context of higher education institutions, specifically regarding their efforts to make changes in institutional environments as better workplaces, Blumenfeld's social ecology of bullying framework and social reproduction theory place the responsibility on colleges and universities to determine, understand, and, if necessary, institute procedures that prevent workplace bullying. Walton (2005) urges that bullying prevention efforts very often focus instead merely "on statistics, characteristics, psychological profiles, and measurable events . . . [that] leave unclear and unconsidered the ways in which bullying is a manifestation of larger power relations in society" (p. 113). Higher education needs to consider those institutional identities and characteristics that lead to reproducing bullying behaviors and seek to change society. In this chapter, we contextualize this notion into higher education institutional characteristics, including but not limited to geography (Hardy & Katsinas, 2006, 2007; Katsinas, 2003), student services (Castañeda, Katsinas, & Hardy, 2008; Moeck, Katsinas, Hardy, & Bush, 2008), gender, and academic programs (Reid, 2006).

Institutional Identity

To understand the context of community colleges and their significance within the higher education landscape, a few facts are in order. In the 2009–2010 academic year, there are approximately 4,500 degree-granting postsecondary institutions in the United States (National Center for Education Statistics [NCES], 2010). Public two-year institutions (as we define as community colleges) constitute 22.2% (or 1,000) of the postsecondary institutions. In fall 2009, community colleges enrolled over 7.1 million credit students, 57% of whom were female students and 40% of whom were ethnic minority students (NCES, 2010).

In particular, students of Hispanic heritage were, by far, the fastest growing student population. The U.S. Census Bureau (2008) notes, the Hispanic population between 15 and 24 years of age is projected to grow from 8,483,000 in 2010 to 21,384,000 in 2050, an increase of more than 152%. It is expected that the enrollment of ethnic minority students will continue to grow at community colleges.

We have also learned that students attend community colleges for many different reasons. It seems that students choose community colleges because of these institutions' offering of diverse programs. For example, adult students who were recently unemployed and need extra academic preparations to attend college, can take remedial education at community colleges. These students have options of advancing to Career and Technical Education (CTE) programs to obtain successful employment, or moving on to transfer programs at a four-year institution to obtain a baccalaureate degree. Some of them may take advantage of completing both programs to pursue their own educational goals. To serve these student populations, community colleges offer curricular functions that are complex, thus creating a unique workplace as compared to other segments of educational institutions, such as secondary schools and four-year institutions.

Curricular Functions and Classifications of Community Colleges

Cohen and Brawer (2008) provide four curricular functions to help researchers, educators, and policymakers to organize and categorize complex programs at community colleges. The authors acknowledge that the following curricular functions are intertwined and hardly distinct. In fact, these defined functions are provided "primarily for funding agents and classification systems as a way of understanding events" (Cohen & Brawer, 2008, p. 24). These four curricular functions are:

1. Academic Transfer and General Education: Academic transfer, or collegiate, studies were meant to fulfill several institutional purposes: a popularizing role to have the effect of advertising higher education, democratizing pursuits as the community colleges became the point of first access for people entering higher education, and a function of conducting lower-division courses for the universities.
2. Vocational-Technical Education: Originally conceived as an essential component of terminal study—education for students who would not go on to further studies, designed to teach skills more complicated than those taught in high schools.
3. Continuing Education and Community Service: This function often serves as the cultural center for a community offering spectator events sponsored by the colleges but open to the public as well as to students.
4. Developmental (remedial) Education: Also known as remedial, compensatory, preparatory, or basic skills studies—has grown as the percentage of students poorly prepared in secondary schools has increased (Cohen & Brawer, 2008, pp. 20–24).

We believe that the above curricular functions will help us to see institutional identity and set the foundation to understand the unique workplace in community colleges. Utilizing the notion of social ecology of bullying, we conceive these curricular functions as institutional organisms that react and respond to the surrounding environment. We then take principles of the Carnegie Classifications™ to help us describe the immediate social environment of these curricular functions, such as geography, institutional size, and control.

The Carnegie Classification™ system takes into account four general principles of community colleges, including (a) institutional control (whether institutions are governed privately or publicly); (b) geographic location (rural, suburban, or urban); (c) size; and (d) governance (single or multi-campus) to organize and categorize diverse and complex institutions (Katsinas, 2003; The Carnegie Foundation for the Advancement of Teaching, 2005). There are numerous studies (Castañeda et al., 2008; Hardy & Katsinas, 2006, 2007; Moeck et al., 2008; Reid, 2006; Roessler, 2006) that utilized the Carnegie Classifications™ for public 2-year institutions to examine diverse issues and challenges that community colleges are facing. We firmly believe that this classification system will help community colleges to understand their social environment and how it interacts with their curricular functions, and to develop their institutional identity and thus interact to reproduce workplace bullying.

How the Curricular Functions and Classification Interact

In the following section, we are going to discuss how the curricular functions and classification system interact within the frameworks of social ecology of bullying and the social reproduction theory. We depict this phenomenon as a model in Figure 5.1.

It is critical to note that there are numerous limitations as we present our conceptual model of social ecology of bullying in community colleges in a two-dimensional figure. First, it is difficult to depict the intertwined nature of four curricular functions on paper. Though they are illustrated in four distinct circles, readers need to be aware that the relationship among these functions can be fluid (directional) and multiple dimensional. Second, the relationships among the curricular functions and the principles of the Carnegie Classifications™ are also complex; thus, it is possible that those relationships possess some directionality and multi-dimensionality. Finally, though factors that cause social inequalities from culture and larger society are illustrated in the figure in six distinct rectangles, we conceive that these factors are also intertwined, and they can relate to any curricular functions and/or principles of the Carnegie Classifications™. Given the limitations mentioned above, how can we utilize the model to understand workplace bullying in community colleges? By reviewing evidence from the literature, we will discuss how the elements in this model can be applied to examine plausible causes of bullying and/or enabling structures for bullying (Lester, 2009)

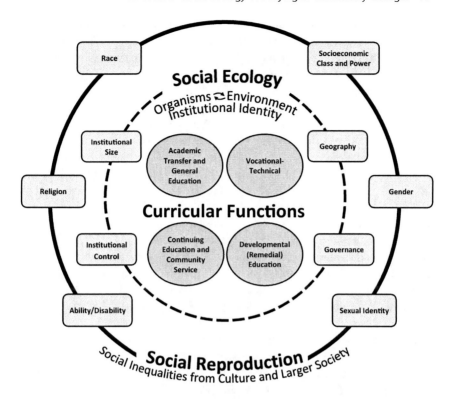

FIGURE 5.1 Starobin & Blumenfeld Model of Social Ecology of Bullying in Community Colleges

in community college settings. To do this, we pay special attention to issues that can be generated from particular geography and gender, because these are two distinct institutional identities that are also relevant in social reproduction theory and are unique characteristics of community colleges, as will become clear in the following section.

Plausible Causes of Bullying Based on Geography

In this chapter, we argue that there is a scarcity of evidence-based or empirical research on workplace bullying in community colleges. There is another area, among many, of community college research that deserves more attention from researchers. In particular, we argue that community colleges in rural areas have been the forgotten majority (as measured by the number of campuses) with regard to research in the field of higher education, and may play a role in the prevalence of workplace bullying. Recently, Some scholars (Hardy & Katsinas, 2007; Katsinas, 2003; Moeck et al., 2008) have advocated the critical role that these institutions play in the nation's most economically distressed and remote communities.

Based on their classification analysis, Hardy and Katsinas (2007) found that by the numbers of enrollment, two-thirds of all community college students were enrolled in urban and suburban colleges. However, by the number of campuses, rural community college campuses represent 59% of all community college campuses. Among those colleges, 25% were classified as rural small colleges (less than 2,500 annual unduplicated head count). The authors (Hardy & Katsinas, 2007) further argue that these rural colleges are more likely to serve larger percentages of full-time students, as compared with colleges in urban and suburban areas. The high percentage of full-time enrollment reflects the curricular functions of rural small colleges—they serve selected programs, such as nursing, allied health, and career and technical education programs and illustrate the relationship between classification and curricular functions (Hardy & Katsinas, 2007; Reid, 2006). Hardy and Katsinas (2007) also argue that it is possible for rural small colleges to focus on traditional transfer curricular programs that enroll full-time students. It is also likely that these colleges serve less diverse academic programs, which leads the colleges to hire a higher percentage of full-time faculty and staff members to serve such programs. Further, rural small colleges are more likely to serve a high percentage of Caucasian students (more than 70%, compared with less than 50% in urban colleges). This unique institutional identity, based on curricular functions and principles of the classification, lead us to think the institutional organisms (curricular functions) are interacting within an extremely homogeneous environment—both socially and institutionally. Through personal communication, a human resources director in a rural small college indicated that such homogeneity in a workplace can create a sense of "oneness" or "one big family," in which faculty and staff members *bite their tongues* to avoid behaviors and/or attitudes that are undesirable and harmful to others. A lack of anonymity in a small community can also serve as a threat to faculty and staff members for possible retaliation if they *don't bite their tongues* or act differently from their institutional or surrounding social norms. This can create a potential surge in and perpetuation of workplace bullying that is forced from the reproduction of social inequalities.

The homogeneous social and work environment can also create a potential harm where *differences* exist. One of the obvious differences in the curricular functions is the difference between traditional transfer curricular programs and vocational/career technical education programs. In case of the State of Iowa, to teach at a community college in traditional transfer curricular programs, faculty must have a Master's degree in the teaching field. However, for career and technical programs, an instructor with more than 6,000 contact (teaching) hours in a vocational program in high school can teach welding classes at community colleges. Again, rural small colleges have seen tensions and unspoken bullying behaviors among faculty members based on their *differences* in educational background, which can be translated as social power differences. Another instance can be found in the student services area. Rural colleges (in various sizes) are more likely to have residence halls (Moeck et al., 2008) and intercollegiate athletics (Castañeda et al., 2008), as compared with colleges in suburban and urban areas. This implies that these colleges enroll students who may not be familiar with surrounding (or majority) culture, custom, religion, and other factors that can create inequality.

Plausible Causes of Bullying Based on Gender

Community colleges have served favorably both for women who enroll in colleges as students and those who work at colleges as faculty and staff members. Of the estimated 301,000 faculty throughout the United States, women comprise 48.7% of total faculty at community colleges, compared with 36.3% at four-year institutions. Townsend (1995, in Hagedorn & Laden, 2002) argues that women have attained administrative managerial positions more often within community colleges than within four-year institutions, primarily because there is a greater presence of women role models serving in leadership positions. Yet researchers have found a greater gender inequity measured by salaries exists in community colleges than in four-year institutions, despite the outnumbered women serving in key leadership positions, including departmental and college-level administrations and faculty unions (Castro, 2000; Hagedorn & Laden, 2002; Townsend, 1995). Hagedorn and Laden (2002) conclude that while conditions appear somewhat better for women faculty and administrators within community colleges, that "with the knowledge that we continue to live in a gendered world (Wood, 1997), but that the gender politics may be a shade softer at community colleges where equality is embedded in the institutional mission" (p. 76).

Going beyond the institutional-level study of women faculty and administrators in community colleges, Lester (2009) looked at gendered culture differences between academic and vocational disciplines. The author found that bullying occurs more often between male and female colleagues, as well as between students, within "male-dominated vocational departments where women faculty faced challenges to their credibility and authority as female instructors in a 'man's job'" (p. 458). This is precisely how we conceive that workplace bullying could emerge based on a relationship between curricular functions in community colleges and social (gender) inequalities.

Most of the existing literature on gender issues in the workplace in community colleges focuses on gender differences (regardless of how women representation appears as dominant or non-dominant in a workplace), but we suggest broadening such gender perspective on workplace bullying in community colleges by considering some other curricular functions of community colleges. For instance, numerous educational programs offered at community colleges are female dominant, including nursing, paralegal, and cosmetology, to list a few. These educational programs typically contain elements from academic transfer and general education and continuing education curricular functions. We choose nursing programs at community colleges to discuss the utilization of the model of social ecology of bullying, as community colleges play a significant role in nursing education in the United States.

The U.S. Department of Health and Human Services (HHS), Health Resources and Services Administration (HRSA) has conducted the National Sample Survey of Registered Nurses (NSSRN) every four years since 1980 (Health Resources and Services Administration [HRSA], 2010). The results of the 2008 NSSRN revealed some demographics, educational background, and other information about a sample of 55,151 actively licensed RNs across the 50 states and the District of Columbia, as of March 10, 2008. Since the beginning of the national survey, HRSA has seen dramatic growth in the percentage of RNs whose initial education program in the Associate Degree in Nursing (ADN) was at community colleges. The percentage of RNs prepared in ADN programs grew from 18.7% in 1980 to 45.4% in 2008 (HRSA, 2010). It is also notable that the 2008 female representation of the sample was 93.4% (or 51,511 by the number of females).

We reviewed several more-recent research studies that focus on bullying at both educational and work (clinical and/or practicum experiences) environments in nursing programs (Cleary, Hunt, & Horsfall, 2010; Hogh, Gomes Carneiro, Giver, & Rugulies, 2011; Hutchinson, Wilkes, Jackson, & Vickers, 2010; Randle, 2003). These studies acknowledge that bullying has been found to be commonplace, especially in the transition to becoming a nurse (Randle, 2003). Nursing students are in a vulnerable position that carries a high risk of exposure to nursing norms (being bullied and witnessing patients being bullied by qualified nurses, who could be their instructors). Randle (2003) notes that such internalization of nursing norms leads students to reproduce bullying to others. It is critical that bullying behaviors among nursing instructors could directly (e.g., students' lower self-esteem) and indirectly (e.g., reproduction of bullying to others) influence nursing students. Put differently, negative implications of nursing faculty workplace bullying can be identified not only among faculty themselves, but among students as well. We further argue that the degree of such internalization of nursing norms in gendered educational and work environments can differ based on geography and size of the respective institutions (e.g., community colleges, hospitals, etc.).

In the context of nursing programs, race also could interact with gender as a plausible cause of bullying. A survey study that resulted in 5,696 respondents of Danish health care workers who received educational credentials in 2004 revealed significant findings regarding immigrant health care workers at rick of being bullied (Hogh et al., 2011). A logistic regression analysis controlled for gender, age, type of job, and type of education revealed that the non-Western immigrants were more than six times more likely to be bullied than were the Danish respondents during their health care education. Implications from this study include that the higher risk among non-Western immigrants of being bullied during their health care education could be explained by language and communication difficulties that include mastery of grammar and vocabulary, accent, and nonverbal communication (Hogh et al., 2011). Similar results were found in a study of black and ethnic minority nurses in a study in England (Alexis & Vydelingum, 2004).

Another plausible cause of bullying in nursing programs can be seen as related to exercises of both formal and informal uses of power identified in Lester's study

(2009), specifically between the female-dominated ranks of administrators (nursing deans and program directors) and the male-dominated faculty members who teach general science courses (biology, chemistry, etc.) that are required in nursing curriculum. Moreover, these science faculty members are typically predominantly White males. Thus, we hypothesize that there might be some complex relationship between the administrators who could formally exercise their bureaucratic, hierarchical, and political power and the faculty members who could informally exercise their power that can be genderized and racialized.

Conclusions and Implications

In this chapter, we proposed a model of social ecology of bullying to advance our knowledge and understanding of workplace bullying at community colleges. For those who are new to the study of community colleges, we provided Cohen and Brawer's (2008) curricular functions of community colleges to understand community colleges as unique educational postsecondary institutions. Though four unique curricular functions of community colleges are listed in this chapter, we are in agreement with Cohen and Brawer that these functions are rarely exclusive, and interweave to best serve in their community. We also postulated that the utilization of the Carnegie Classifications™ could allow researchers to discover holistic measurements of institutional characteristics and identity. In other words, we found the application of this classification system strengthens our understanding of the workplace bullying in community colleges.

We hope that the discussion of the intersection between the curricular functions and the Carnegie Classifications™ provided the readers ways to better understand the existing literature including, but not limited to, Hagedorn and Laden (2002), Lester (2009), and Townsend (1995, 2009). In particular, our review of the literature and discussion of the utilization of the model of social ecology of bullying in community college advance the knowledge of "enabling structures for bullying" that were generated from Lester's work. Looking ahead, we see possible uses of our model to respond to areas of investigation, such as intersection of gender and race as well as role of subculture, as suggested by Lester (2009). We further suggest that future research on workplace bullying in community college take a look at community colleges, including but not limited to (a) historically Black two-year colleges, (b) tribal colleges, and (c) Hispanic Serving Institutions (HSIs). These two-year publically controlled institutions are rich in their institutional history and surrounded by community where race plays a critical role.

Finally, it is our great hope that our proposed frameworks, a model of social ecology of bullying, implications, and recommendations for future research will generate critical discourse on workplace bullying at community colleges. Most importantly, we continue to examine the plausible causes of the emergence and perpetuation of workforce bullying, so that all members of workplaces at community colleges, including administrators, faculty, staff, and students can work toward the prevention and avoidance of workplace bullying to protect the rights and dignity of individuals.

References

Alexis, O., & Vydelingum, V. (2004). The lived experience of overseas black and minority ethnic nurses in the NSH in the south of England. *Diversity in Health and Social Care*, 13–20.

Blumenfeld, W.J. (1995). Gay/straight alliances: Transforming pain to pride. In G. Unks (Ed.), *The gay teen: Educational practice and theory for lesbian, gay, and bisexual adolescents* (pp. 211–224). New York: Routledge.

Blumenfeld, W.J. (2006). Christian privilege and the promotion of "secular" and not-so "secular" mainline Christianity in public schooling and the larger society. *Equity and Excellence in Education, 39*(3), 195–210.

Blumenfeld, W.J. (2010). The social ecology of bullying. Presentation at the International Bullying Prevention Conference, Seattle, Washington.

Bowles, S., & Gintis, H. (1976). *Schooling in capitalist America*. London: Routledge and Kegan Paul.

The Carnegie Foundation for the Advancement of Teaching. (2005). *The Carnegie classification of institutions of higher education*. Stanford, CA: Author.

Castañeda, C., Katsinas, S.G., & Hardy, D.E. (2008). Meeting the challenge of gender equity in community college athletics. *New Directions for Community Colleges, 142*, 93–105.

Castro, C.R. (2000). Community college faculty satisfaction and the faculty union. In L.S. Hagedorn (Ed.), *What contributes to job satisfaction among faculty and staff*. New Directions for Institutional Research, 105. San Francisco, CA: Jossey-Bass.

Cleary, M., Hunt, G.E., & Horsfall, J. (2010). Identifying and addressing bullying in nursing. *Issues in Mental Health Nursing, 31*, 331–335.

Cohen, A. M., & Brawer, F.B. (2008). *The American community college* (5th ed.). San Francisco: Jossey-Bass.

Cohen, J. (2006). Social, emotional, ethical, and academic education: Creating a climate for learning, participation in democracy, and well-being. *Harvard Educational Review, 76*(2), 201–237.

Davis, L. (2006). *The disability studies reader*. New York: Routledge.

Gilligan, C. (1977). In a different voice: Women's conceptions of self and of morality. *Harvard Educational Review, 47*, 481–517.

Hagedorn. L.S., & Laden, B.V. (2002). Exploring the climate for women as community college faculty. *New Directions for Community Colleges, 118*, 69–78.

Hardy, D.E., & Katsinas, S.G. (2006). Using community college classifications in research: From conceptual model to useful tool. *Community College Journal of Research and Practice, 30*, 339–358.

Hardy, D.E., & Katsinas, S.G. (2007). Classifying community colleges: How rural community colleges fit. *New Directions for Community Colleges, 137*, 5–17.

Health Resources and Services Administration (HRSA). (2010). *The registered nurse population: Findings from the 2008 national sample survey registered nurses*. Washington, DC: U.S. Department of Health and Human Services. Retrieved from http://bhpr.hrsa.gov/healthworkforce/rnsurveys/rnsurveyfinal.pdf

Hogh, A., Gomes Carneiro, I., Giver, H., & Rugulies, R. (2011). Are immigrant health care workers subject to increased risk of bullying at work? A one-year prospective study. *Scandinavian Journal of Psychology, 52,* 49–56.

Hutchinson, M., Wilkes, L., Jackson, D., & Vickers M.H. (2010). Integrating individual, work group and organizational factors: testing a multidimensional model of bullying in the nursing workplace. *Journal of Nursing Management, 18,* 173–181.

Katsinas, S.G. (2003). Two-year college classifications based on institutional control, geography, governance, and size. *New Directions for Community Colleges, 122,* 17–28.

Lester, J. (2009). Not your child's playground: Workplace bullying among community college faculty. *Community College Journal of Research and Practice, 33,* 444–462.

McNaron, T.A.H. (1997). *Poisoned ivy: Lesbian and gay academics confronting homophobia.* Philadelphia, PA: Temple University Press.

Merriam-Webster. (2003). *Collegiate dictionary* (11th ed.). Springfield, MA: Author.

Miller, J.B. (1976). *Toward a new psychology of women.* Boston: Beacon Press.

Moeck, P.G., Katsinas, S.G., Hardy, D.E., & Bush V.B. (2008). The availability, prospects, and fiscal potential of on-campus housing at rural community colleges. *Community College Review, 35*(3), 237–249.

National Center for Education Statistics (NCES). (2010). *Digest of education statistics.* Retrieved from http://nces.ed.gov/programs/digest/d10/

Randle, J. (2003). Bullying in the nursing profession. *Journal of Advanced Nursing, 43*(4), 395–401.

Rankin, S., Weber, G., Blumenfeld, W.J., & Frazer, S. (2010). *2010 state of higher education for lesbian, gay, bisexual, & transgender people.* Charlotte, NC: Campus Pride.

Reid, M.B. (2006). Rural community colleges and the nursing shortage in severely distressed counties. *Dissertation Abstracts International, 66*(11), 3952. (UMI No. AAT 3196174.)

Roessler, B. C. (2006). A quantitative study of revenues and expenditures in U.S. community colleges, 1980–2001. *Dissertation Abstracts International, 67*(4), 1200A. (UMI No. AAT3214494.)

Schlosser, L.A. (2003). Christian privilege: Breaking a sacred taboo. *Journal of Multicultural Counseling and Development, 31,* 44–51.

Schmidt, P. (2010, June 8). Workplace mediators seek a role in taming faculty bullies. *The Chronicle of Higher Education.* Retrieved from http://chronicle.com/article/Workplace-Mediators-Seek-a-/65815/

Schmidt, P. (2011, February 18). Ohio U. is found to have unfairly branded a professor a bully. *The Chronicle of Higher Education.* Retrieved from http://chronicle.com/article/Ohio-U-Is-Found-to-Have/126461/

Sears, J. (2002). Institutional climate for lesbian, gay, and bisexual education faculty: What is the pivotal frame of reference? *Journal of Homosexuality, 43*(1), 11–37.

Townsend, B.K. (1995). Women community college faculty: On the margins or in the mainstream? In B.K. Townsend (Ed.), *Gender and power in the community college* (pp. 39–46). New Directions for Community Colleges, 89. San Francisco: Jossey-Bass.

Townsend, B.K. (2009). Community college organizational climate for minorities and women. *Community College Journal of Research and Practice, 33,* 731–744.

Twale, D.J., & De Luca, B.M. (2008). *Faculty incivility: The rise of the academic bully culture and what to do about it.* San Francisco, CA: Jossey-Bass.

U.S. Census Bureau. (2008, August 14). Projections of the Hispanic population (any race) by age and sex for the United States: 2010 to 2050. Table 20. (NP2008-T20.)

Population Division, U.S. Census Bureau. Retrieved from http://www.census.gov/population/www/projections/summarytables.html

Walton, G. (2005). "Bullying widespread": A critical analysis of research and public discourse on bullying. *Journal of Social Violence, 4*(1), 91–115.

Wood, J.T. (1997). Discordant voices in the community colleges. In L.S. Zwerling & H. London (Eds), *First-generation students: Confronting the cultural issues*. New Directions for Community Colleges, 80. San Francisco: Jossey-Bass.

6

WORKPLACE BULLYING IN HIGHER EDUCATION

Some Legal Background

Kerri Stone

The United States Supreme Court has recognized that "[t]he college classroom[,] with its surrounding environs[,] is peculiarly the 'marketplace of ideas'" (*Healy v. James*, 1972, p. 180). Academic freedom is the cornerstone of higher education. It enables professors to effectively educate their students, using independence and their own judgment, and to contribute to the marketplace of ideas. Professors engage in unique activities, such as the publishing of original scholarship and faculty governance, which demand that they be unmoored from most restraints regarding their thoughts on any number of topics and how they choose to express those thoughts. The free, unfettered exchange of ideas, and constant rigorous, if not rancorous, debate, are seen by some as hallmarks of an institution that is flourishing. This makes allegations of bullying in the context of higher education particularly thorny and difficult to negotiate.

Additionally, in many situations, by virtue of their placement on lecturer review or promotion and tenure committees, professors find themselves situated to evaluate and make recommendations about the employment status or situation of those who used to be their peers. In other situations, a chairperson or dean with decision-making power resigns from that post to rejoin her teaching faculty fulltime and finds herself on the same level as those over whom she used to wield power. This type of fluidity in structure, hierarchy, and decision making differs from the more fixed structure typically found in an office, factory, or other workplace context, in which people work for progressive promotions and function at well-defined varying gradations of status and power. This, too, can complicate employment decisions and internal adjudications that follow interpersonal struggles and blowups in the workplace.

This chapter is about some of the legal considerations underlying workplace bullying that might occur in the context of higher education. When an employee is bullied in the workplace, a host of legal ramifications can ensue. Despite the fact that bullying behavior, per se, is not currently unlawful under federal or state law (Harthill, 2011; Healthy Workplace Bill), depending on the specifics of the behavior and how it is characterized, it may form the basis for one or more federal or state claims (Chamallas, 2007; Harthill, 2011; Stone, 2012). As such, any employer who is on notice of bullying behavior ought to be on guard and proactive, but also be careful, for several reasons.

In the first place, the bullying victim may, as mentioned, bring one or more federal or state claims against the employer (Chamallas, 2007; Harthill, 2011; Stone, 2012). However, disciplining or attempting to fire the alleged bully, especially if he or she holds a tenured position, may be troublesome, as well. Specifically, one who feels that she is unfairly fired or treated unfairly with respect to the terms, conditions, or privileges of her employment, may not see herself as a bully, but rather, believe that she is the victim of unlawful discrimination or retaliation. So, for example, in the midst of an interpersonal workplace dispute, an employee may see herself as the victim of a supervisor's bullying behavior. That employee might complain to management, resulting in discipline or firing of that supervisor. The supervisor, believing that she was not bullying the employee, might argue to the court that she was not fired for bullying behavior, but for some other and unlawful reason, such as retaliation or discrimination. To the extent that a person is asked to leave or is somehow disciplined for what the employer considers bullying behavior, she may argue to a court that it was not her own behavior, but rather retaliation for her own complaints or allegations of harassment or discrimination that got her fired.

Employment is presumed to be at will. This means that individuals may be hired or fired for any reason at all—or no reason—and that, absent a dictate (via legislation or via common law) engrafted atop this background presumption, this presumption remains intact. Moreover, even sweepingly broad remedial antidiscrimination statutes like Title VII of the Civil Rights Act of 1964 are not, as numerous courts have intoned over decades, "civility codes" designed to compel civility, kindness, or even decency in the workplace (*Burlington Northern v. White*, 2006; *Davis v. Coastal Int'l Sec., Inc.*, 2002; *Oncale v. Sundowner Offshore Servs., Inc.*, 1998). Rather, they exist to combat class-based discrimination with respect to the terms and conditions of one's employment (*Burlington Northern v. White*, 2006; *Oncale v. Sundowner Offshore Servs., Inc.*, 1998; *Ricci v. DeStefano*, 2009). To the extent that behavior termed "bullying" actually amounts to or may be seen as amounting to discrimination based on a protected class such as race, religion, sex, age, disability, etc., the behavior may be seen as actionable (Fitzpatrick, 2011). Moreover, to the extent that the behavior might fall within the definition of an actionable tort, such as assault or defamation, it may very well result in individual and/or employer liability (Chamallas, 2007).

Bullying, itself, though, as stated, is not unlawful. Despite efforts by the Workplace Bullying Institute to endorse the Healthy Workplace Bill, a model statute drafted by Professor David Yamada, no state has yet enacted anti-bullying legislation for the workplace (Workplace Bullying Institute, 2011; Healthy Workplace Bill). There are, however, currently 21 states that have introduced versions of the bill, and there are now 16 bills active in 11 states (Healthy Workplace Bill; Workplace Bullying Institute, 2011). If the movement gains more traction and some of these bills pass, employers will need to pay closer attention to their potential liability for workplace bullying. In the meantime, this chapter will detail some of the extant federal and state claims that those who have experienced various forms of bullying at work might be able to make presently.

Federal Statutes and Claims

There are several federal statutes that prohibit workplace discrimination based upon protected class status. Examples of some of the most commonly invoked statutes in lawsuits brought today are Title VII of the Civil Rights Act of 1964, which prohibits discrimination with respect to the terms, conditions, or privileges of employment on the basis of race, color, religion, sex, or national origin; the Age Discrimination in Employment Act of 1967, which prohibits employment discrimination because of age and protects those 40 years old and older; and the Americans with Disabilities Act of 1990, which prohibits workplace and other discrimination based on one's status as disabled.

There are three primary causes of action that a plaintiff can make under each statute. The first of these is a claim for disparate treatment, whereby a plaintiff alleges that she was treated differently than others with respect to the terms and/or conditions of her employment, such as pay, title, work assignments, etc., on the basis of her protected class status (Civil Rights Act of 1964, § 2000e-2). Where this occurs, a court will expect the plaintiff to allege that she suffered an adverse action because of her protected class status (*Texas Dept. of Cmty. Affairs v. Burdine*, 1981). The court will then typically turn to the defendant employer to proffer a legitimate, nondiscriminatory reason for the action (*Texas Dept. of Cmty. Affairs v. Burdine*, 1981). Then, it will turn back to the plaintiff to assist it in ascertaining whether the proffered reason was the defendant's true reason for acting as it did, or a mere pretext for unlawful discrimination (*Texas Dept. of Cmty. Affairs v. Burdine*, 1981). A plaintiff may also allege that a defendant had both a lawful and an unlawful reason for acting as it did, and the defendant will still be liable (Civil Rights Act of 1991, § 2000e-2). So, for example, a terminated plaintiff alleging discrimination based on sex may encounter a response from her employer that it was her excessive tardiness, and not her sex, that resulted in her firing. Even if the defendant employer can document this and show that this consequence is consistent with those that befall similarly situated men, inasmuch as the plaintiff can proffer persuasive evidence (like remarks or admissions) that her sex was also a substantial motivating factor in the termination, the employer will be liable for the discrimination, although damages will be limited.

To the extent that one complains of bullying that is tinged with protected class-related animus such as racism, sexism, ageism, etc., an employer should realize that any real or perceived concrete or palpable effects of that bullying, like a demotion, change in work assignments, or even a subsequent firing, may be framed as the basis for a statutory disparate treatment claim (Stone, 2009). A plaintiff bringing suit against her employer in such a circumstance could certainly argue persuasively that the adverse employment action was "because of" her protected class status.

The second type of claim that might be made is one of disparate impact, whereby a plaintiff alleges that a facially neutral policy or practice engendered a disparate effect on her protected class (*Griggs v. Duke Power Co.*, 1971). So, for example, a company that chooses to consider for promotion only those who can attend meetings on Sundays (where Sunday is not a necessary meeting day) may not be trying to exclude observant Christians from consideration, but it may nonetheless disproportionately be screening out candidates on the basis of their religion. Thus, a neutral practice, whether or not it was conceived with discriminatory intent, will be seen as conferring a disparate impact on a protected class (*Griggs v. Duke Power Co.*, 1971).

Once a plaintiff has demonstrated a disparate impact, the defendant is given the opportunity to show that there is a business necessity behind its practice or policy (Civil Rights Act of 1991, § 2000e-2). Even then, the plaintiff is given the chance to counter this by showing that there is an equally valid, less-discriminatory alternative to that practice or policy being challenged (Civil Rights Act of 1991, § 2000e-2). So, referring to the example given above, even if the employer could argue successfully that Sunday *was*, in fact, the only day on which meetings could be held, the plaintiff would be given an opportunity to proffer a viable alternative, like meeting at night. Such a claim is unlikely to be tied to workplace bullying, because the type of deliberate, humiliating behavior that typically underlies allegations of bullying is not likely to be classified as a neutral practice that happens to create a disparate effect.

The third type of claim that may be made is one for supervisory harassment based on protected class status, and this type of claim is most likely to be levied in connection with a complaint of bullying behavior. Perhaps the best-known variety of protected class-based harassment is sexual harassment, where one is deemed to have had her work environment permeated by harassment "because of" her sex. The cause of action for harassment was deemed cognizable by the U. S. Supreme Court in 1986 in the context of a sexual harassment case (*Meritor Sav. Bank v. Vinson*, 1986). The Court recognized the claim as a legitimate derivative of Title VII's prohibition against discrimination "because of," among other things, sex, with respect to the terms or conditions of an individual's employment (*Meritor Sav. Bank v. Vinson*, 1986). Further, although the cause of action was derived in the context of an interpretation of Title VII, courts have recognized harassment that occurs "because of" a status protected by other statutes, like the ADEA (age) and the ADA (disability) (*Arrieta-Colon v. Wal-Mart Puerto Rico, Inc.*, 2006; *Mojica v. El Conquistador Resort and Golden Door Spa*, 2010).Additionally, harassment claims that stem from bullying behavior have been made in the higher education context (*E.E.O.C. v. Univ. of Phx., Inc.*, 2007). Such claims can be made in the context of any workplace environment, so long as the claim of harassment may be anchored to the plaintiff's protected class status.

While the required elements of a claim will vary slightly from jurisdiction to jurisdiction, to make out a claim of harassment, a plaintiff must typically establish:

> (1) that she . . . is a member of a protected class; (2) that she was subjected to unwelcome . . . harassment; (3) that the harassment was based upon [that protected class]; (4) that the harassment was sufficiently severe or pervasive so as to alter the conditions of plaintiff's employment and create an abusive work environment; (5) that . . . [the] objectionable conduct was both objectively and subjectively offensive, such that a reasonable person would find it hostile or abusive and the victim in fact did perceive it to be so; and (6) that some basis for employer liability has been established. (*Agusty-Reyes v. Dept. of Educ. of Puerto Rico*, 2010, p. 53)

Factors that a court will look to when evaluating behavior alleged to be harassing include whether the harassment was intimidating, humiliating, or physically threatening; whether it unreasonably interfered with the plaintiff's performance at work; whether it became physical at any point, and if so, to what extent; and whether it pervaded the plaintiff's professional environment, effectively altering it with the number and impact of insults, ridicule, or even advances (*Harris v. Forklift Sys., Inc.*, 1993).

It is important to remember that if a plaintiff alleges behavior that would otherwise rise to the level of harassment, but is unable to show a nexus between the harassment and her protected class status (sex, race, religion, etc.), there can be no cognizable Title VII harassment claim (*Farpella-Crosby v. Horizon Health Care*, 1996).Therefore, generalized or so-called "status neutral" bullying will not support a claim of workplace harassment (*Farpella-Crosby v. Horizon Health Care*, 1996).

Additionally, as stated, in order for an employer to be found liable for discrimination, a basis for that liability must first be established. If a plaintiff alleging harassment can point to a tangible employment action in which her supervisor's harassment culminated—something along the lines of a firing, demotion, tenure denial, pay decrease, etc.—then the defendant enterprise/employer will be found vicariously liable once she has established that the harassment took place (*Faragher v. City of Boca Raton*, 1998). However, if the supervisory harassment did not culminate in a tangible employment action, the defendant enterprise may interpose a two-pronged affirmative defense to ward off liability (*Faragher v. City of Boca Raton*, 1998). This defense requires the employer to show that it had a reasonable policy in place and that it "exercised reasonable care to prevent and correct promptly any . . . discriminatory behavior," and "the plaintiff employee unreasonably failed to take advantage of any preventive or corrective opportunities provided by the employer or to avoid harm otherwise" (*El-Hakem v. BJY Inc.*, 2003, p. 1151). To the extent that a plaintiff endured actionable harassment at the hands of nonsupervisors, like coworkers or clients, that plaintiff may still sue her employer, but the standard to which the employer will be held will not be one of vicarious liability (*Faragher v. City of Boca Raton*, 1998). Instead, a court will ask whether the employer was negligent in permitting the abusive behavior to occur (*Faragher v. City of Boca Raton*, 1998). This essentially would mean that the employer knew or should have known about the behavior, but still failed to act in a way to attempt to remedy it as a reasonably prudent employer would (*Ocheltree v. Scollon Prods.*, 2003).

It is hard to imagine that there could exist today an institution of higher education that would not have promulgated a university or school policy on harassment and what constitutes harassment. It is important to remember that where the institution is a public institution, as a federal court has explained, "[b]ecause overbroad harassment policies can suppress or even chill core protected speech, and are susceptible to selective application amounting to content-based or viewpoint discrimination, the overbreadth doctrine may be invoked in student free speech cases" (*DeJohn v. Temple Univ.*, 2008, p. 314). A speech regulation is said to be impermissibly overbroad when it "reaches too much expression that is protected by the Constitution" (*DeJohn v. Temple Univ.*, 2008, p. 314). The drafting of such policies, whether at a public or at a private institution, should be done with the input of counsel who can foresee and preempt problems and challenges.

Finally, employers must be cognizant of how they handle allegations of bullying with regard to disciplining or firing employees. It may be the case that one who complains about a bully in some context is either later disciplined or fired for unrelated reasons or is disciplined or fired in connection with what she believes to be the bullying behavior. It may also be the case that one who is accused of bullying is subsequently disciplined or fired. In any event, an adverse employment action that befalls either an accuser or an accused bully may also be alleged by that person to be retaliatory.

Retaliation may be alleged for anything that either the common law or statutory law deems "protected activity." So, for example, Title VII and the other pieces of federal legislation discussed in this chapter have embedded anti-retaliation provisions contained within them that renders it unlawful for an employer to retaliate by discriminating against an employee who (1) "has opposed any practice made an unlawful employment practice by this subchapter"; or (2) "has made a charge, testified, assisted, or participated in any manner in an investigation, proceeding, or hearing under this subchapter" (Civil Rights Act of 1964, § 2000e–3(a)). Thus, once any employee has engaged in protected activity, which could be anything from filing an EEOC claim to complaining internally about an occupational safety issue, among countless other things, anything that happens to that employee going forward may be viewed in the context of a retaliation suit as suspect (*Hochstadt v. Worcester Found.*, 1976). Factors that a court will look to when determining whether an action taken was retaliatory include the surrounding circumstances (with a focus on the plaintiff's performance record and employee files) and the temporal lapse between the protected activity and the adverse action (*McCray v. Wal-Mart Stores, Inc.*, 2010; *Pham v. City of Seattle*, 2001; Weiner, 2003). The shorter the lapse, the stronger the inference may be that the former motivated the latter (*McCray v. Wal-Mart Stores, Inc.*, 2010; *Pham v. City of Seattle*, 2001).

State Statutes and Claims

Both states and localities have antidiscrimination laws that regulate discrimination in the workplace on the basis of both classes that are protected by federal statute, like race, sex, and religion, and classes that are not, like weight, appearance, and sexual orientation (Institute of Real Estate Management, 2007; Kristen, 2002). These laws will vary from jurisdiction to jurisdiction, but they will often draw on or mirror the adjudicatory frameworks used under federal law, like that for harassment (Institute of Real Estate Management, 2007; Kristen, 2002; Langan & Ritts, 2011).

Moreover, there are also a variety of state law tort claims (meaning claims for civil wrongs) that a bullying victim may bring against her bully, employer, or both. These claims, too, will vary somewhat from jurisdiction to jurisdiction in terms of how they are defined and precisely how they must be made out. These claims will be viable so long as the behavior alleged (and ultimately proven) falls within a given jurisdiction's definition for or requirements of the given tort. It is important to keep in mind that intentional torts that stem from circumstances surrounding the work of an employee may render the employer vicariously liable (especially where the offensive conduct was done within the scope of another employee's employment, i.e., in his furtherance of his employer's goals or interests) *and* the tortfeasor (the person who committed the civil wrong) liable (Campbell, 2005).

Intentional infliction of emotional distress is a claim that may be levied in most jurisdictions against one whose "extreme and outrageous" conduct causes another "extreme emotional distress" (Restatement (Second) of Torts § 46 (1965)). Extreme emotional distress has been defined as constituting "among other things, mental suffering, mental anguish, nervous shock, and other highly unpleasant mental reactions" (86 C.J.S. *Torts* § 78 (2011); *Young v. Allstate Ins. Co.*, 2008, pp. 429, 692). It is the case that the threshold for liability is extremely high in these cases, though, because "[e]ven if a defendant's conduct is unjustifiable, it does not necessarily rise to the level of atrocious and beyond all possible bounds of decency that would cause an average member of the community to believe it was outrageous" (38 Am. Jur. 2d *Fright, Shock, Etc.* § 8 (2011)).

In the employment context, courts have held that claims for intentional infliction of emotional distress do not apply to ordinary employment disputes, stating that

> [t]he range of behavior encompassed in "employment disputes" is broad, and includes at a minimum such things as criticism, lack of recognition, and low evaluations, which, although unpleasant and sometimes unfair, are ordinarily expected in the work environment. Thus, to establish a cause of action for intentional infliction of emotional distress in the workplace, an employee must prove the existence of some conduct that brings the dispute outside the scope of an ordinary employment dispute and into the realm of extreme and outrageous conduct. Such extreme conduct exists only in the most unusual of circumstances. (*GTE Southwest, Inc. v. Bruce*, 1999, p. 613)

Therefore, "[i]t is neither extreme nor outrageous for an employer to ask an employee to share information concerning allegations made against a coworker, even if it is an unpleasant experience" (*Wal-Mart Stores, Inc. v. Canchola*, 2003, p. 738). Similarly, there was no extreme and outrageous conduct where an employee was yelled at and forced to endure an "exit parade" during the busiest time of the day (*Sebesta v. Kent. Elecs. Corp.*, 1994, pp. 463–464). Hence, unless the bullying described is truly beyond the pale in the context of other successful intentional infliction of emotional distress claims brought in that jurisdiction, this type of claim is not likely to succeed. In fact, one court has stated that "[a]s inappropriate and repulsive as workplace harassment is, such execrable behavior almost never rises to the level of outrageousness . . . as to reach the high threshold invariably applicable to a claim of intentional infliction of emotional distress" (*German v. Akal Sec., Inc.*, 2011, p. 6).

A jurisdiction may recognize the intentional tort of outrage, which typically requires that

> (1) the defendant intended to inflict emotional distress or knew or should have known that emotional distress was the likely result of its conduct; (2) the conduct was extreme and outrageous, was beyond all possible bounds of decency, and is "utterly intolerable in a civilized community; (3) the actions of the defendant were the cause of the plaintiff's distress; and (4) the emotional distress sustained by the plaintiff was so severe that no reasonable person could be expected to endure it." (*Davenport v. Bd. of Trustees of the Univ. of Ark. at Pine Bluff*, 2011, p. 4)

Bullying behavior may create liability for this tort, as well.

Assault is another intentional tort that is often defined as "any intentional, unlawful offer of corporal injury to another by force, or force unlawfully directed toward the person of another, under such circumstances as to create a well-founded fear or reasonable apprehension of imminent peril or an immediate battery, coupled with the apparent present ability to effectuate the attempt if not prevented" (6A C.J.S. *Assault* §1 (2011)). This means that a successful assault claim may be made out even where no physical contact has occurred. All that must be present is a well-founded apprehension of an imminent battery. In determining whether the fear was reasonable, the supervisor's accompanying words may be crucial (*Carter v. Virginia*, 2005, p. 841). The analysis will boil down to whether a judge can discern a reasonable, well-founded apprehension.

Battery is another intentional tort, generally defined as "unlawful, harmful, or offensive contact with the person of another," or as "the unlawful striking or beating of the person of another, no matter how slight" (6A C.J.S. *Assault* §3 (2011)). Thus, while this tort does require physical contact, it generally need not be violent, so long as it is reasonably perceived as harmful or offensive, and it can be something that, in another context and/or coming from another person, would have been perceived as welcome and benevolent, like a hug or a kiss. To the extent that such behavior, or the engenderment of reasonable apprehension of such behavior, is part of bullying behavior, it may thus give rise to an intentional tort claim.

A claim for defamation may be engendered where one publishes (by informing others of) false information about another that injures the other's reputation, usually thereby causing the other emotional distress (53 C.J.S. *Libel and Slander; Injurious Falsehood* §2 (2011)). Most jurisdictions have certain categories of defamatory speech that are so strongly presumed to injure one's reputation that harm need not be proven (Restatement (Second) of Torts §§570–574 (1977)). Inasmuch as bullying behavior involves intentionally humiliating someone by revealing false information about her to others, whether through the written or the spoken word, liability for defamation may be engendered. Defenses to defamation, however, include truth and privilege, which may be invoked in certain circumstances in which the law wants to encourage candor (Restatement (Second) of Torts §581A (1977)). This is why a jurisdiction may recognize, for example, a qualified privilege of an employer to provide a truthful reference letter (*Birch v. JP Morgan Chase & Co.*, 2010; *Senisch v. Carlino*, 2011). Even where information discovered or revealed is not false, a bully might commit a privacy tort in a given jurisdiction if he intentionally intrudes or brings to public light "a matter which the plaintiff has a right to keep private by the use of a method which is objectionable to the reasonable person" (62A Am. Jur. 2d *Privacy* §39 (2011)). Inasmuch as bullying may involve the deliberate humiliation of its target through behavior that might constitute a privacy tort, those who act as agents for and/or employers of those who engage in this type of humiliation should be aware of this type of tort's existence.

Another intentional tort claim that might be made by a bullying victim is one of tortious interference with employment or tortious interference with contract

(30 C.J.S. *Employer-Employee* § 281 (2011)). In order to make out such a claim, a plaintiff typically must demonstrate "(1) an advantageous employment relationship; (2) the defendant's knowledge of such relationship; (3) the defendant's interference, in addition to being intentional, was improper in motive or means; and (4) the plaintiff suffered economic harm as a result of the defendant's conduct." (30 C.J.S. *Employer-Employee* § 281 (2011)).

Based on traditional principles of agency law, an employer may be held liable for the negligence of its agents acting within the scope of their employment in addition to their intentional acts (Restatement (Second) of Agency § 213 (1958)). Where, for example, an employer hires someone who poses a danger to others, it may be liable for the tort of negligent hiring (*Hutcherson v. Progressive Corp.*, 1993; *Tichenor v. Roman Catholic Church of Archdiocese of New Orleans*, 1994). To make out such a claim, a plaintiff must allege that the employer hired someone whom it knew or whom it ought to have known was unfit, and that the hiring situated the unfit employee such that her incompetence or dangerous traits proximately caused harm to another (*Hutcherson v. Progressive Corp.*, 1993; *Tichenor v. Roman Catholic Church of Archdiocese of New Orleans*, 1994). The problem with trying to bring such a cause of action, however, is that many states impose very high standards on plaintiffs wishing to make such claims, with some requiring that the hiring create a palpably foreseeable or unreasonable risk of harm to others, which is often impossibly difficult to prove (Williams, 2007). So, for example, to the extent that the unfit employee did not have a record that would undeniably put an employer on notice that he had previously engaged in virtually the precise behavior that later renders him unfit, a plaintiff seeking to hold the employer responsible may not be successful. Often, an employer must actually have evidence that an employee has behaved in a specifically violent or harmful way previously before a court will find that it was negligent in hiring or retaining the employee.

Relatedly, while there is also a cause of action for negligent retention of an unfit employee, this, too, is often a very difficult claim to bring successfully. An employer who negligently hires an unfit employee remains obligated to exercise reasonable care to prevent her from harming others, even if the employee is acting outside the scope of her employment, provided that the employee is on the employer's premises or on premises upon which the employee may enter only as an employee (*Hutchison v. Luddy*, 2000).

Application

The fact of the matter is that in the context of higher education, many decisions, like those related to the promotion and tenure process, for example, will receive great deference from courts asked to disturb them. The Fourth Circuit Court of Appeals, for example, has spoken of its "consistent admonition against interfering with a university's tenure process" (*Sawicki v. Morgan State Univ.*, 2005, p. 12). This deference, combined with the fact that generalized, non-class-premised bullying is, in most of its typical iterations, lawful, and the very high standards that courts have applied to the available causes of action, discussed previously, makes it very difficult indeed for a plaintiff to recover after having been bullied, or perhaps victimized by an adverse employment action stemming from the bullying.

Obviously, to the extent that anyone—either an accused bully or an accuser—suffers an adverse employment action, like a demotion, nonselection, termination, or a constructive discharge (meaning that workplace conditions were made so objectively intolerable that anyone in her shoes would feel compelled to resign), a host of claims may be engendered. These may include wrongful termination claims, which, if you are dealing with a person with tenure or under contract, will be governed by the standard set forth in whatever agreement is in place between the parties (*Otero-Burgos v. Inter-Am. Univ.*, 2009). These may also include discrimination claims, inasmuch as the individual alleges that whatever action was directed toward her was motivated by her protected class status (Age Discrimination in Employment Act of 1967; Americans with Disabilities Act of 1990; Civil Rights Act of 1964).

However, even in a scenario in which an employer is contractually bound to show some level of "cause" for terminating an employee, where an employee engages in bullying, harassing, disruptive, or sabotaging behavior, such a showing may be relatively simple for the employer to make (White, 2000, p. 29). Moreover, where employment is at will, an employer typically need not show anything more than a nondiscriminatory reason for the action (like, for example, poor performance or excessive tardiness) and the fact that other, non-class members were not treated in a disparate fashion (Corbett, 2009). Further, while many people who believe they have been bullied may also believe that they have been constructively discharged, the standard of proving that any reasonable person in one's shoes would feel compelled to resign is one that many plaintiffs have found impossible to meet (Wolf, 1999).

The fact also remains that generalized bullying is not actionable under employment discrimination laws. For example, in a 2006 federal lawsuit, a computer technician who had worked for a college alleged that the bullying behavior that he suffered at the hands of his supervisor supported claims for, among other things, racial discrimination and harassment (*Lewis v. Ivy Tech State Coll.*, 2006). The court, however, found that while the plaintiff clearly "did not get along with his supervisor . . . whom he believes to be a tyrant, a bully, passive aggressive in his style of management, dishonest, and disrespectful-to everyone he worked with[,] . . . Title VII 'does not guarantee a utopian workplace, or even a pleasant one,' and the plaintiff could not demonstrate actionable discrimination" (*Lewis v. Ivy Tech State Coll.*, 2006, p. 3).

Employers should not feel overly constrained when dealing with bullies, although provisions in employment contracts and collective bargaining agreements that deal with discipline or termination should not be ignored or overlooked. Generally, however, firing or otherwise disciplining a bully where the bullying and disruptive behavior is amply documented has been viewed by courts as a legitimate action. For example, in a recent (2011) employment case in New York, the plaintiff alleged racial discrimination after she was progressively and repeatedly disciplined, transferred, and eventually terminated in the face of well-documented allegations that her "inappropriate behavior continued and even escalated, to the point that her coworkers repeatedly complained to supervisors about plaintiff's bullying conduct, and the tension and loss of morale that it had created" (*Coley-Allen v. Strong Health*, 2011, p. 2). The court rejected her allegations of discrimination because it found

> no evidence that the progressive discipline to which plaintiff was subjected was motivated by discriminatory animus. Plaintiff does not dispute that she engaged in the unacceptable and unprofessional behavior for which she was disciplined, or deny that she failed to substantially comply with the requirements of her performance improvement plan. In fact, at her deposition, plaintiff repeatedly admitted prior incidents of unprofessional conduct, complaints by coworkers, and failing to sign out of the . . . Lab. (*Coley-Allen v. Strong Health, 2011*, p. 3)

In a 2007 federal case, a professor filed a complaint alleging discrimination based on her national origin (Spanish) (*Recio v. Creighton Univ.*, 2007). The commission found no reasonable cause, so that complaint did not go far (*Recio v. Creighton Univ.*, 2007). However, a year later, the professor filed another complaint, alleging that the university had retaliated against her for the filing of her national origin discrimination charge (*Recio v. Creighton Univ.*, 2007). The professor alleged that she suffered numerous adverse actions, including denial of privileges, unfair discipline, and termination (*Recio v. Creighton Univ.*, 2007).

The university, defending its treatment, discipline, and eventual termination of the professor, proffered nonretaliatory reasons for each thing that it stood accused of doing (*Recio v. Creighton Univ.*, 2007). The university cited the professor's own "pattern of obsessive, aggressive and retaliatory behavior" and "long-standing unprofessional behavior" contributing to "a dysfunctional and hostile academic environment for the entire department that continues constantly to be addressed by the administration" (*Recio v. Creighton Univ.*, 2007, p. 1). Members of her department "describe[d] her as 'obsessive, a bully, aggressive, irrational, demanding, creates conflict, stalking, retaliates, rages, verbal violence, explosive, etc.'" (*Recio v. Creighton Univ.*, 2007, p. 2).

The court, persuaded by the rationales proffered by the university, concluded that the plaintiff had not suffered a materially adverse employment action (*Recio v. Creighton Univ.*, 2007). Observing that the law did not permit the professor to "make her claim based on personality conflicts, bad manners, or petty slights and snubs," the court found that she had experienced no actionable retaliation (*Recio v. Creighton Univ.*, 2007, p. 6).

The distinction created by the law between actionable discrimination and a legitimate response to bullying is perfectly encapsulated by the court in a 2007 case out of Washington State (*Turner v. Univ. of Wash.*, 2007). Here, a black, Ethiopian-born female, Director of Education and Outreach for the University of Washington's Engineered Biomaterials program, sued the university and an individual director alleging race and national origin disparate treatment discrimination, hostile work environment harassment, retaliation pursuant to Washington's Law Against Discrimination, and other federal civil rights claims:

> Fanaye Turner and Buddy Ratner should have been friends for life. They shared a commitment to science education, a hope to extend the joy of science professions to under-served groups such as women and minorities and a zest for life away from UW that led to Ms. Turner participating in Dr. Ratner's wedding ceremony. Instead, they find themselves avoiding each other's glances sitting in opposing tables in an employment discrimination civil trial in the United States District Court for two weeks. How did this close professional and social relationship disintegrate over time? That is the question the Court must answer in determining whether plaintiff has met her burden of proof in this trial.
>
> It is clear that in 1997 Fanaye Turner arrived at the UWEB program as a talented and valued member of an extraordinary team of scientists, educators and staff people embarked on an important project with tremendous value to the community. It is also apparent that she departed UW in 2004 as a depressed, shaken individual who was a shell of her former self. This trial is about what happened between her arrival and departure and what caused the serious emotional and economic damages Fanaye Turner suffered as a result of leaving her job under duress in 2004. Was Fanaye Turner a victim of discrimination by a series of managers and fellow employees who treated her unfairly because of her race or Ethiopian background? Or was her downfall a matter of her own making fueled by her bursts of anger at colleagues and an inability to see that while her motives may always have been good, her behavior became unbearable in the workplace? That it was these actions of Fanaye Turner that led to the employment actions she later complained about, not any bias or prejudice by the defendants? (*Turner v. Univ. of Wash.*, 2007, p. 1)

The court ultimately concluded that the plaintiff's professional deficiencies and "bouts of unprofessional behavior," both well-documented by the university, were what really gave rise to any adverse employment actions that she faced (*Turner v. Univ. of Wash.*, 2007, p. 6). The court also found that she had not, consequently, adequately demonstrated unlawful discrimination or that other, similarly situated, individuals were treated differently than she was in a way that would suggest class-based disparate treatment or disparate discipline (*Turner v. Univ. of*

Wash., 2007, p. 6). Based on these findings, the court was also able to dismiss the plaintiff's federal claims (*Turner v. Univ. of Wash.*, 2007). Had the plaintiff been able to demonstrate that others, similarly situated, who had exhibited behavior and shortcomings similar to her own, had been disciplined or somehow treated differently than she had been, a legitimate inference of discrimination might have been raised. This underscores the importance of an employer's institutional consistency when it comes to disciplining employees who are accused of bullying.

The court further concluded the plaintiff was unable to sustain her claim of workplace harassment pursuant to state law, because the facts that she alleged simply did not rise to a level of offensiveness or pervasiveness sufficient to alter the terms and conditions of her employment (*Turner v. Univ. of Wash.*, 2007). Moreover, while the court found that the plaintiff had suffered adverse employment actions and that she had engaged in protected activity by complaining of discrimination, she had not established a legally tenable nexus between the protected activity and the adverse actions because she

> failed to prove that [her] opposition to what she reasonably believed to be discrimination based on race or national origin, or participation in [a legal] proceeding, was a substantial motivating factor in the adverse employment actions. . . . The Court finds more credible defendants' explanation that the actions were motivated by plaintiff's unprofessional, abrasive, and brusque management style and plaintiff's performance problems. . . . In particular, the Court finds that defendant [Director] Ratner credibly testified that his attitude toward plaintiff changed not because of plaintiff's opposition to race or national origin discrimination, but because his superior, Engineering School Dean Denise Denton gave him an 'order' that she did not want to have to intervene in any future personnel issues at UWEB caused by plaintiff's actions. (*Turner v. Univ. of Wash.*, 2007, p. 8)

The court also noted that many of the plaintiff's professional and interpersonal problems were brought to her attention well before she engaged in any protected activities (*Turner v. Univ. of Wash.*, 2007). The court's conclusion as to the plaintiff's retaliation claims highlights the fact-intensive nature of credibility-based queries, and the importance of understanding from the outset that when a university or any other employer takes an action against someone who has raised a complaint of discrimination or otherwise engaged in protected activity, that action may or may not look like an unlawful retaliatory act, depending on how the trier of fact in a case processes and interprets the surrounding circumstances.

The court concluded by noting:

> This was not an easy case for the Court to decide. Fanaye Turner is a likeable woman who brings an admirable passion to all her endeavors. Throughout

the course of her employment at UWEB, however, plaintiff failed to accept that her colleagues' perception of her was not the product of race, national origin, sex discrimination, stereotyping, or retaliation, but rather was a reasonable reaction to her brusque and abrasive management style.... Although defendants' response to plaintiff's behavior may not have been artful, defendants' actions were not the product of discrimination or retaliation. . . . For individuals who could handle Ms. Turner's blunt and direct style, she was a joy to work with. But she could not see that for other individuals, she needed to use a more diplomatic style and when she crossed the line into bullying and abusive behavior, she had an extremely negative influence on the workplace. (*Turner v. Univ. of Wash.*, 2007, p. 10)

The problem of workplace bullying and negotiating how to handle it from a human resources perspective is undoubtedly exacerbated by its occurrence in the context of higher education. Unless and until legislation is passed that makes the behavior unlawful, employees who wish to sue after having been victimized will struggle to fit their claims into viable frameworks and contexts.

References

6A C.J.S. *Assault* (2011).

30 C.J.S. *Employer-Employee* (2011).

38 Am. Jur. 2d *Fright, Shock, Etc.* (2011).

53 C.J.S. *Libel and Slander; Injurious Falsehood* (2011).

62A Am. Jur. 2d *Privacy* (2011).

86 C.J.S. *Torts* (2011).

Age Discrimination in Employment Act of 1967, 29 U.S.C. §§ 621–634 (2006).

Agusty-Reyes v. Dept. of Educ. of Puerto Rico, 601 F.3d 45, 53 (1st Cir. 2010).

Americans with Disabilities Act of 1990, 42 U.S.C. §§12101–12213 (2000).

Arrieta-Colon v. Wal-Mart Puerto Rico, Inc., 434 F.3d 75 (1st Cir. 2006).

Birch v. JP Morgan Chase & Co., 685 F. Supp. 2d 350 (E.D.N.Y. 2010).

Burlington Northern v. White, 548 U.S. 53 (2006).

Carter v. Virginia, 606 S.E.2d 839 (2005).

Chamallas, M. (2007). Discrimination and outrage: The migration from civil rights to tort law. *William and Mary Law Review*, 48, 2115–2187.

Civil Rights Act of 1964, 42 U.S.C. §§ 2000e—2000e17 (2006).

Civil Rights Act of 1991, 42 U.S.C. §§ 2000e—2000e17 (2006).

Coley-Allen v. Strong Health, No. 09-CV-6036L, 2011 WL 5977792 (W.D.N.Y. Nov. 29, 2011).

Corbett, W.R. (2009). Fixing employment discrimination law. *Southern Methodist University Law Review*, 62, 81–116.

Davenport v. Bd. of Trustees of the Univ. of Ark. at Pine Bluff, No. 5:10CV00023 BSM, 2011 WL 900095 (E.D. Ark. Mar. 14, 2011).

Davis v. Coastal Int'l Sec., Inc., 275 F.3d 1119 (D.C. Cir. 2002).

DeJohn v. Temple Univ., 537 F.3d 301 (3d Cir. 2008).

E.E.O.C. v. Univ. of Phx., Inc., 505 F. Supp. 2d 1045 (D.N.M. 2007).

El-Hakem v. BJY Inc., 262 F. Supp. 2d 1139 (D. Or. 2003).

Faragher v. City of Boca Raton, 524 U.S. 775 (1998).

Farpella-Crosby v. Horizon Health Care, 97 F.3d 803 (5th Cir. 1996).

Fitzpatrick, R.B. (2011). Advanced employment law and litigation: Bullying in the work-place. *American Law Institute*, SS032, 1551.

German v. Akal Sec., Inc., Civil No. CCB-11–142, 2011 WL 5974619 (D. Md. Nov. 29, 2011).

Griggs v. Duke Power Co., 401 U.S. 424 (1971).

GTE Southwest, Inc. v. Bruce, 998 S.W.2d 605 (Tex. 1999).

Harris v. Forklift Sys., Inc., 510 U.S. 17 (1993).

Harthill, S. (2011). Workplace bullying as an occupational safety and health matter: A comparative analysis. *Hastings International and Comparative Law Review, 34*, 253–301.

Healthy Workplace Bill, http://www.healthyworkplacebill.org.

Healy v. James, 408 U.S. 169 (1972).

Hochstadt v. Worcester Found., 545 F.2d 222 (1st Cir. 1976).

Hutcherson v. Progressive Corp., 984 F.2d 1152 (11th Cir. 1993).

Hutchison v. Luddy, 742 A.2d 1052 (Pa. 2000).

Institute of Real Estate Management (2007). Laws prohibiting discrimination based on sexual orientation and sexual identity, http://www.irem.org/pdfs/publicpolicy/Anti-discrimination.pdf

Kristen, E. (2002). Addressing the problem of weight discrimination in employment. *California Law Review, 90*, 57–109.

Langan, K.W. & Ritts, K.A. (2011). Labor and employment. *Syracuse Law Review, 61*, 831–77.

Lewis v. Ivy Tech State Coll., No. 1:04-CV-459-TS, 2006 WL 1408398 (N.D. Ind. May 18, 2006).

McCray v. Wal-Mart Stores, Inc., 377 F. App'x 921 (11th Cir. 2010).

Meritor Sav. Bank v. Vinson, 477 U.S. 57 (1986).

Mojica v. El Conquistador Resort and Golden Door Spa, 714 F. Supp. 2d 241 (D.P.R. 2010).

Ocheltree v. Scollon Prods., 335 F.3d 325 (4th Cir. 2003).

Oncale v. Sundowner Offshore Servs., Inc., 523 U.S. 75 (1998).

Otero-Burgos v. Inter-Am. Univ., 558 F.3d 1 (1st Cir. 2009).

Pham v. City of Seattle, 7 F. App'x 575 (9th Cir. 2001).

Recio v. Creighton Univ., No. 8:06CV361, 2007 WL 1560323 (D. Neb. May 29, 2007).

Restatement (Second) of Agency (1958).

Restatement (Second) of Torts (1965).

Restatement (Second) of Torts (1977).

Ricci v. DeStefano, 129 S.Ct. 2658 (2009).

Sawicki v. Morgan State Univ., No. WMN-03–1600, 2005 WL 5351448 (D. Md. Aug. 2, 2005).

Sebesta v. Kent. Elecs. Corp., 886 S.W.2d 459 (Tex. App. 1994).

Senisch v. Carlino, 2011 WL 5984785 (N.J. Super. Ct. App. Div. Dec. 1, 2011).

Stone, K.L. (forthcoming 2012). The so-called "Equal Opportunity Bully's" effect on women in the workplace. In S. Fox & T. Lituchy (Eds), *Gender and the dysfunctional workplace* (pp. 121–141). Cheltenham: Edward Elgar Publishing.

Texas Dept. of Cmty. Affairs v. Burdine, 450 U.S. 248 (1981).

Tichenor v. Roman Catholic Church of Archdiocese of New Orleans, 32 F.3d 953 (5th Cir. 1994).

Turner v. Univ. of Wash., No. C05–1575RSL, 2007 WL 4365789 (W.D. Wash. Dec. 11, 2007).

Wal-Mart Stores, Inc. v. Canchola, 121 S.W.3d 735 (Tex. 2003).

Weiner, P.I. (2003). Equal employment retaliation cases—Whistle blowing. *Practicing Law Institute, 693,* 189–221.

White, L. (2000). Academic tenure: Its historical and legal meanings in the United States and its relationship to the compensation of medical school faculty members. *Saint Louis University Law Review Journal, 44,* 51–80.

Williams, K.A. (2007). Employing ex-offenders: Shifting the evaluation of workplace risks and opportunities from employers to corrections. *UCLA Law Review, 55,* 521–558.

Wolf, R.M. (1999). Recent decisions: The United States Court of Appeals for the Fourth Circuit. *Maryland Law Review, 58,* 1280–1303.

Workplace Bullying Institute. (2011, May 6). Minnesota is 21st state to introduce anti-bullying Healthy Workplace Bill, http://www.workplacebullying.org/2011/05/06/mn-21/

Young v. Allstate Ins. Co., 119 Haw. 403, 198 P.3d 666 (2008).

7

THE ETHICAL DIMENSIONS OF BULLYING

Tricia Bertram Gallant

> As an assistant professor at a nondescript liberal arts college, I was relentlessly bullied by one of my higher ranked colleagues. She harassed me with phone calls to my home about my failings, egged students on to challenge my grading system, ranted at me in the corridors about trivial matters, and unleashed her temperamental disapproval of me in front of my pupils. I complained to an administrator, who told me to forget it. It turned out that the colleague and the supervisor were having an affair. Needless to say, I resigned as soon as I could. (Dulce)

Dulce's comment above, in response to a *New York Times* health column entitled "Have you been bullied at work?" (Pope, 2008), dramatically paints a portrait of workplace bullying in the halls of the academy. Earlier chapters in this volume support this portrait and clearly establish bullying as a wrongful behavior that involves at least one victim and one perpetrator. When a wrongful behavior is identified, the typical organizational response is to establish rules that articulate prohibited behaviors and create policies that delineate the process for dealing with perpetrators. This emphasis on the "victim-perpetrator dimension" (LaVan & Martin, 2008) may, however, encourage a focus on achieving compliance rather than on facilitating and supporting individual and organizational ethicality. Articulating shared standards and establishing policies for dealing with undesirable behaviors can be helpful, but to be successful, they need to be part of a larger organizational strategy to support ethical "conduct that is honest, transparent, and accountable to higher-order principles (such as do more good than harm)," even "when there may not be a law or rule to guide behaviors, or when there may be no known resolution to conflicting interests, needs, or demands (Bertram Gallant, Beesemyer, & Kezar, 2009, p. 201).

In this chapter, I position bullying as an ethical issue for the organization, one that demands new and expansive responses beyond compliance. To do this, I first examine bullying through an ethical lens. I then examine the systemic factors that shape the bullying problem and establish the organization as an actor. Finally, I propose a systemic response to bullying, that is the creation of an ethical academy in which bullying will find no place to thrive.

Positioning Bullying as an Ethical Issue

The study of ethics in higher education (herein referred to as academic ethics) is decades old, enhancing our understanding of what shapes misconduct and how to reduce and manage it (Bertram Gallant & Goodchild, 2011). Academic ethics is grounded in fundamental ethical theories or principles for determining the appropriate (What ought I to do?) and inappropriate (What should I not do?) actions in a particular situation (Bertram Gallant & Kalichman, 2011). There are three ethical principles distinctly useful for understanding academic ethics: virtues, utilitarianism, and deontological ethics (Goodchild, 2011; LaVan & Martin, 2008). See Table 7.1 for an overview.

Virtues ethics informs us that a behavior is inappropriate in a particular situation if it undermines widely shared values. In the academy, there are five fundamental values: honesty, trust, responsibility, respect, and fairness (Center for

TABLE 7.1 Three Ethical Principles

	Virtues Ethics	*Utilitarianism*	*Deontological Ethics*
Description	Ethical choices can be made by analyzing the character or value of an action	Ethical choices can be made by analyzing the effects or consequences of acting	Ethical choices can be made by analyzing the rules, codes, or maxims of a situation
Illustration of ethical behavior	Behavior is ethical if it is in accordance with widely held virtues like honesty, trustworthiness, respect, responsibility, and fairness	Behavior is ethical if it creates more good than harm (preferably for the greatest number of people)	Behavior is ethical if it is aligned with shared norms, rules and codes
Illustration of bullying as unethical	Bullying is unethical because it is a form of disrespect, and creates a hostile workplace in which trust is dissipated	Bullying is unethical because it results in harmful consequences for the direct victim, as well as on the larger organization	Bullying is unethical in organizations where there are well-known rules or codes prohibiting such behavior

Academic Integrity, 1999). These values are fundamental because of the obligations higher education has to society: the discovery of new truths, the production of new knowledge, the generation of solutions for societal ills and systemic wrongs, and the education and certification of the next generation of citizens and professionals. So, for example, if we deliver research findings that are not honest or trustworthy because the research was conducted fraudulently, then we are not fulfilling our obligation to produce new knowledge.

It is easy to categorize bullying as inappropriate behavior and therefore unethical when viewing it through a virtues ethics lens. Bullying is a form of disrespect, most often used by one person or group of people to exert power over another in order to make the other feel inferior (LaVan & Martin, 2008). Bullying will create an environment that lacks trust and a sense of fairness, and this in turn will "negatively impact teaching, scholarship, service, and relations with other members" of the community (Cassell, p. 36).

This leads us to the second useful ethical perspective known as utilitarianism, which suggests that ethical choices can be "determined by their effects or consequences" on others (Goodchild, 2011, p. 137). The academy has obligations it must meet, but will only be able to do so if people perform their roles, all of which are highly interdependent. If students are to learn, teachers must teach. If teachers are to fairly evaluate student learning, students must honestly demonstrate their learning. In other words, the actions of one person will have rippling effects or consequences on others. From this perspective, the act of bullying is clearly unethical, because it results in harmful consequences for others (Cassell, 2011; Harvey et al., 2007; Soares, 2002). The target of the bullying experiences harmful consequences, such as stress-related illnesses (e.g., cardiovascular), emotional distress, depression, fatigue, guilt, high blood pressure, and low self-esteem (Yamada, 2008). However, there are harmful effects of bullying on the larger campus as well in the form of high employee turnover rates, hostile work environments, decreased productivity or performance, increased workers compensation or disability claims, and low morale (LaVan & Martin, 2008; McKay, Arnold, Fratzl, & Thomas, 2008; Yamada, 2008). In other words, bullying is unethical because it harms the ability of individuals to perform their roles, thereby harming the ability of the college or university to fulfill its obligations.

Finally, the deontological ethics perspective informs us that what is appropriate to do in a situation can be determined by the "rules, norms or maxims" inherent in that situation or context (Goodchild, 2011, p. 137). For example, I only know that it is appropriate for me to drive at 65 miles per hour on the freeway because the speed limit signs tell me so. In other words, people look to external signs or behavioral standards for guidance on how to act. If there are no explicit rules, then people often turn to norms for information on appropriate behavior; if I am driving in a new area with no speed limit signs, I will observe the speed of fellow drivers and match my speed to theirs. Explicit behavioral standards are necessary in diverse colleges and universities, because we cannot assume that people from varied backgrounds share an understanding of what are appropriate and inappropriate behaviors in a particular context. Research has demonstrated this to be true in the case of bullying; bullying behaviors are less prevalent in workplaces that have codes of conduct that clearly establish bullying as unethical (Bulutlar & Oz, 2008; LaVan & Martin, 2008; McKay, et al., 2008).

Highlighting the role of situation in establishing bullying as an ethical issue is not to imply an ethical relativism where "anything goes." Rather, it is to emphasize that ethical issues are complex, often presenting "competing interests, goods, and rights," none of which may be inherently wrong but yet requiring a person to choose one at the expense of the others (Bertram Gallant & Kalichman, 2011, p. 32). Ethics may also suggest that sometimes a moral wrong might be the appropriate thing to do in a particular situation. For example, although "thou shall not kill" is a widely held moral norm, utilitarianism might suggest that it is the right thing to kill one person if it will save many more people from harm (say, in a situation where you must choose to shoot an armed robber in the interest of defending your family).

Although it is difficult to imagine bullying ever as an appropriate action, one could easily see how bullying might persist in higher education, given its ethical complexity. For illustration, let's consider Molly, an undergraduate student working in a campus office that raises funds for scholarships for underrepresented students. Molly has repeatedly overheard the director verbally harass and intimidate one of the full-time staff members; she believes the staff member is being bullied. Molly also knows, however, that the director has been cultivating a relationship with a potential donor whose gift could endow a scholarship that would serve thousands of underrepresented students for years to come. Molly also knows that a key obligation of the college is to serve underrepresented students and without the work of this particular director, it might be more difficult to meet that obligation. What are Molly's choices? Using a virtues ethics lens, Molly might choose to report the director for the "bullying," because she can see that the behavior is disrespectful and is creating an unfair work environment for the bullied employee. However, using a utilitarianism lens, Molly might justify not reporting the director, because the harm caused to one employee is outweighed by the great benefits to be gained by thousands of students. While the solution to this ethical dilemma is not so dichotomous, the scenario is used to illustrate that bullying, like most other forms of academic misconduct, is a complex ethical issue best understood from a lens that encompasses the entire system, not just the individuals involved.

Understanding Bullying as a Systemic Ethical Issue

Much of the problem is systemic, not only in academe but in this particular region: Georgia has traditionally had an authoritarian culture that values pecking orders, and a "merit" pay system has bred distrust and resentment among faculty. (Anon)

Anon's quote, written in response to the *New York Times* column (Pope, 2008), highlights what research has discovered—workplace bullying is systemic, shaped and reinforced by forces emanating from outside the particular individuals involved (Bulutlar & Oz, 2008; Cassell, 2011; LaVan & Martin, 2008; McKay et al., 2008; Salin, 2003; Von Bergen, 2006). It is the system, or the environment, that allows bullying to exist because bullying is not a single negative act but "persistent, repeated and continuous behavior" (Salin, 2003, p. 1215). To be sure, some individuals may be more prone to bullying-type behaviors than are others, but without environmental supports, single negative acts committed by such individuals are unlikely to devolve into bullying. Thus, bullying is clearly an ethical issue for the system, rather than simply for the individual perpetrator. In this section, then, we will explore the ethical dimensions of bullying at all four levels of the system: individual, organizational, educational, and societal (Bertram Gallant & Kalichman, 2011; LaVan & Martin, 2008).

The Ethical Dimensions at the Individual Level

Although individual personality traits (e.g., narcissism) may be antecedents of bullying behavior, these cannot be altered by higher education institutions, and so will not be addressed here (for those interested, see Hoel & Cooper, 2001). Instead, this section will focus on the ethics of the other individuals involved in creating an environment where bullying can thrive—the observers and bystanders.

Students, staff, and faculty largely conduct their work unregulated and unsupervised. Students complete their assignments primarily in private, and faculty conduct their research and teaching responsibilities under the watchful eye of only a handful of others. The majority of college and university staff members are also professionals who are expected to self-regulate. Thus, the individual has primary responsibility to recognize ethical issues and then act to resolve them. In the scenario described earlier, for example, the director's bullying was enabled by the inactions of Molly and other possible bystanders. There could be many individual reasons why Molly chose not to respond (e.g., fear, age, lack of perceived power, to protect her own self-interests, to protect the interests of future potential scholarship recipients), but the most pertinent may be a lack of ethical decision-making skills.

Individuals often do not know how to recognize an ethical dilemma when they are faced with one, or if they do, they often do not have the skills necessary to resolve it (Kidder, 2003). This ability requires more than just a superficial knowledge of ethical principles (like virtues, utilitarianism, and deontological), but the actual steps one can take to get to an ethical action (Goodchild, 2011). We could see in Molly's story, for example, that she might have been paralyzed by her inability to define the interaction she saw as bullying, to realize her ability to ethically act in response to the bullying, or to pinpoint the answer to the question "what ought I to do in this particular situation?" In other words, bullying can persist because individuals within the organization lack the ethical skills necessary to respond.

The Ethical Dimensions at the Organizational Level

Organizational inaction as a result of "organizational culture or organizational structure issues" (McKay et al., 2008, p. 78) seems to be a major force in shaping bullying. According to McKay and colleagues, toxic ethical cultures are particularly influential, because in such cultures, ethical values are espoused but not acted upon or non-ethical values (like wealth or prestige) take precedence over ethical values (like honesty, trust, responsibility, fairness, and respect). For example, if Molly's college knew about the director's bullying behaviors but decided not to act, this could create a toxic culture. Organizational members might interpret the inaction as a sign that the college values the cultivation of donor money over the welfare of an employee, and bullying behaviors might spread (Salin, 2003), ultimately undermining trust and institutional integrity and the ethics of the organization. However, again this presents an ethical dilemma for the organization because the bully may be "serving an organizational purpose [even] while being destructive to individuals within the organization" (McKay et al., 2008, p. 81).

Organizational leadership, then, is another force to either support or refute bullying and other unethical behaviors. Organizational leaders, especially those in positions of formal authority (e.g., president, high-level administrators, department chairs), occupy a unique position to shape ethical environments (Kezar & Sam, 2011). Such leaders, for example, have the power to define "the behaviors that are acceptable or unacceptable in an organization" (Kezar & Sam, 2011, p. 156); in other words, to define the culture. And, according to years of organizational research, "the establishment of an ethical culture in an institution is a necessary component in building an ethical academy, and should be foremost in the minds of leaders at the institution" (Kezar & Sam, 2011, p. 153). Bullying researchers agree; attending to an ethical culture is necessary to address workplace bullying (Cassell, 2011; McKay et al., 2008; Twale & DeLuca, 2008; Yamada, 2008).

Ethical climate, or the perception of normative behavior, is also an extremely powerful force in shaping individual ethical (or unethical) decision making and behavior (Victor & Cullen, 1988). Thus, bullying can either thrive or be stymied on a college or university campus, according to the campus ethical climate. Bulutlar and Oz (2008), in their study of non-academic organizations in Turkey, found that instrumental climates (those in which self-interest and organizational profits take precedence over "altruistic and caring behavior") shape bullying behavior, because it is acceptable "for people to act without considering others' well-being" (p. 288). In such climates, competition is often fierce and "bullying behavior becomes widespread" (Bulutlar & Oz, 2008, p. 289). In their book on faculty incivility, Twale and DeLuca (2008) agreed that higher education climates nourish a fertile ground for bullying, because competition is inherent in the tenure and promotion process, as well as in the securement of funds (which are increasingly coming from competitive sources).

Thus, it is apparent that what organizational leaders do is more important than what they say. After all, espousement without evidence of action can actually create toxic cultures (as mentioned earlier). However, if employees see those with formal authority and power acting ethically and treating others with respect, they are more likely to do the same (Kezar & Sam, 2011; Yamada, 2008). It is not just the actions of those with positional authority that matter. When bullying occurs in the open and no one does anything to stop it, "the bully feels he or she has the blessing, support, or at least, the implicit permission of superiors and other coworkers to behave in this manner" (Harvey et al., 2007, p. 119). In addition, the non-action of others institutionalizes bullying into the academy (McKay et al., 2008) and, as a result, victims are further silenced because they "feel that since nobody will stand up for them or to the bully, there is nothing they can do about the situation" (Lipsett, 2005, ¶6). Jan Look, in response to the *New York Times* article "Have you ever been bullied at work?" reinforces this with her personal story:

> I learned a lot. Sadly, it was to confirm the saying, "Bad things happen when good people do nothing." Many staff, academic collaborators and community partners recognized my bosses horrible behavior, and of all who saw what she did, only one stood by me to say she would go the course to defend my case.

When bullying remains "unchallenged," it will "thrive" because it is "encouraged in an indirect way" (McKay et al., 2008, p. 81) and, as a result, "the socially accepted norms of civil behavior can quickly change to incivility and bullying behaviors" (Harvey et al., 2007, p. 119).

The Ethical Dimensions at the Educational Level

Forces emanating from the educational systems level (including academic, research, athletic, and funding functions) transcend organizational boundaries and commonly impact many individual campuses (Bertram Gallant & Kalichman, 2011). Bullying is exacerbated by forces at this level because it is utilized as a way to regain a sense of control when there is a feeling of being out of control (Harvey et al., 2007; Salin, 2003).

Competition is a particularly salient force at this level: competition in athletics for the "best" coaches and athletes; competition for a diminishing number of state monies and federal (or other) grants; competition for entry into college and university; and, competition for publishing in the "top" journals, to name just a few. Competition need not breed unethical behavior like bullying, but it might if people perceive that the competition cannot be won fairly or "winners" actually won using bullying-type methods (Salin, 2003). Also, in highly competitive environments, "employees may thus try to elevate their own status by lessening other employees' prestige through" bullying (Salin, 2003, p. 1225). Competition can also prevent people and the organization from acting ethically in response to bullying. Endowed scholarships are hard to come by, especially in times of economic hardship as competition for available funds increases; thereby placing Molly's college in a terribly difficult situation.

A real or perceived sense of injustices in the education system can also be a shaper of unethical conduct in the academy. There are two types of injustices that may shape environments in which bullying will occur: procedural and distributive (Harvey et al., 2007). Procedural injustices are perceived when funds are (or appear to be) distributed or allocated in an unfair or haphazard way; for example, if the Department of Education awards grants based on unarticulated criteria or personal favoritism. Distributive injustices involve the perception that there is a lack of coherent, transparent, or trustworthy decision-making processes and outcomes; for example, if the NCAA issues a decision that seems to favor Big-10 schools over other member schools. These injustices will be particularly powerful shapers of bullying in times of intense competition for dwindling funds or if the decision requires organizational change; when people feel that their livelihoods or work are threatened, they are more likely to act in an unethical manner (Salin, 2003; Soares, 2002).

The Ethical Dimensions at the Society Level

The systemic nature of bullying may be shaped, in part, by the systemic nature of other forms of unethical conduct in the larger society, for example, racism, sexism, ageism, homophobia (Salin, 2003). This can be in part because legal and regulatory changes have shifted "isms" and "phobias" from overt manifestations (like physical abuse) to more covert mechanisms, like bullying (Fox & Stallworth, 2005). Bullying is often characterized by power imbalances (e.g., a supervisor bullying a subordinate), but the power imbalances may emerge not just from organizational positionality but from societal positionality, like the "power differences associated with traditional gender roles and minority status" in which it is "assumed that women and minorities are perceived to have less power and status" (Salin, 2003, p. 1219). If someone is the lone female, African American, Hispanic, or gay employee in a department, for example, they will have less power than those who are members of the dominant group, and may therefore be more subject to bullying (Harvey, Treadway, Heames, & Duke, 2009).

Another powerful force at the societal level may be technology, specifically the internet. In *Academic Integrity in the Twenty-First Century: A Teaching and Learning Imperative*, I write that technology has greatly shaped academic misconduct by students because acts like plagiarism are easier with technology but also because technology has changed our conceptions of what is right and wrong (Bertram Gallant, 2008). Likewise, technology makes bullying easier and likely has changed some notions of what is and what isn't bullying (Jackson et al., 2008). The features of technology also allow people to ignore normal behavioral constraints, which makes bullying more likely to happen online than face-to-face:

> the elements of perceived anonymity on-line, and the safety and security of being behind a computer screen, aid in freeing individuals from traditionally constraining pressures of society, conscience, morality, and ethics to behave in a normative manner. (Hinduja & Patchin, 2008, p. 134)

Overall, the forces emanating from the society level of the system should not be ignored even if they cannot be controlled or affected, because they can be mediated. Salin (2003) notes that there is a growing recognition among bullying researchers that "larger societal forces, such as globalization and liberalizing markets, an ever increasing struggle for efficiency, and performance-related reward systems" will impact bullying (p. 1228). These forces may shape bullying because they can decrease organizational members' feelings of trust, cause sacrifices within institutional integrity, and increase stress. Colleges and universities can mediate the effects of societal forces, as well as the effects of organizational and educational forces, by creating an ethical academy.

Addressing Bullying Systemically by Creating an Ethical Academy

In this chapter, I have established that while one person bullying another may be unethical or wrong, the phenomenon of bullying is complex, with multiple ethical dimensions. Thus, relying on a strategy that enforces compliance with anti-bullying rules will have "little to no effect" (McKay et al., 2008, p. 95). As such, the phenomenon of bullying is best addressed by countering the forces that shape an environment that allows bullying behaviors to repeat, persist, and continue. This can best be done by creating an ethical academy. In this last section of this chapter, I offer recommendations for how this can be accomplished.

Recommendation 1: Conduct an Ethical Audit

The first step any college or university should take in addressing bullying is also useful for addressing other forms of academic misconduct—conducting an ethical audit to asses the prevalence and role of ethics within organizational structures, processes, climates, and cultures (Bertram Gallant et al., 2009). According to Navran (n.d.), such an audit goes beyond assessing whether the organization is in compliance with laws or policies, to an analysis of how ethics is integrated in the culture, structures, and procedures of the organization. At the cultural level, an audit assesses how organizational members feel about or perceive the behaviors and ethics of the organization. As already discussed, bullying is shaped by toxic ethical cultures in which people feel that the organization is willing to sacrifice ethical virtues (like honesty, trust, respect, responsibility, and fairness) for other values, such as wealth or prestige. Bullying also thrives in ethical climates that are more instrumental rather than rule-based (Bulutlar & Oz, 2008). A cultural audit will inform a college or university if organizational cultural change is necessary to create an environment in which bullying is less likely to thrive.

An audit should also be conducted of structures and procedures and the relationships within and between them, to assess whether espoused ethics are aligned and integrated (Navran, n.d.). For example, are sufficient resources allocated to ensure that ethical principles can be enacted on a daily and task-by-task basis? Are ethical principles modeled by those in positions of power and influence? How are rewards and status allocated? Are organizational members recruited, promoted, or fired based on ethical principles? What structures, policies, and processes tell organizational members what bullying is and what to do when they see it occurring?

An ethical audit should be conducted once to "benchmark the nature and prevalence of particular behaviors" (McKay et al., 2008, p. 95), as well as the nature and prevalence of attitudes.[1] Then, these audits should be conducted every two to five years hence to determine if cultural and systemic changes made have had the desired effect. Without this data, it is difficult to determine the necessary next steps.

Recommendation 2: Create an Integrous, Caring, and Cooperative Culture

As illustrated earlier, bullying is shaped in part by a culture that is unethical, instrumental, and competitive. Organizational members need to see that the larger institution at least attempts to do what it promises to do; that is, that the institution lives with integrity according to its espoused values (Bertram Gallant & Kalichman, 2011). So, for example, if a college promises that it will prepare students for transfer to universities but then does not implement the structures, policies, and procedures to make that happen, it will be seen to lack institutional integrity. It is easy to see how in such a culture, stress, and employee dissatisfaction may be prevalent, thereby fertilizing a breeding ground for bullying behaviors.

Organizational leaders should also strive to create climates of cooperation rather than competition "by clarifying goals and roles, not creating too much pressure around meeting goals, and being careful about the messages they send related to competition" (Kezar & Sam, 2011, p. 161). Organizational members may need to be reminded that they are interdependent and their ability to reach their goals and perform their roles depends on mutual cooperation rather than competition. Also, the organization should find ways to reward cooperation. Do faculty earn greater tenure and promotion points for projects and research that they have done with others or for those they completed independently? Are students graded on a curve (that is, in competition with other students) or on their own efforts and accomplishments? Are campus departments encouraged and rewarded for working together to solve issues or does the campus encourage operational silos?

Because of the systemic forces shaping competitive rather than cooperative cultures in higher education, competition can never be eliminated completely from colleges and universities. However, regular dialogues about the importance and value of cooperation, allowing members to openly discuss the challenges to being cooperative in what is inherently a competitive education system, may be helpful. Such a "participative communication environment" gives employees a sense that they have a "voice" to "question and debate ethical issues," and can also open doors between employees and supervisors or central administration so reports of bullying and other unethical behaviors are more likely (Kezar & Sam, 2011, p. 162). Finally, ethicality can be encouraged if employees know that they are expected to resist competitive pressure by looking for "alternatives or solutions" that favor ethical actions over unethical actions and cooperation over competition (Kezar & Sam, 2011).

Recommendation 3: Articulate Ethical Standards

Colleges and universities are composed of individuals from diverse backgrounds, perhaps with varied understandings of appropriate and inappropriate behaviors. Thus, campuses have an ethical responsibility to articulate shared values and ethical standards; otherwise, we cannot expect people to be able to make appropriate assessments of "what is right or wrong to do in *this situation.*" And, because individuals in the academy largely work in private and unsupervised, shared standards help to create mutual trust (Harvey et al., 2009), a necessary condition to refute bullying.

Bulutlar and Oz (2008) found that bullying is less likely to thrive in a virtues or deontological ethical climate, and creating a code of ethical conduct can help achieve such a climate. To create the virtues climate, the code should articulate the virtues desired in students, staff, and faculty. For a good example of how this has been done to counter student academic cheating, see the Fundamental Values document created by the Center for Academic Integrity online at www. academicintegrity.org. The document lists the virtue (e.g., honesty) and then describes how that should be enacted by students, faculty, and staff. Such a document not only articulates the virtues standards by which people are expected to act, but it also communicates that these virtues are important to the college or university. This can help establish a virtues climate.

The code should also articulate the rules that follow from the virtues; this can help create a deontological ethical climate in which people feel duty bound to act accordingly. To do this, the code should describe the virtue, how that virtue can be manifested (as described previously), and then the corollary prohibited behaviors. A sample code statement might sound something like this: "Trust is a critical virtue for Western College. When we can trust that others are doing their work according to shared standards and expectations, we can maintain the privilege to do our work independently and unregulated. In order to sustain trust, Western College supervisors must not make belittling remarks about an employee either in private or in front of others."

Codes should obviously include the rules that prohibit bullying behaviors. However, codes should also prohibit bystander behaviors because single, negative acts can only become bullying if they repeat and persist. As we saw in the Molly example, the actions and inactions of bystanders (those who witness the bullying behaviors) can either sustain or end bullying. However, potential bystanders need to know that they will be supported by the organization if they do or say something to stop bullying, and that doing or saying something is aligned with organizational values. So, to continue with the above sample code statement, a statement for bystanders might look something like this: "Those who witness belittling remarks being made must address the behavior either in the moment or within a reasonable amount of time to ensure these behaviors does not persist." Such a statement written for bystanders may enhance their ability to identify what is the appropriate action to take in their particular situation.

Recommendation 4: Create Ethical Infrastructures

In his article on *Workplace Bullying and Ethical Leadership*, Yamada (2008) reminds us that if bullying is not addressed, it will proliferate. Bullying is best addressed in an organization that has an established ethical infrastructure designed to address all forms of unethical conduct, not just bullying. An ethical infrastructure provides the foundation on which to build an ethical academy and is made up of two main components: structures and policies. Structures can be physical (e.g., ethics or academic integrity office), virtual (e.g., website), or human (e.g., oversight committee, coalition, working group); they are identifiable resources to which people can turn if they are being bullied or are observing bullying. Also, implementing structures to enhance campus ethics or address bullying conveys the message that ethics and ethical conduct are important to the college or university.

An anti-bullying policy is also important (McKay et al., 2008). Policies provide fair and just mechanisms for addressing violations of the ethical codes of conduct. Without (clear) policies, organizational members who observe bullying cannot be expected to know how to respond. Policies can help reinforce virtue principles because organizational members see how the principles are enacted in practice. For example, if fairness is an articulated virtue, a policy that allows due process for the accused and achieves efficacy in procedures enacts that virtue.

A good anti-bullying policy, like other conduct policies, will have four main sections:

1. An introduction or preamble. Articulates the ethical standards or virtues mentioned earlier, as well as details the purpose of the policy.
2. Definitions. Defines what are prohibited behaviors, but prefaces the definitions with the statement "including, but not limited to."
3. Consequences. Detail the consequences for the bully, the bystander(s), and the organizational unit.
4. Process. The process for addressing behaviors or complaints, as well as the process for appealing decisions. Identify the people involved in the process, and to whom complaints should be reported. Indicate how long the process takes on average, with specific timelines for each part of the process, as well as how relevant parties are notified of the outcomes. Duffy (2009) also suggests that alternative resolutions should be detailed. Can the bully accept responsibility for the behaviors and end the process, thereby accepting accountability and the consequences? Are mediation, negotiated agreements, or restorative justice possible resolution processes (Whitney, 2009)? Is there a formal process with a board of peers if an informal resolution cannot be reached?

There are many resources available to help colleges and universities craft their anti-bullying policies. A good first step is to review your existing campus policies that cover other ethical issues (e.g., academic or research misconduct). A second step is to review actual anti-bullying policies used by other colleges or universities[2] and even interview the authors of those policies and the staff that enact the policies to assess what are the policy weaknesses and strengths.

Recommendation 5: Educate Students, Staff, and Faculty

Once the ethical conduct code, structures, and policies are in place, organizational members need to be educated about the change occurring on campus. There are changes in expectations (perhaps employees were not previously expected to report bullying when they observed it) that need to be communicated, but also expectations that always existed (bullying is unacceptable) need to be reinforced. A major one-time educational campaign should be launched to inform campus members that changes have occurred. This campaign could include visits to departmental meetings, guides for supervisors on creating bully-proof cultures, campus notices pointing organizational members to online resources, and the socialization of new students and faculty to the new culture. Information can be delivered in a variety of formats (electronic, face-to-face, workshops, flyers, posters, and presentations) in order to reach everyone—especially on large campuses. McKay and colleagues (2008) recommend that anti-bullying training "help individuals understand that particular behaviors, in person or through email, are unacceptable in the work environment and . . . encourage witnesses to speak up when such behaviors occur" (p. 95). Training should cover the code of ethical conduct standards and rules, as well as educate members on the policy so they know how bullying will be addressed.[3] This training can help reinforce the virtues and deontological ethical climates.

Students, staff, and faculty need to be educated, not just on appropriate behavioral standards and the consequences of bullying (McKay et al., 2008), but also on how to make ethical decisions when they are faced with a bullying situation. Lester Goodchild in *Creating the Ethical Academy* suggests that responding ethically to unethical situations (like bullying) requires not just a superficial knowledge of ethical principles (like deontology or utilitarianism) but skills to identify the situation as an ethical one requiring a response and what the appropriate responses ought to be (Goodchild, 2011). We could see in Molly's story, for example, that she was paralyzed by her inability to define the interaction she saw as bullying, identify her ability to ethically act in response to the bullying, and pinpoint the answer to "what ought I to do in this particular situation?" Such ethics education should be infused throughout the education pipeline so that the individuals joining colleges and universities as employees will already be ethically skilled, sensitive to individual responsibility, and ready to act to support ethical environments (Keller, 2011). However, colleges and universities can implement ethical decision-making training for their employees, specifically how to identify bullying when they see it and how to intervene.

Workplace anti-bullying education and training will not need to be too different than that provided on other ethical conduct issues, such as sexual harassment. Most institutions tend to lean toward online tutorials, which can be an efficient way to cover all of the material. However a newer, more engaging approach to training is the use of live "freeze-frame" theater.[4] Through theater, trainees watch actual scenarios that illustrate key concepts and ideas, as well as model inappropriate and appropriate ways of acting in a particular situation. The "freeze-frame" part is the engaging part—actors or audience members can stop the action to discuss or even change the scene. So, for example, actors could be acting out the Molly example discussed earlier. The actor playing Molly could freeze the frame to ask the audience for their thoughts or ideas on choices of action. By staying in character, the actor can engage the audience in thinking about the complexity of the issue and the possible action resolutions. In such theater training, there is always a moderator or narrator who will actually cover institutional policies and procedures at appropriate times.

Concluding Thoughts

Bullying, like other forms of misconduct in the academy, is a complex ethical issue shaped by multiple forces emanating from multiple levels of the system: individual, organizational, education system, and societal. Although colleges and universities can do little to change individual characteristics or external forces that may lead one to bully or be bullied, they do have an ethical obligation to create cultures in which bullying will not be tolerated and to institute mechanisms to help their employees respond ethically to pressures emanating from the education and societal levels. Thus, organizational leaders, particularly those with positional authority, must assess their own campus culture and climate and how it might be undermining an ethical academy. Does the campus favor competition over collaboration? Are employees pressured to meet external goals "at all costs," even if it means sacrificing ethical norms and values? Do employees trust one another and if not, why not? Does the campus do what it promises to do and does it have the mechanisms in place to respond to unethical conduct when it occurs?

Colleges and universities also have the ethical obligation to give their people the necessary tools to deal with bullying when it occurs and to address local environment conditions that may be shaping a breeding ground for bullying behaviors. Organizational leaders must ensure that there are stated (and followed) normative expectations for ethical behaviors, structures for responding to misconduct when it occurs, and mechanisms for employees to report bullying when they see it. In addition, colleges and universities must infuse ethics education into the curriculum from elementary school to workplace/professional training so that individuals can develop the skills and knowledge to make ethical decisions and to act ethically, especially when they see situations that may be influencing bullying behaviors or people that are bullying others.

Notes

1. For more information on conducting ethics audits, readers can consult the following references: Bertram Gallant et al. (2009), May (1990), and Navran (n.d.).
2. Colleges and universities in the UK and other commonwealth countries seem further ahead in terms of anti-bullying policy development. For some good example policies, see: University of Wollongong (http://www.uow.edu.au/about/policy/UOW066134. html), University of Portsmouth (http://www.port.ac.uk/accesstoinformation/policies/ humanresources/filetodownload,13116,en.pdf), and Northumbria University (http:// www.northumbria.ac.uk/sd/central/hr/azpolicy/antiharassment/).
3. There are numerous training resources available online that readers can consult for assistance on developing training. To begin, readers might want to consult: www.shrm.org/ TemplatesTools/Samples/PowerPoints/Pages/ConfrontingWorkplaceBullying.aspx, and The Workplace Bullying Institute at www.workplacebullying.org.
4. See, for example, Life Theatre Services at www.lifetheatre.com.

References

Bertram Gallant, T. (2008). *Academic integrity in the twenty-first century: A teaching and learning imperative.* San Francisco: Jossey-Bass.

Bertram Gallant, T., Beesemyer, L. A., & Kezar, A. (2009). A culture of ethics in higher education. In D. Segal & J. Knapp (Ed.), *The business of higher education volume 1: Leadership and culture* (pp. 199–226). Santa Barbara: Praeger.

Bertram Gallant, T., & Goodchild, L. F. (2011). Introduction. In T. Bertram Gallant (Ed.), *Creating the ethical academy: A systems approach to understanding misconduct and empowering change in higher education* (pp. 3–12). New York: Routledge.

Bertram Gallant, T., & Kalichman, M. (2011). Academic ethics. In T. Bertram Gallant (Ed.), *Creating the ethical academy: A systems approach to understanding misconduct and empowering change in higher education* (pp. 27–44). New York: Routledge.

Bulutlar, F., & Oz, E. U. (2008). The effects of ethical climates on bullying behavior in the workplace. *Journal of Business Ethics, 86,* 273–295.

Cassell, M. A. (2011). Bullying in academe: Prevalent, significant, and incessant. *Contemporary Issues in Educational Research, 4*(5), 33–44.

Center for Academic Integrity. (1999). *Fundamental values of academic integrity.* Durham, NC: Duke University Press.

Duffy, M. (2009). Preventing workplace mobbing and bullying with effective organizational consultation, policies, and legislation. *Consulting Psychology Journal: Practice and Research, 61*(3), 242–262.

Fox, S., & Stallworth, L. E. (2005). Racial/ethnic bullying: Exploring links between bullying and racism in the US workplace. *Journal of Vocational Behavior, 66,* 438–456.

Goodchild, L. F. (2011). Enhancing individual responsibility in higher education: Embracing ethical theory in professional decision-making frameworks. In T. Bertram Gallant (Ed.), *Creating the ethical academy: A systems approach to understanding misconduct and empowering change in higher education* (pp. 135–152). New York: Routledge.

Harvey, M. G., Buckley, M. R., Heames, J. T., Zinko, R., Brouer, R. L., & Ferris, G. R. (2007). A bully as an archetypal destructive leader. *Journal of Leadership & Organizational Studies, 14*(2), 117–129.

Harvey, M., Treadway, D., Heames, J. T., & Duke, A. (2009). Bullying in the 21st century global organization: An ethical perspective. *Journal of Business Ethics, 85,* 27–40.

Hinduja, S., & Patchin, J. W. (2008). Cyberbullying: An exploratory analysis of factors related to offending and victimization. *Deviant Behavior, 29*(2), 129–156.

Hoel, H., & Cooper, C. L (2001). Origins of bullying: Theoretical frameworks for explaining workplace bullying. In N. Tehrani (Ed.), *Building a culture of respect: Managing bullying at work* (pp. 3–20). London: Taylor & Francis.

Jackson, L. A., Zhao, Y., Qiu, W., Kolenic, A., Fitzgerald, H. E., Harold, R., & von Eye, A. (2008). Morality in cyberspace: A comparison of Chinese and U.S. youth's beliefs about acceptable online behavior. In *Proceedings of the 41st Hawaii International Conference on System Sciences* (pp. 1–10).

Keller, P. A. (2011). Integrating ethics education across the education system. In T. Bertram Gallant (Ed.), *Creating the ethical academy: A systems approach to understanding misconduct and empowering change in higher education* (pp.169–182). New York: Routledge.

Kezar, A. J., & Sam, C. (2011). Enacting transcendental leadership: Creating and supporting a more ethical campus. In T. Bertram Gallant (Ed.), *Creating the ethical academy: A systems approach to understanding misconduct and empowering change in higher education* (pp. 153–168). New York: Routledge.

Kidder, R. M. (2003). *How good people make tough choices: Resolving the dilemmas of ethical living.* New York: Harper Collins.

LaVan, H., & Martin, W. M. (2008). Bullying in the U.S. workplace: Normative and process-oriented ethical approaches. *Journal of Business Ethics, 83,* 147–165.

Lipsett, A. (2005, September 16). The university of hard knocks and heartaches. *The Times Higher Education Supplement.* Retrieved from http://www.timeshighereducation.co.uk/story.asp?storyCode=198413

May, W.W. (1990). *Ethics and Higher Education.* New York: American Council on Education/Macmillan.

McKay, R., Arnold, D., Fratzl, J., & Thomas, R. (2008). Workplace bullying in academia: A Canadian study. *Employee Responsibilities and Rights Journal, 20,* 77–100.

Navran, F.J. (n.d.). *Ethics audits: You get what you pay for.* Retrieved from http://www.navran.com/article-ethics-audits.html

Pope, T. P. (2008, March 24). Have you been bullied at work? *New York Times.* Retrieved from http://well.blogs.nytimes.com/2008/03/24/have-you-been-bullied-at-work/

Salin, D. (2003). Ways of explaining workplace bullying: A review of enabling, motivating and precipitating structures and processes in the work environment. *Human Relations, 56*(10), 1213–1232.

Soares, A. (2002). *Bullying: When work becomes indecent.* Retrieved from http://www.angelosoares.uqam.ca

Twale, D. J., & DeLuca, B. M. (2008). *Faculty incivility: The rise of the academic bully culture and what to do about it.* San Francisco: Jossey-Bass.

Victor, B., & Cullen, J. B. (1988). The organizational bases of ethical work climates. *Administrative Sciences Quarterly, 33,* 101–125.

Von Bergen, Z. (2006). Legal remedies for workplace bullying: Grabbing the bully by the horns. *Employee Relations Law Journal* (Winter), 14–41.

Whitney, M. (2009). *Workplace bullying policies: A policy template for organizations.* Retrieved from http://suite101.com/article/workplace-bullying-policies-a162445

Yamada, D. C. (2008). Workplace bullying and ethical leadership. *Journal of Values-Based Leadership, 1*(2), 49–62.

8

HIGHER EDUCATION HUMAN RESOURCES AND THE WORKPLACE BULLY

*Linda H. Harber, Patricia L. Donini,
and Shernita Rochelle Parker*

Throughout the chapter you will find a variety of case studies, which are meant to be thought-provoking and to serve as starting points for conversations with colleagues or training discussions as you consider how to handle the workplace bullies on your campus.

Higher education is by its very nature an environment where voicing one's opinion, arguing one's perspective, and challenging the views posited by others is "all in a day's work." To some degree, we encourage those who are aggressively curious and reward those who are outspoken. And, because the emphasis is often on the individual contribution (whether research or publications), there is little communication that conveys the importance of how the individual acts within a community. David Damrosch (1995) explored this in *We Scholars: Changing the Culture of the University*, suggesting the modern university exists on a foundation of "alienation and aggression" (p. 78). However, universities and colleges are communities, so it is important to think of how the behavior of faculty and staff shapes the culture of an institution. Human Resources (HR) has a responsibility to address behavior that is destructive, intimidating, negative, or harassing, as in the Dr. Trouble vignette below.

Dr. Trouble

A female, tenure-track faculty member has been told to keep her mouth shut in faculty meetings so as not to alienate any of the tenured faculty who will have to vote on her tenure case in a few years. An issue arises over which she is passionate and she cannot hold back her opinion, which is the opposite of the department Chair. For months after this event, she is labeled as trouble.

> *She is excluded from prime committee assignments, given several courses to develop without ample time, assigned to teach heavily enrolled basic classes, and finds no time for her research and scholarship. Eventually, she verbally explodes over this treatment and her label shifts from "trouble" to "angry" and "crazy."*

If HR is to be successful in combating workplace bullying, it is important to determine how it will define the behavior. Adopting the commonly used definition provided on the Workplace Bullying Institute's website, workplace bullying is "repeated, health-harming mistreatment of one or more persons (the targets) by one or more perpetrators that takes on one or more of the following forms: verbal abuse; or offensive conduct/behaviors (including nonverbal) which are threatening, humiliating, or intimidating; or work interference—sabotage—which prevents work from getting done."

As human resources (HR) professionals, we find ourselves referring to this definition as we have more of our employees seeking assistance and support in dealing with and responding to this behavior. That we are hearing about these incidents more from employees is not surprising, as the results of the second representative U.S. Workplace Bullying Survey (Workplace Bullying Institute, 2010) illustrate. The survey continued the collaboration between the Workplace Bullying Institute (WBI) and Zogby International researchers and supported the 2007 survey's findings—with 35% of workers having experienced bullying firsthand and an additional 15% having witnessed it. While limited, the research supports our desire to not only be responsive to our employees, but also proactive in tackling this disturbing phenomenon.

Specifically, in the arena of higher education, the HR professional may face some of the same challenges as their private-sector colleagues in dealing with workplace bullying. However, they may not have the same tools available to address the issue. If HR is to be successful in confronting the problem, we need to take a closer look at how the academy's structure, priorities, and values can present a challenge for HR as it battles workplace bullying.

In seeking to stem workplace bullying, some may advocate instituting a zero-tolerance policy. This can seem like the correct approach because it sends a good message and makes decision making easy. But, in higher education, where the diverse categories of employees complicate the environment, a one-size-fits-all doctrine does not work well. For instance, a staff manager who acts as a bully at work is disciplined or fired. When a million-dollar research scientist or patient-saving physician bullies his or her staff, there are more complications. The academic playing field is not level. The award-winning researcher or a long-tenured professor do not have the same employment rules or separation implications as does the physical plant supervisor. With tenure, different employment rules and rights, the HR leader must consider all of the complexities in coming to the best solution. In the higher education workforce, where everyone is special, some groups are just "more special."

Only in higher education does one find cultural discrepancies that prevent consistent treatment of bullying in the workforce. For instance, in an environment where credentials support hierarchy, it should be no surprise that the result is domination by some and victimization of others—despite many people's belief of higher education being an environment where equity and inclusion are valued, prized, even heralded. Or, consider how an entrepreneurial faculty member or another with significant research revenue is able to exert more power—or is afforded a certain political "clout" as a result of introducing a more corporate-inspired thinking into the academic culture, causing the shift of "learning as a competitive right to learning as a purchasable commodity" (Gould, 2003, p. 72).

Another example of higher education's cultural discrepancies lies in the role tenure plays in the distribution of power in the academic community (see Chapter 2 in this book for additional discussion of tenure). Introduced to ensure faculty could not be summarily dismissed for expressing controversial or unpopular opinions, tenure may handcuff us and limit the ability to address behavior that can be categorized as workplace bullying. Tenure provides a free and open environment for some of the university community's members, but not all. Fogg (2008) writes, "In academe, where tenure allows bad apples to stick around longer, bullying can be particularly debilitating" (p. 1).

Higher education's complexities, both natural and unnatural, create hierarchies that make a zero-tolerance policy an ineffective approach. HR leaders must be more creative. We must open ourselves to solutions that may be more effective in working with the individuals involved and that may have long-term transformative results for our campuses. Our focus becomes identifying and creating resources that will be instrumental in supporting victims, transforming the behavior of bullies, and creating a campus environment that promotes civility and does not tolerate bullying. Our focus is no longer on who gets in trouble, or who is punished.

The Problem Has Been Identified, Now What?

As an HR professional, while the phenomenon of workplace bullying is what everyone may be focused on, we are always drawn to look at not only the problem, but also the people who are involved in the problem, as in the tortured tenure-track faculty member mentioned above. So, it is important that we take a critical eye to the individuals involved and what role they may play as we work to create effective strategies. In most workplace bullying situations, three primary "players" have been identified: (1) the bully, (2) the victim/target, and (3) the observer or witness. On occasion, two additional "players" may be involved (to varying degrees): (4) the ally/supporter and (5) the defender. In breaking down the different roles, it helps us to better understand the dynamic and becomes part of the consideration for the strategy we implement. To look more closely at each individual involved allows us to determine the type of bully we are dealing with and how we can best serve the victim/target.

The Tortured Tenure-Track

A male, tenure-track faculty member calls from a cell phone outside of his office space. He does not know who to talk to but feels chronically bullied by a female faculty member from his unit. He is called into her office and berated fairly often, sometimes in front of others. He is challenged in meetings and made to feel like an outsider. He feels isolated and confused because some days she is "good" to him and some days she is not. He never knows what to expect when he comes to work, and is now thinking about leaving.

Gary and Ruth Namie's 2009 edition of *The Bully at Work: What You Can Do to Stop the Hurt and Reclaim Your Dignity on the Job* suggests, "people arrive at bullyhood by at least three different paths: through personality development; by reading cues in a competitive, political workplace; and by accident" (p. 45). The Namies go on to discuss the chronic bully whose personality leads him or her to seek to dominate or control in all areas of life, and the opportunistic bully who bullies as a tactic to "win" or succeed—and is, therefore, more likely the bully encountered in the workplace.

With a better sense of what type of bully you are dealing with, HR can begin to consider how to best address the bully. For instance, if a tenured faculty member who has strong relationships with several donors the university is courting is a chronic bully, how HR approaches the bully and moves forward to address the behavior may require a different approach than if the same faculty member is merely an accidental bully.

In determining the type of bully you are dealing with, the best source of information will be the victim/target. Most often, it is the victim who has suffered as a result of the bully's aggression, sabotage, verbal assault, or some other targeted and vicious behavior for an extended period of time, and has reached the critical point of seeking help to get the behavior to stop. In a one-on-one meeting with HR, the victim will typically have a number of stories to share to provide examples of the bully's behavior; in many cases the victim may have begun to keep a log or journal of the incidents.

However, on some occasions, the victim does not come forward to discuss the bully's behavior; instead, one of the other "players," who has determined HR needs to be made aware of the behavior because it has intensified or has been going on for a long period of time, addresses the issue. This person may be a bystander or observer, an ally or supporter of the victim, or even a defender who has actively engaged in helping the victim. In all three of these cases, HR professionals will be able to gather information of past accounts of the bully "in action" that are useful in determining what type of bully they are dealing with and what next steps should be taken.

Referring to the *Yelling Match* example, let's presume you have spoken with the student or someone who is aware of and may have even witnessed the exchange. As you work to address the behavior, HR should shift its perspective and change the language used in dealing with bullying behavior. Simply put, if we stop viewing bullying as a "problem," then we will be less focused on placing blame and carrying out some "punishment" or enacting some consequence. The *No Blame Approach* which was developed in Europe and migrated to the United States, represents another opportunity for human resources professionals. Despite the fact that the approach has been implemented in the K–12 setting only, it has the potential to be effective in a higher education workplace setting, as well. In this approach, instead of focusing bullies, bystanders, and targets on negative consequences, the *no blame approach* emphasizes constructive conflict resolution. Impressive results from a 2006 to 2009 effort using this approach included 192 cases (87.3%) of bullying that could be stopped—despite the fact that half of those cases had a long-standing and gridlocked history (Maines & Robinson, 2010). Additionally, in these cases, the bullying behavior was stopped and did not reemerge.

Yelling Match

A graduate student challenges her grade on an exam and the faculty member adjusts her score by several points. It appears the matter has been resolved. A week or so later, the individuals pass each other in the hallway of a campus building. The faculty member has just left a doctor's appointment at which he was given some upsetting news. He sees the student and loudly yells at her that she is a liar and a cheat. She is startled and yells back that he is a lousy teacher. Observers witness this uncivil display.

Supporting the Victim

In working to support the individual who is the target of the bully's behavior, the most important thing to do is to listen to the victim. More than likely, you will find them grateful and very appreciative that you have taken the time to listen to them. As they share their experience, many people often remark "how good it is to talk to someone about it," "how they were beginning to feel a little crazy, but talking about it with someone else really helps," and a variety of other statements that will give you a better idea of how great an impact being listened to has had on them. Life may have changed for the *Angry E-mailer* if someone had listened to her early on. Each victim is different and it is important to determine what he or she wants or expects as an outcome from meeting with you.

Angry E-mailer

An office manager is severely chastised routinely by certain senior faculty. Future interaction with these faculty members cannot be avoided, so the office manager puts up with uncivil, disrespectful, critical language for a long time. The stress takes a toll on some of her other office relationships, and some colleagues complain about her, as well. Meanwhile, she receives extraordinary performance evaluations annually from her department Chair. Finally, she has had it. She sends an angry e-mail communication to all, warning them of the consequences of continued disrespectful behavior. For the most part, the bad behavior stops, but she has been alienated from the group.

Due to the effect that bullying has on a victim, it is important to provide them with resources that help them manage stress, strengthen their coping skills, and engage in constructive conflict resolution. Recognizing the stress a victim has been under is critical, as its effects are wide ranging and can be quite debilitating. The WBI (formerly known as the Work Place Bullying and Trauma Institute, WBTI) conducted a survey in 2003 of self-described targets of workplace bullying, which found that "stress effects range from severe anxiety (76%), disrupted sleep (71%), loss of concentration (71 %), PTSD (post-traumatic stress disorder, 47%), clinical depression (39%), and panic attacks (32%)." With stress manifesting in myriad ways and possibly resulting in other physical ailments, a victim may need to utilize the employee assistance program (EAP), as well as be interested in other opportunities to manage the stress. For instance, campus fitness facilities provide a great opportunity to "burn" off stress, while helping to maintain or improve physical health. Or, perhaps an on-campus yoga or meditation class might be helpful and provide some important stress management tools.

Next, learn more about how the victim deals with conflict. This is important because even victims who consider themselves able to deal well with conflict in other circumstances may find themselves at a loss when dealing with a bully. Other victims may simply be self-proclaimed as conflict avoidant and more apt to "take flight" than to fight. So, in learning how each person engages in conflict, the human resources professional can work with the individual to create a new dynamic for how they participate in conflict and help them begin to view conflict as an opportunity. Cloke and Goldsmith (2011) assert, "By experiencing our conflicts as opportunities, we automatically increase our capacity to listen and resolve our disputes, thereby strengthening our relationships and improving the way we approach conflicts in the future. Listening is therefore the 'opportunity of opportunities' because it is through listening that it becomes possible to increase trust and collaboration, gain deeper insights, act with greater self-awareness, prevent conflicts from escalating, and begin to see how we can shift our communications and relational dynamics in a more constructive direction" (p. 15). Now, it has to be recognized that this shift in perspective is not easy when research has shown "targets of workplace bullying endure their pain, on average, for 22 months" (Namie, 2003, p. 3). But, in shifting to view conflict as an opportunity, eschewing blame, and promoting listening, human resources professionals can help the victim confront the bully's behavior in a manner that is not aggressive and that lessens the chances for an aggressive response. This shift helps to break the cycle of escalating aggression in the workplace.

However, some victims will not feel comfortable engaging the bully in any way without some intermediary. In these cases, despite the coaching human resources professionals may have provided the victim, they may find themselves in the role of facilitator—helping the victim to have a conversation with the bully to address the behavior and establish a dialogue aimed at ending the behavior. Or, it may be worthwhile to consider recent efforts discussed in an article in *The Chronicle of Higher Education*, to involve a mediator or arbitrator in university workplace bullying situations. The American Arbitration Association and the ADR (Alternative Dispute Resolution) Consortium teamed up in 2010 to advocate intervention by a mediator or arbitrator to turn situations of workplace bullying around, while the Institute of Human Resources and Industrial Relations at Loyola University, Chicago has been conducting research on the potential of using alternative dispute resolution, even requiring it, to address higher education bullying (Schmidt, 2010). The question remains as to whether introduction of a mediator or arbitrator would significantly improve these situations or make things worse. Keeping in mind the power imbalances and other unique characteristics of the higher education environment, human resources professionals will need to weigh the costs and benefits of adopting this approach.

When focused on the victim, the human resources professional settles into more of a coaching role providing feedback, connecting him or her to resources, and encouraging the individual as he or she works to create a better work environment. The victim's needs may fluctuate and be ongoing for a while, so it may be helpful to ensure they have a support network. Many victims will have an ally—sometimes a coworker, often a friend or family member with whom they can brainstorm possible solutions and from whom they seek advice and encouragement. As part of their *no blame approach*, Maines and Robinson advocate a support group approach in which the target is interviewed first and alone. A group is then convened of individuals suggested by the target. This group includes the bully(ies), bystanders, and ally(ies). The group is not accused or made to feel guilty. Instead, group members are invited to problem solve in order to help a person who is having trouble. Opportunities for check-in and follow-up are built in—and the victim then has an established community with whom he or she can confer and work in dealing with, addressing, and stopping the bully's behavior. Since the bully (who has remained unidentified to the others) is included in the group, a subtle monitoring system has been created.

Problem-Solving to Manage Workplace Bullying

A great deal of time and attention is deservedly given to the victim in workplace bullying situations. Yet, HR professionals must involve others in the problem solving, as well. HR must work with managers, bystanders, and allies to address this issue. As human resources professionals, it is vital that we remain focused on educating our managers about workplace bullying and providing training on how to deal with these types of situations.

At George Mason University, we have begun to offer these types of opportunities to our faculty and staff. In a collaborative effort with the Office of the Provost's Center for Teaching Excellence, the Human Resources' learning and professional development professionals created a series of development sessions with department chairs. These sessions were called *Conversations with Chairs* and provided a forum for faculty to share best "management" practices and an opportunity for them to role play difficult conversations, including a confrontation with a bully. Another Mason initiative, *Leadership Legacy*, is a leadership development program where cohort members participate in several self-assessments and a 360-degree feedback instrument focused on emotional intelligence. Each member is given an opportunity to work with an executive coach, utilizing information from these tools to work on areas where improvement is desired. Through the coaching experience and self-reflection, cohort members are better able to identify where their own behavior may be categorized as bullying and work to change that behavior. Cohort members also participate in a session entitled *Constructive Engagement in Conflict*, and practice a step-by-step format for negotiating difficult conversations. These examples recognize the importance of higher education HR collaborating with other university administrators to help managers and ensure they are able to constructively engage in conflict, as well as help others in conflict seek a resolution. But, it is just as important that managers value conflict resolution skills and are willing to invest the time necessary to attend training. An endorsement from senior leadership can be very helpful. Randall (1997) emphasizes higher management should communicate the importance of these skills to all managers and supervisors and ensure they know how highly prized they are within the organization (p. 144). This helps increase the likelihood managers will get the necessary training and prioritize attaining these skills as highly as they do the skills and technical training they need to function in their jobs.

Reversal of "Bullying Fortune"

A long-term support employee has created an environment in which she controls both the time she gives to work and the tasks she chooses to do. She has slowly—with facial expressions, terse words, staring, and anger—"trained" her supervisor not to ask her for anything more than she is willing to give. She closes her door when asked not to do so, refuses to attend certain meetings, and berates colleagues who ask for help or even offer to help. Finally, when her supervisor has "had it" and initiates corrective action, she (the bully) accuses her supervisor of bullying her. Sigh. . .

Providing managers with coaching skills can also be instrumental in helping ensure they are better prepared to work with the victim and the bully. In *School Bullying, A Crisis or an Opportunity?*, Frey, Edstrom, and Hirchstein (2010) discuss several components of an elementary school-age anti-bullying program *Steps to Respect* (Committee on Children, 2001). Two of these, in particular, appear to translate well as significant opportunities for human resources professionals in higher education. One is the creating of "practice" opportunities around assertive responses to bullying (p. 405). The other, perhaps even more appealing, is their description of individual coaching sessions with perpetrators and with targets of bullying (p. 407). Coaching sessions may focus on behavior, individual and collective responsibility, problem solving, empathy, recognition, strategies to avoid future bullying episodes, appropriate social skills, and effective interventions. The authors recommend this coaching model instead of the more reactive approach suggested by zero-tolerance policies. Higher education human resource professionals could train both faculty and staff in this type of coaching, as well as conduct their own sessions with both perpetrators and targets. Even though these types of intervention programs typically have been focused on children, little work has been done on bullying in the higher education setting; therefore we need to be innovative and creative as we seek to address the issues on our campus. Borrowing a "best practice" from middle or high school environments, and reframing it for higher education, can provide HR professionals with a straightforward way to begin.

In Human Resources, our awareness of bullying on our campus begins with the individual in our office sharing an account of the behavior he/she has either experienced or witnessed. Therefore, our first reaction or first actions are focused on helping the individual. This makes sense and it is a necessary part of combating bullying. To make a more significant impact, we have to shift our focus from the individual and embrace a more strategic outlook. It is imperative we work to institute change and to carry out initiatives that are far-reaching across our campus. We must think about what needs to be done to create and sustain a culture of civility to make it more difficult for workplace bullies to have a place in our organization. For some universities, this will require major institutional and cultural change, but in some cases, the changes are far less sweeping and may begin with a simple, intentional reframing of the "way we want to be with each other."

A Strategic Look at Bullying

After a few meetings and phone calls with faculty and staff, you may have a better sense of some of the bullies on your campus, but not necessarily enough information to help determine if the problem is localized to certain areas—creating "pockets" of workplace bullying—or more widespread and even systemic. It is necessary to gather more information to assess or "take the university's temperature." This process is important, because you may find that what you have are a few isolated incidents to deal with, and you can turn your attention and direct your energy elsewhere. Or, you may find the campus outside your office is a virtual jungle, with everyday interactions fueled by aggression, conflict, and abuse. More than likely, you will determine your campus falls somewhere in the middle of these two extremes and can then go about working to influence and guide positive change.

With a better sense of the workplace environment on your campus, human resources will want to begin to look more closely at identifying what factors may contribute to protecting and, perhaps, creating bullies on your campus. As Twale and DeLuca (2008) suggest, the world of academe naturally lends itself to bullying behavior.

> With the specialization of academic disciplines and professions and the rise of the corporate culture, faculty members may inadvertently dismiss aggressive behaviors as typical of the times or treat them as a trade-off for the personal autonomy they enjoy. In time, such behaviors become accepted as necessary to accomplish tasks or perhaps for senior faculty to increase their power or move up the administrative ladder. Bully behaviors become institutionalized within the culture, strengthen it negatively, and are transmitted to the next generation of faculty. (p. 149)

Yet, with further examination, HR may identify additional factors that foster a bully culture on campus. Some of these can include things such as budget cuts, competition for resources, or changes in leadership. Any of these types of changes across an institution will impact faculty and staff (to varying degrees), and may result in behavior that is more aggressive, competitive, and uncivil. Changes may create a more politicized environment, result in ideological clashes, or simply threaten a faculty or staff member's role and perceived value to the institution. All of these types of scenarios may create a culture where bullies dominate.

One of the best ways to begin an assessment of the work environment on campus as it relates to workplace bullying is to conduct a survey. By giving employees an opportunity to respond to questions about their experience with workplace bullying (either as a target or observer), human resources will garner a sense of the prevalence of this phenomenon on their campus and can begin to create a strategy to proactively raise awareness, provide education and resources, and establish and maintain a more civil workplace on campus.

In January 2010, we sent out a bullying survey at George Mason University. We assessed being bullied or witnessing bullying by type of benefitted employee (instructional faculty, research faculty, administrative/professional faculty, and classified staff). Questions were asked about whether the work unit found bullying acceptable and whether such behavior was rewarded. We asked questions about whether incidents of bullying were reported and found that 60% of those who were both bullied and witnessed bullying did report it. The majority of those who reported it did not experience negative repercussions. One of the findings from the survey was that while survey respondents did report bullying they experienced or witnessed, they often did so to different people. What we learned was faculty and staff identified multiple places to report bullying, but this often left them confused as they tried to determine the process and appropriate person with whom to raise the issue.

Once an executive summary was prepared and communicated to university leadership and staff, the Human Resources Employee Relations staff started an educational campaign to help Mason faculty and staff learn more about bullying, provide them with the tools to address bullying in their work setting, and heighten awareness of everyone's responsibility to ensure the Mason workplace is bully-free.

Specifically, as part of our annual *Faculty and Staff Enrichment Day* (a day where a variety of learning opportunities are offered to faculty and staff), two workshops were offered: *So What Is All of This Talk About Workplace Bullying?* and *Empowering Yourself to Deal With A Workplace Bully.* The sessions were well attended, attendees were highly engaged, and the feedback was very positive. Both at these sessions and during other meetings throughout the university, we have shared handouts with tips on how to deal with a bully, to help faculty and staff feel better prepared for encounters that often leave most people feeling harassed, overwhelmed, and ill equipped to respond appropriately. In sharing information about workplace bullying, discussing the characteristics of bullying behavior, and "arming" faculty and staff with tools to help them, HR's efforts against workplace bullying are strengthened.

At Mason, these activities have become part of our educational awareness campaign. In sharing information with faculty and staff, we heighten their awareness of workplace bullying, engage in interesting and thought-provoking conversations about the issue, and create opportunities to partner with others as we work to build and sustain a civil work environment on our campus. In this way, human resources is able to spur change not only in one department, college or unit, but campus-wide. Human Resources can then facilitate a more far-reaching institutional cultural change in the university. Fried and Sosland (2009) advocate the role of the "Change Agent"—an active individual whose goal is culture change and total community involvement in the change process. With many "Change Agents" working together, human resources may have more success in guiding the culture change needed.

Adopting this approach represents another opportunity for the human resources professional in higher education. Working with collaborative teams across campus, human resources is able to bring a variety of perspectives and ideas to the conversation of how to eliminate workplace bullying. This may include discussion of creating anti-bullying language for the community. Perhaps this anti-bullying language could be positively framed as a campus code of conduct, even personal goals such as "I will show respect to others, property, and myself" (Fried & Sosland, 2009, p. 89). This may also encourage exploration of whether the creation of new policies or enhancement of existing policies is necessary as a means of elevating the importance of the issue and communicating more widely that workplace bullying will not be tolerated. At George Mason University, we considered these approaches and decided to incorporate bullying into our current policy on workplace violence. According to Mason Policy 2208, "violence and threats of violence are defined as any direct or indirect threat, behavior or action which suggests personal violation or endangers a person's safety, including but not limited to sexual assault, stalking, domestic violence, verbal and non-verbal threats, bullying, intimidation, or harassment of any nature, in person, through electronic media, or by phone" (Section III).

Another initiative we are working on at Mason is a civility statement. The goal is aspirational in nature, keeping in mind the resistance of the academic community to anything that may be deemed to restrict or curb freedom of speech. As we are reminded by the American Association of University Professors' (AAUP) *Statement on Freedom of Expression and Campus Speech Codes,* "Free speech is not simply an aspect of the educational enterprise to be weighed against other desirable ends. It is the very precondition of the academic enterprise itself" (1994, p. 38). Therefore, crafting civility statements or some similar guiding statements of principle require faculty and staff involvement, support, and even endorsement.

Civility statements, policies, and trainings are all important in helping human resources professionals foster an environment where civility can flourish and workplace bullies do not have an opportunity to grow or thrive. However, even with these measures in place, bullying will go unaddressed if targets, bystanders, or others don't report the incidents. It is important to look more critically at why the incidents were not reported. Paperclip Communications sponsored a webinar with the Senior Associate Legal Counsel for the Colorado State University System and the Special Advisor for Support and Safety Assessment for Colorado State University as the panelists. The webinar, *Workplace Violence & Bullying on Campus: Prevention, Recognition and Resolution* (Schutjer & Burke, 2011) explored a number of issues related to workplace bullying and suggestions for organizational strategies to lead universities to effective resolution of this problematic issue. In offering what could be used as a checklist for HR professionals, they encourage a thoughtful review of organizational culture and climate, followed by critical questions such as, "Is feedback solicited?" "Are employees encouraged to report concerns?" and "Are there grievance resolution processes?" (p.13, PowerPoint presentation). These types of questions help us to assess the mechanisms we may or may not have in place to encourage and facilitate faculty and staff reporting workplace bullying incidents. Next, if we don't have the mechanisms in place, we should work to create them. If we do have the mechanisms in place, it is imperative to assess whether we have communicated widely enough across campus to ensure that everyone is familiar with the mechanics should there be a need to utilize them.

Communication of reporting mechanisms is another opportunity for human resources professionals to collaborate with managers. In particular, managers and those in supervisory roles may be helpful in "getting the word out" on campus—essentially marketing the reporting mechanism and serving as a first point of contact for employees (where appropriate). With managers and HR working together in this capacity, a very powerful partnership is formed, which can be instrumental is creating and maintaining systemic change.

Next Steps for HR Professionals: HR as Leaders

The HR professional gets many leadership opportunities in higher education. Those opportunities may range from providing strategic direction, managing downsizing, budget reductions and compensation initiatives on a variety of budgets, to handling serious Employee Relations situations. Yet leading the course for civility in the workplace is one of the most important leadership roles. The HR leader sends an important message to the university community about whether or not bullying behavior is acceptable.

Often, as it relates to workplace bullying, human resources professionals may feel they are in a reactive mode. In some cases, HR may not be aware of the bully until the target or a bystander comes forward to report the behavior. Or, HR may be aware of the behavior via the campus "network," but lack corroboration from a target or someone else who has observed the behavior and, therefore, is ill equipped to address it. Yet this dynamic should not limit the role of human resources in addressing workplace bullying. Despite how and when HR becomes involved, there are numerous opportunities for a leadership role.

First, in order for faculty and staff to feel comfortable approaching human resources, it is critical for HR to communicate its commitment and dedication to fostering an environment where civil behavior is the expectation. This proves to be critical, as "researchers have also noted that a company's HR department is seldom portrayed as a center of support and advice for either the targets of bullying or for the bullying manager" (Daniel, 2009, p. 101). This is further substantiated by the 2010 Workplace Bullying Survey, in which 36.9% of respondents stated they were "not sure" about their employer's activities to prevent or correct workplace bullying. Clearly, it is not enough for human resources professionals to simply go about the work of coaching targets, providing trainings, and interceding where necessary. It is also important to communicate these and all the other resources available to the campus community, while encouraging faculty and staff to share thoughts and ideas on what the university is doing well and what it can do better to combat the issue.

As important as it is to keep the dialogue going on campus, human resources professionals should connect with and engage their colleagues at other institutions (as well as in the private sector) to discuss how they are handling the issue of workplace bullying. Higher education human resources has a reputation for open sharing of best practices and learning across institutions. In "tapping into" this network, human resources professionals can gain the benefit of learning more about other institutions' successes and failures and determine what they may be able to implement on their campus for the benefit of their university community. In sharing best practices, HR arms itself with the tools to proactively combat workplace bullying, not merely sit back and wait for an incident to which it has to respond or react. Anderson (2011) speaks to "Post-Bystanderism" in this way: "Traditionally, when we as educators observe a bullying interaction, we have private conversations with everyone involved and try to protect everyone's confidentiality. This is not working" (p. 116).

With a commitment to be a leader in addressing workplace bullying, human resources catapults itself into an active and engaged role. Anderson (2011) recommends stopping the bullying immediately with one's words. She advocates five steps in moving from bystander to effective intervener.

> Step 1: Noticing That Something Unusual or Inappropriate Is Occurring
> Step 2: Deciding If Help Is Needed
> Step 3: Feeling a Responsibility to Help
> Step 4: Having the Ability to Help
> Step 5: Intervening (pp. 122–123)

Implicit throughout the five steps is personal recognition that HR, in fact each person, has a part to play, a responsibility to notice and stop the bullying behavior. And that is where the human resources professional can lead the way via communications, collaborative steering committees, reward programming, expectations and accountability built into performance evaluation, explicit standards written into university policies and procedures, and training opportunities built around noticing bullying behavior and learning to do something about it.

In working to engage all members of the campus community to eradicate workplace bullying and promote a more civil institutional culture, human resources professionals (often working with legal counsel) may seek some legal "footing" to help them address the issue more completely and effectively. However, to date, what will be found instead is that the law is slow to catch up not only in defining this behavior, but also recognizing it as legally actionable. Though there are conversations being held that have proven instrumental in shaping antibullying legislation, most of them are aimed once again at the K–12 arena. Therefore, their impact and protection does not extend to higher education.

In Closing

The higher education work environment has many unique qualities, and creates a dichotomy that makes working in higher education fulfilling and flexible, while also intense and challenging. As higher education HR professionals seek to understand and address workplace bullying, it will serve them well to fully take advantage of an environment where spirited dialogue and aggressive inquiry can offer new and interesting ways to tackle this troubling phenomenon.

Clearly, it is important to think about the many different scenarios as HR professionals work with the leadership in their university or college. In particular, before creating a "one-size-fits-all" policy with zero tolerance in higher education, please consider and work through the following questions:

1. How will the policy treat any "special" classes of university citizens? Think specifically about tenured faculty, entrepreneurial faculty whose outside partnerships provide significant revenue stream for the university, sometimes referred to as your "high rollers," or the superstar researchers whose grants not only bring prestige to the university, but fill the coffers as well.
2. Will there be a (or perhaps several) review board(s) of diverse community members to review the impact—helping to ensure a variety of perspectives are considered?
3. How will confidentiality be handled for the parties involved?
4. What, if any, impact does your state's FOIA laws have on how you document these incidents?

These questions help draw attention to some sensitive or potentially complicated aspects of workplace bullying in the realm of higher education. They serve as reminders of the complexity of the academic community and the importance of taking these things into consideration when determining the best course of action to confront, control, and eliminate workplace bullies within the university community.

Throughout this chapter we have endeavored to address some of the unique challenges facing human resources professionals in higher education. In exploring some of the qualities that are unique to higher education, we get an opportunity to better understand how they may impact and sometimes encourage bullying in academe.

Higher education human resources professionals have a special role to provide both support and leadership in building a workplace of civility and respect for all faculty and staff. With all of the resources available to us, we have the opportunity to "blaze a new path." HR should remain dedicated to fostering positivity and civility as a means of eliminating bullying and improving the learning and working environments on our campuses. Higher education HR must be committed to these goals to ensure higher education environments are "Employers of Choice" for everyone in all segments of the workforce.

References

American Association of University Professors (AAUP). (1994). *Statement on freedom of expression and campus speech codes.* Retrieved from http://www.aaup.org/AAUP/pubsres/policydocs/contents/speechcodes.htm

Anderson, S. (2011). *No more bystanders = no more bullies: Activating action in educational professionals.* Thousand Oaks, CA: SAGE.

Cloke, K., & Goldsmith, J. (2011). *Resolving conflicts at work. Ten strategies for everyone on the job.* San Francisco, CA: Jossey-Bass.

Committee on Children. (2001). *Steps to respect: A bullying prevention program.* Seattle, WA: Author. Retrieved from http://www.cfchildren.org/steps-to-respect.aspx

Damrosch, D. (1995, April 3). *We scholars: changing the culture of the university.* Cambridge, MA: Harvard University Press.

Daniel, T.A. (2009). *Stop bullying at work: Strategies and tools for HR & legal professionals.* Alexandria, VA: Society for Human Resource Management.

Fogg, P. (2008, 12 September). Academic bullies. *The Chronicle of Higher Education, 55*(3), B10.

Frey, K., Edstrom, L., & Hirchstein, M. (2010). School bullying: A crisis or an opportunity? In D. Espelage, S. Jimerson, & S. Swearer (Eds), *Handbook of bullying in schools: An international perspective* (pp. 403–416). New York: Routledge.

Fried, S., & Sosland, B. (2009). *Banishing bullying behavior: Transforming the culture of pain, rage, and revenge.* Lanham, MD: Roman & Littlefield.

Gould, E. (2003, April 10). *The university in a corporate culture.* New Haven, CT: Yale University Press.

Maines, B., & Robinson, G. (2010). *The support group method training pack: Effective anti-bullying intervention.* Thousand Oaks, CA: SAGE.

Namie, G. (2003, November/December). Workplace bullying: Escalated incivility. *Ivey Business Journal.* Retrieved from http://www.iveybusinessjournal.com/topics/the-workplace/workplace-bullying-escalated-incivility

Namie, G., & Namie, R. (2009). *The bully at work: What you can do to stop the hurt and reclaim your dignity on the job.* Naperville, IL: Sourcebooks.

Randall, P. (1997). *Adult bullying: Perpetrators and victims.* New York: Routledge.

Schmidt, P. (2010, June 8). Workplace mediators seek a role in taming faculty bullies. *The Chronicle of Higher Education.* Retrieved from http://chronicle.com/article/Workplace-Mediators-Seek-a/65815/

Schutjer, L., & Burke, D. (2011, 10 November). *Workplace violence & bullying: Prevention, recognition & resolution.* Webinar presented at the November 10, 2011. Webinar, PaperClip Communications.

Twale, D.J., & Luca, B.M.D. (2008). *Faculty incivility: The rise of the academic bully culture and what to do about it*. San Francisco: Jossey-Bass.

Workplace Bullying Institute. (2010). Results of the 2010 and 2007 WBI U.S. workplace bullying survey. Retrieved from http://www.workplacebullying.org/wbiresearch/2010-wbi-national-survey/

9

MOVING BEYOND AWARENESS AND TOLERANCE

Recommendations and Implications for Workplace Bullying in Higher Education

Carrie Klein and Jaime Lester

Higher education institutions, at their best, are environments in which individuals engage in respectful discourse in order to expand perspectives and further knowledge and learning within and beyond their communities. However, the nature, structure, and context of higher education, particularly the competition and confrontation inherent in the academy, can often work against this collegial ideal, fostering an environment in which bullying behavior can thrive. As stated repeatedly in this text, reporting of bullying in higher education is on the rise. In the last 20 years, researchers have explored the types, meaning, and motivations involved in the bullying process. The purpose of this book is to take that research further by providing academic managers, administrators, and human resources professionals with the information and tools they need not only to understand the nature and impact of bullying behavior within the academic setting, but also to underscore both the legal and ethical issues surrounding it and the historical and current practices utilized to address bullying behavior.

As Keashly and Neuman (Chapter 1) note, "bullying appears to be an unfortunately familiar aspect of academic settings," and its victims and perpetrators can fall anywhere on the institutional scale, including tenure, tenure-track, and non-tenure-track faculty, administrators, and staff. The effects of workplace bullying have an equally broad impact, according to Taylor, including reducing organizational learning and creativity; imperiling financial efficiency; reducing productivity; creating an "unhealthy and revolving workforce"; and acting, in extreme and rare cases, as a precursor toward workplace violence. To limit liability, improve organizational effectiveness and efficiency, and foster employee well being, higher education leaders must understand the causes, impacts, and possible solutions to workplace bullying.

By delving further into the realm of workplace bullying in academe, leaders can begin to reimagine and refocus their institutions toward greater understanding, engagement, and civility. This chapter will review the strategies and best practices proffered by the book's authors for addressing workplace bullying on the individual, unit, and institutional levels. Recommendations for future research will be suggested and a listing of resources that offer information on new policies and practices will be provided.

Institutional Strategies

Regardless of how bullying is defined (as repeated and persistent harassment, torment, abuse, or criticism) or whether it is perpetrated by a single person or by a group (mobbing), the practice has a negative impact on all levels of an institution. Because of the broad impact of bullying, it is the responsibility of everyone—the individual, the unit, and the organization—to work to ensure that opportunities for bullying are minimized and that a climate of respect is promoted. The literature suggests a number of strategies that can be employed to reduce the incidents and impacts of bullying, which are reviewed throughout this book. Among the most effective of these practices are those that focus on education, support, and transformation of climate and culture, versus those that place blame, punish, or ignore bullying behavior. The following section reviews the authors' recommendations for what works in understanding and addressing workplace bullying in higher education. We also provide additional recommendations that were not included in the book chapters, but are worthy of consideration.

The Individual

Bullying often begins with the individual. The actor (bully) commits repeated negative acts, including criticism, torment, harassment, abuse, etc., that work to belittle, distress, or demean the target (victim) of the actor's aggression. The bullying process involves both the actor and the target, but the target feels the impact of bullying most prominently. Additionally, any individuals witnessing this behavior are also impacted. Keashly and Neuman note that targets of bullying behavior and those who witness such behavior often engage in a number of interventions to ameliorate their situations, with varying degrees of success. Surprisingly, the strategy that has traditionally been supported by human resources (HR) professionals and leaders, formal reporting, was found, along with direct confrontation, to be the least effective way to manage the actor's aggression. Furthermore, those in positions of power or influence had little impact in reducing or ending the negative behavior. So what strategies do work on the individual level? The most effective means of coping with workplace bullying is for targets to use their own support systems to process what is happening to them, reduce stress, and avoid the actors involved in the bullying event. Although this may be easier said than done, partnerships between academic leadership and higher education HR professionals can aid this process through collaborative education and support of the individuals involved.

Education and support should include clear definitions of what constitutes workplace bullying, its causes, and the resources available for combating it. Taylor recommends that HR professionals become well versed on American Association of University Professors (AAUPs) definitions and limitations of collegiality, tenure, and academic freedom, so that they can convey the distinctions between "collegial debate, conflict and bullying." These distinctions are especially important for faculty and staff to understand, so that they can appreciate the difference between healthy academic debate and civil discourse, which furthers knowledge, versus unhealthy instances of harassment and bullying, which can emerge when debate and conflict are allowed to go unchecked. The statements may also serve to promote discussion within and across constituent groups. Higher education institutions are often structurally and culturally divided, with varying expectations for behavior. These discussions can help to bridge cultural divides and help to define the differences between respectful and collegial debate and bullying behaviors. By learning more about the nuances of the academic workplace, both the actors and targets involved in potential bullying are able to recognize and label the behavior, so that it can be effectively addressed.

Supporting the individual and helping to create a common understanding is important to address bullying; yet, the individual who is victimized has immediate needs. Harber, Donini, and Parker recommend the "no blame approach" to bullying interventions—bringing witnesses, actor(s), and the target together to work collectively and anonymously (in the case of the actor) to address the situation and support the target. This work, in conjunction with direct support of the targeted individual, allows the target support from a number of angles, provides the chance to "talk out" the issue in a group and in private, and gives the HR professional a better understanding of how the individual deals with conflict, so that they can provide them with better resources for future interactions with workplace aggressors.

Understanding what resources are available and how to use them is another key strategy for individuals wanting to address bullying in the workplace. Gallant states that, while the primary responsibility to address bullying lies in the individual, they often do not have the needed skills or understanding of what to do, what resources are available, and to whom they should talk. HR professionals can steer actors, targets, and witnesses toward resources available to combat some of the causes and repercussions of workplace bullying—competition for resources, organizational uncertainty, and stress, to name a few. Beyond offering clear lines of communication and policies related to workplace bullying, Harber, Donini, and Parker recommend using the "no blame approach" with counseling and coaching by HR staff. The coaching model provides tools that can help individuals rethink conflict as opportunity, reduce stress related to bullying circumstances, develop a plan for dealing with conflict, establish support networks, and understand their rights (Harber, Donini, & Parker, Chapter 8). Coaching can also extend beyond the target's experience. Including actors and witnesses of workplace bullying in the coaching process is vital to changing how bullying is viewed in higher education.

Witnesses are, by definition, involved in bullying events and are often part of a target's support system. Most importantly, when they know how to handle workplace bullying, witnesses are key to curtailing it. This "power of the peer" (Keashly & Neuman, Chapter 1), to step in to limit bullying behavior and act as a sounding board, helps targets make sense of their experiences. Furthermore, with each buffering act, report, or denouncement of inappropriate behavior, individuals help shape the culture and climate of their departments and campuses toward a more civil and collegial state of being. Conversely, when witnesses do not assist, the campus climate suffers. To empower both the witness and the target and to engage everyone—actor, target, and witness—in civil interactions, Gallant recommends a code of conduct that "articulates shared values and ethical standards" be employed for all members of a campus community. Sallee and Diaz support this perspective and would add the necessity of training for individuals in diversity, inclusion, and campus climate to support campus codes, as members of marginalized groups are bullied at higher rates than non-marginalized members of the academic community. An effective code of conduct requires leadership by individuals who do not stand by while abuse occurs (despite the shifting and fluid nature of academic management). Gallant espouses this view, stating that in order to have an ethical culture and climate of social justice, "what leaders do is more important than what they say" and that addressing bullying immediately "affects societal forces by creating an ethical academy."

The Unit and Its Leadership

Workplace bullying, while felt most prominently by the individuals involved, also impacts institutional units. Again, education and support are vital to counteracting bullying in the various departments in colleges and universities, as are unit leaders. Thus, unit leadership must work to be aware of workplace bullying; to develop the skills to address it from a managerial perspective; to provide training and resources to their faculty and staff members; to diminish its occurrence and force; and to, as Harber, Donini, and Parker state, " walk the walk" and set a standard of civility for their campuses.

Leadership at the unit level in higher education, especially in academic departments, is challenging. Tenure and the shifting nature of departmental leadership, especially, make addressing instances of workplace bullying difficult. As Lester (2009) noted, organizations with a high rate of leadership change, like those of academic departments, are often ripe for workplace bullying to emerge. The independent nature of faculty, coupled with a management system in which department chairs move in and out of authority roles, creates a hierarchy that lacks stability and promotes uncertainty both for management and subordinates. Compounding the consistent change and organizational uncertainty inherent in academic units is the lack of management expertise held by most faculty chairs and the highly competitive nature of a system in which prestige, resources, and promotions are limited. These pressures can create an environment in which individuals begin to engage in bullying behavior for their own perceived survival.

Indeed, at its core, bullying is a survival mechanism. Actors engaged in bullying behavior are often driven by aggression, a primal strategy on the fight-or-flight spectrum for negotiating an environment that is plagued with stress, intimidation, and lack of resources. Given the "elitist, hierarchical," decentralized, pressure-filled and increasingly resource-deprived structure of higher education (Fratzl & McKay, Chapter 4), workplace bullying as response by certain members of the academic community is not surprising. However, there are ways to mitigate the occurrence and impact of this response.

Department leads must address bullying directly, taking reports of incidents seriously and working with those involved—actor, target, and any witnesses—to ameliorate the situation. As Taylor notes, managers may be reluctant to report bullying, as they are disinclined to admonish other autonomous faculty members, may worry that such reports may reflect poorly on their management, or because they have not been trained in policies and procedures related to bullying. Department chairs (who are generally plucked from the ranks of their colleagues to fill the role, regardless of their management experience) often receive little to no management training in human resources-related issues. Yet, despite a lack of management education or support, these individuals are tasked with leading colleagues (whose ranks to which they will eventually return), with a limited understanding of how to approach and resolve workplace bullying issues or the resources available to them or those they supervise.

Therefore, to overcome these aspects of academic unit leadership, chairs must work collaboratively with the HR professionals of their institutions. Through these collaborations, leaders can not only gain a greater understanding of how bullying affects individuals and organizations, how it is often the structure and context of higher education that allows for workplace bullying to emerge, and the legal ramifications of bullying left unchecked, but can also build the confidence to deal effectively with acts of bullying that may occur under their watch. When department leaders receive training, Harber, Donini, and Parker argue that they are more likely to understand the difference between bullying and a lack of collegiality, as well as the limits of academic freedom. Additionally, when unit leaders and HR professionals have a clear grasp of both AAUP's and their institution's policies and procedures regarding bullying, they will have the tools to appropriately address instances of workplace bullying and view these occurrences, not as a reflection on their management but as opportunities to improve the academic discourse and culture of their units and institutions (Taylor, Chapter 2).

This education and support regarding the limits of academic freedom, the effects of workplace bullying, and the resources to combat unacceptable behavior on campus should extend not only to members of each department, but should also be promoted and presented during faculty senate or academic council meetings, and in staff senate and union meetings, so that the responsibility of addressing and reducing workplace bullying becomes a shared endeavor by all members of the institution. Gallant notes that by engendering an environment of cooperation versus competition, specifically among faculty, the overall institutional culture can begin to shift toward a more ethical state of being and the propensity for workplace bullying will be reduced (Gallant, Chapter 7).

Equally important to the training unit members receive related to workplace bullying is the consistency with which they apply what they have learned. As Stone points out, the ability to be consistent when dealing with workplace bullying is critical. When implementing action against the actor in a bullying event, especially when claims of retaliation come into play in a legal scenario, the courts look to consistency of action toward employees by the institution and its departments when determining liability (Stone, Chapter 6). Stone states that employment contracts should specifically outline the institution's policies related to bullying, tenure, and academic freedom. Having a clearly articulated anti-bullying policy provides institutions and its members with a "fair and just mechanism for addressing violations to codes of conduct" (Gallant, Chapter 7). Although there is currently no federal law prohibiting bullying in the workplace, institutions can use state anti-bullying laws to help guide the construction of their anti-bullying policies and codes of conduct (Stone, Chapter 6; Harber, Donini, & Parker, Chapter 8). Among federal laws that are useful in informing policy creation are the Civil Rights Act of 1964, American with Disabilities Act of 1993, Age Discrimination Act of 1967, and Occupational Safety and Health Act, all of which work to protect special classes and members of marginalized groups that have historically been the target of bias or harassment (Stone, Chapter 6; Harber, Donini, & Parker, Chapter 8). This is particularly important, as the targets of bullying are often members of marginalized groups.

In order to limit bullying of marginalized individuals in the workplace, Sallee and Diaz encourage establishing a climate and culture of inclusivity. Unit heads should provide training on different identity groups to all of its members and for faculty, in particular, to actively participate on diversity committees and consider cluster hires of members of marginalized groups (Sallee & Diaz, Chapter 3). Sallee and Diaz also support the promotion of faculty instruction in the area of social justice, whether explicitly a part of or woven into the context of their courses.

When department chairs and campus administrators act as role models, they are pivotal in reducing instances of workplace bullying in their institutions for all members of the community. Their action sets the climate and shapes the social and cultural structure on their campuses (Gallant). HR professionals can support the work of these individuals by promoting inclusive thought and action through cross-departmental collaborative efforts (Sallee & Diaz, Chapter 3). When working in concert, individuals change the climate and cultures of their institutions, creating a more just climate and culture and an environment in which workplace bullying is diminished institution-wide.

The Institution

The theme of creating a more socially just climate and culture to combat workplace bullying is relevant to the individual, to the unit, and to the university as a whole. Although institutions of higher education are often viewed as bastions of social justice, they often "reproduce the social inequalities stemming from the larger society, especially in terms of socioeconomic class and race" (Starobin & Blumenfeld, Chapter 5). Furthermore, Starobin and Blumenfeld argue that the characteristics of institutions (community college, research university, residential campus, etc.) and their circumstance (geography, homogeneity, etc.) play a role in the inequities, biases, and propensity for bullying to emerge on campus. Therefore, institutional leaders should understand the interplay between their school's structure and its climate when working to understand workplace bullying.

Gallant; Harber, Donini, and Parker; Taylor; Sallee, and Diaz; and Keashly and Neuman all strongly recommend the importance and effectiveness of shifting campus culture toward a climate of civility and ethicality. Education and support are again important for institutional-level change. Civility or anti-bullying campaigns appear to be effective, shifting perspectives in how community members are (or are not) to be treated. Yet, as effective as these campaigns can be, they are often limited by their scope. Many civility campaigns on university campuses are developed in student affairs offices and geared toward student-to-student interactions. A cursory review online of campus civility campaigns shows that most are housed in offices of residence life or deans of students offices. Among the campaigns with a large online presence are those at Rutgers University, CalPoly, SCU San Marcos, and the University of Memphis, which do include members of the campus community beyond students in order to change the conversation regarding bullying on their campuses. However, these campaigns are limited in that, despite campus-wide participation (via committees), the images and focus of these campaigns are still heavily weighted toward student populations. This biased focus can limit a campaign's impact, as it is possible that faculty and staff will view them as irrelevant to their specific situations.

In order to be truly effective, civility campaigns must be inclusive of faculty at staff at their inception. Civility campaigns should be developed in concert with human resources, student affairs, deans of students, and ombudsman offices, and with the support of faculty and staff senates, so that they are not deemed as a student-only issue. Furthermore, the creation of these campaigns should be backed up by an educational effort geared specifically toward higher education faculty, staff, and leadership. These members of the community should be present, along with students, in images, promotions, and publications related to these campaigns. By underscoring clear policies, procedures and communication lines, faculty and staff, in addition to students, can understand what action to take in the event bullying occurs. Consequently, they become champions of civility on their campuses.

The need for inclusivity extends to the creation of codes of conduct on college and university campuses. Gallant; Sallee; Taylor; Fratzl and McKay; and Harber, Donini, and Parker all recommend instituting a code of conduct to implement and sustain cultural change, as bullying is less prevalent when codes of conduct are promoted on campuses (Gallant, Chapter 7). By creating a code of conduct with rules and policies that forbid bullying and are "honest, transparent and accountable to higher order principles, . . . ethical standards and shared values" are thus articulated. These standards and values guide the frame in which community members view workplace bullying (Gallant, Chapter 7).

As with civility campaigns, to be truly effective, all members of the campus community must see themselves in their institution's code of conduct and understand that the code applies to every individual, not just to a particular group (e.g., students). This "requires faculty and staff involvement, support and even endorsement" (Harber, Donini, & Parker, Chapter 8) of codes of conduct, so that they will be uniformly adopted as official campus policy, introduced at employee orientation and promoted online and through campus civility campaigns. CalPoly, the University of Connecticut, and Cornell University all have codes of conduct that are geared toward and reflective of their communities, as a whole. CalPoly's code, "Statement of Commitment to Community" not only specifically states that it is for faculty, staff, and students and is a clearly articulated code of ethics, but also has been adopted by the institution's academic senate (CalPoly, n.d.).

Implementation of civility campaigns and codes of conduct is a first step in shifting campus cultures toward more ethical and just states of being. However, to understand their effectiveness, campus leaders should periodically get a sense of the climate on their campuses. Sallee and Taylor, and Harber, Donini, and Parker recommend gauging the climate as it relates to workplace bullying through campus audits and using the data collected to develop and augment initiatives related to increasing civility. By gathering data through surveys and reporting records, HR professionals can help shape the conversation with departments and individuals around workplace bullying and work to change the culture of their institutions. Gallant supports the use of ethical audits, which "review the structures, processes, climate and culture" as well as the role and prevalence of workplace bullying, in order to create an "integrous, caring cultural climate."

Through education and support, these best practices can be implemented successfully on college and university campuses. As collaborations, trainings, civility campaigns, codes of conduct, and cultural audits are conducted, the awareness of the perils of workplace bullying will begin to grow. More importantly, the culture of campus communities can begin to shift to a more respectful, civil and ethical state of being. Continued research into the causes and possible solutions to workplace bullying will be vital in supporting this shift.

Future Research

In the past decade, researchers have begun to look at the causes, nature, and frequency of bullying in higher education. Initial information has shed light on how the structure and context of academe can promote bullying behavior. However, more needs to be done to understand how bullying occurs and what are effective means to combat its prevalence on campus. In the beginning of this book, Lester recommends a large-scale study on workplace bullying similar to the work of The Workplace Bullying Institute. This study would examine the nature and prevalence of workplace bullying and fill the gap in the literature found by Keashly and Neuman (Chapter 1). Different definitions, a focus on campus case studies, and small sample sizes do not provide comparative statistics; simply, we do not know how prevalent workplace bullying is in higher education and how bullying differs across institutional types, for example.

Starobin and Blumenfeld argue that campus type plays a significant role in the type of bullying present on college and university campuses. The argument that different institutional types (based on the Carnegie Classification System™) create "enabling structures for bullying" should be further investigated (Starobin and Blumenfeld, Chapter 5). Doing so will help researchers develop models for forecasting potential types of bullying that may be present on a specific type of campus and will aid campus leaders in understanding more fully the social ecology of their schools and the potential biases that are inherently integrated in their institutional structures. A study that compares the factors known to precipitate bullying, such as leadership changes, across multiple institutional types will help to illuminate how bullying manifests and will lead to interventions that are directed toward specific campuses and their unique qualities.

As was discussed earlier, bullying is present in higher education and reporting of bullying has increased. However, whether or not bullying events have increased and what motivates actors in bullying scenarios is still in question. Keashly and Neuman argue that bullying's prevalence and nature "remain empirical questions to be tested," as is the assumption that the structure of higher education creates a hot zone for bullying behavior to flourish (Keashly & Neuman, Chapter 1). In addition to suggesting further research into these areas, they suggest investigation of the link between exposure and experience in a workplace bullying event, as well as further understanding of what motivates or compels an actor to engage in bullying behavior, so that it can be constrained by leadership. Fratzl and McKay encourage this research angle by suggesting that more attention needs to be paid to the catalysts of an actor's aggression and bullying behavior. Greater research into the experiences of witnesses and targets would also be useful, as it would establish a more complete picture of the bullying and could offer insight into how individuals effectively negotiate the experience. Specifically, more information is needed on whether or not allowing the targets involved to label the behavior actually helped improve their outlook.

Finally, Keashly and Neuman also suggest that the effectiveness of techniques used to ameliorate workplace bullying be further investigated. Understanding what responses actually work versus what has been traditionally offered provides a better road map for campus leaders. Researchers should look not only at the formal mechanisms that Keashly and Neuman recommend, but also at what aspects, if any, of civility campaigns, codes of conduct, and anti-bullying policies are successful in managing bullying behaviors. A basic but important question is: do these interventions make a measurable impact in the rates of bullying?

Conclusion

Workplace bullying in the academic community is nothing new, and reports of bullying behavior have increased over the last decade. Left unanswered, these behaviors can negatively impact higher education institutions—driving out qualified members, creating hostile work environments, and reducing productivity. Managers must begin to think and talk openly about how to address instances of workplace bullying on their campuses. This book provides an opening for campus leaders to begin a conversation with their colleagues on how they can work together to create a more open and productive institution with an ethical climate that promotes civil interactions among faculty, staff, and students. This chapter has many recommendations of how campuses can begin to address bullying and how researchers may begin or continue to understand the phenomenon of workplace bullying in higher education.

References

Cal Poly. (n.d.). Campus community commitment statement. Retrieved from http://www.academicprograms.calpoly.edu/academicpolicies/community_commitment_statement.html

Lester, J. (2009). Not your child's playground: Workplace bullying among community college faculty. *Community College Journal of Research and Practice, 33*, 444–464.

ADDITIONAL BULLYING RESOURCES

Associations and Centers

American Association of University Professors (AAUP)
1133 Nineteenth Street, NW, Suite 200
Washington, DC 20036
Phone: 202-737-5900 | Fax: 202-737-5526| www.aaup.org
AAUP Policy Documents and Reports (aka Redbook):

The AAUP Redbook provides information on AAUP's major policy statements, including those related to the limits of academic freedom and tenure as it pertains to workplace bullying. Policies and reports not found in the Redbook can be found on AAUP's site at http://www.aaup.org/AAUP/pubsres/policydocs/

Association for Conflict Resolution (ACR)
12100 Sunset Hills Rd., Suite #130
Reston, VA 20190
Phone: 703.234.4141 | Fax: 703.435.4390 | www.acrnet.org

The ACR is comprised of "mediators, arbitrators, educators and other conflict resolution practitioners," whose organizational conflict management and workplace committees address best practices related to workplace conflict.

Bully Police USA
www.bullypolice.org

Bully Police USA is a volunteer organization that tracks state anti-bullying legislation. The site is geared toward students in P-12 schools, but has links to anti-bullying programs that may be useful for implementation on college and university campuses.

Choose Civility
Howard County Library
6600 Cradlerock Way
Columbia, MD 21045
Phone: 410.313.7750 | Email: info@choosecivility.org | www.choosecivility.org

The Choose Civility campaign was created by the Howard County Library system to act as a role model of "respect, consideration, empathy and tolerance. . .as fundamental values." The program's website provides resources, including reading lists and a "civility store," and information is geared toward everyone—kids, teens, and adults. The program is based on P.M. Forni's book, *Choosing Civility*.

International Ombudsman Association (IOA)
390 Amwell Road, Suite 403
Hillsborough, NJ 08844 USA
Phone: 1+908-359-0246 | Fax: 1+908-842-0376 | www.ombudsassociation.org

IOA is composed of organizational ombudsmen, who work to facilitate conflicts in the workplace. The organization holds annual conferences on workplace bullying and harassment and provides resources for those wanting to learn more about workplace bullying and its impacts, including special journals and webinars on research and best practices related to workplace bullying at http://www.ombudsassociation.org/conferences-professional-development/webinars

Speak Your Peace
Community Foundation of Greater South Wood County
478 East Grand Avenue
Wisconsin Rapids WI 54494
Phone: 715-423-3863 | Email: info@incouragecf.org | www.incouragecf.org

Speak Your Peace is a civility campaign created by the Duluth Superior Area Community Foundation in 2004. The organization provides tools and resources for those organizations seeking to start civility programs and a number of campuses, including Ocean Community College have used Speak Your Peace as their model. As with Choose Civility, Speak Your Peace is based on P.M. Forni's book, *Choosing Civility*.

Student Affairs Administrators in Higher Education (NASPA)
111 K Street, NE, 10th Floor
Washington, DC 20002
Phone: 202.265.7500 | Fax: 202.898.5737 | www.naspa.org

NASPA's Enough is Enough campaign (http://www.naspa.org/enough/default.cfm) was created in 2008 to address issues of youth violence in post-secondary educational institutions.

The Workplace Bullying Institute (WBI)
PO Box 29915
Bellingham, WA 98228
Phone: 360.656.6630 | www.workplacebullying.org

The WBI was created in 1997 as the Campaign Against Workplace Bullying and has grown to include "self-help advice, personal coaching, research, public education, union assistance, training for professionals, employer consulting and legislative advocacy" around the issues of abuse at work. The WBI has extensive resources and publications related to workplace bullying. Among the WBI's initiatives is the Healthy Workplace Bill, part of The Healthy Workplace Campaign (www.healthyworkplacebill.org), which tracks U.S. anti-bullying related laws and state activity related to workplace bullying.

Campus Civility Campaigns

Cal Poly: http://residentiallife.calpoly.edu/rl.cid/civility_campaign.html
University of Memphis: http://www.memphis.edu/respect/
California State University San Marcos: http://www.csusm.edu/civility/
Ocean Community College: http://www.ocean.edu/campus/PAR/civility.htm—program based on Speak Your Peace.

Campus Codes of Conduct

Cal Poly: Statement on Commitment to Community—http://www.academicprograms.calpoly.edu/academicpolicies/community_commitment_statement.html
Cornell: Campus Code of Conduct—http://www.dfa.cornell.edu/cms/treasurer/policyoffice/policies/volumes/governance/upload/CCC.html
UConn: Faculty & Staff Code of Conduct—www.audit.uconn.edu/doc/codeofconduct.pdf
University Ethics Statement—www.audit.uconn.edu/doc/codeofethics.pdf

Books

Baldrige, Letitia. (2007). *Taste: Acquiring what money can't buy.* New York: Macmillan.
Bates, Karen Grigsby, & Karen Elyse Hudson. (1996). *The new basic black: Home training for modern times.* New York: Doubleday.
Bridge, John, & Bryan Curtis. (2006/2012). *50 things every young gentleman should know: What to do, when to do it, and why.* Nashville, NT: Thomas Nelson.
Forni, P.M. (2002). *Choosing civility: The twenty-five rules of considerate conduct.* New York: St. Martin's Press.
Forni, P.M. (2008). *The civility solution: What to do when people are rude.* New York: St. Martin's Press.

Guinness, Os. (2008). *The case for civility: And why our future depends on it.* New York: Harper Collins.

Herbst, Susan. (2010). *Rude democracy: Civility and incivility in American politics.* Philadelphia: Temple University Press.

Holdforth, Lucinda. (2007). *Why manners matter: The case for civilized behavior in a barbarous world.* New York: G.P. Putnam & Sons.

Martin, Judith. (1999). *Miss manners: A citizen's guide to civility.* New York: Three Rivers Press.

Packer, Alex J. (2004). *The how rude! handbook of family manners for teens: Avoiding strife in daily life.* Minneapolis, MN: Free Spirit Publications.

Post, Peggy. (2006). *Excuse me, but I was next: How to handle the top 100 manners dilemmas.* New York: Harper Collins.

Post, Peggy, & Cindy Post Senning. (2005). *Emily Post's* The Gift of Good Manners: *Parent's guide to raising respectful, kind, considerate children.* New York: Harper Collins.

Selzer, Steven Michael. (2000). *By George! Mr. Washington's guide to civility today.* Kansas City, MO: Andrews McMeel Publishing.

Truss, Lynne. (2005). *Talk to the hand: The utter bloody rudeness of the world today, or, six good reasons to stay home and bolt the door.* New York: Penguin Books.

Winkler, Kathleen. (2005). *Bullying: How to deal with taunting, teasing, and tormenting.* Berkeley Heights, NJ: Enslow Publishers.

CONTRIBUTOR BIOGRAPHIES

Warren J. Blumenfeld, EdD, is Associate Professor in the School of Education at Iowa State University in Ames, Iowa, specializing in Multicultural and International Curriculum Studies; & Lesbian, Gay, Bisexual, Transgender, and Queer Studies.

He is author of *Warren's Words: Smart Commentary on Social Justice*; co-editor of *Investigating Christian Privilege and Religious Oppression in the United States*; co-editor of *Readings for Diversity and Social Justice*; editor of *Homophobia: How We All Pay the Price*; co-author of *Looking at Gay and Lesbian Life*; co-editor of *Butler Matters: Judith Butlers Impact on Feminist and Queer Studies*; author of *AIDS and Your Religious Community*; & co-researcher & co-author of *2010 State of Higher Education for Lesbian, Gay, Bisexual, and Transgender People*. He also serves as an editorial blogger for The Huffington Post.

Crystal R. Diaz is the Assistant Director of the Center for Women in Technology at the University of Maryland, Baltimore County, working to recruit and retain women in STEM majors. She earned her MSEd in Higher Education and Student Affairs from Baylor University in Waco, Texas, and is currently working on her PhD in Higher Education Administration at the University of Tennessee. Her research interests include minority and gender issues in higher education. She has previously conducted research on minority students' experiences in a STEM living-learning program. She is particularly interested in understanding women's lived experiences as engineering majors and how those lived experiences can be used to study the institutional culture of engineering within higher education.

Patricia L. Donini has more than 25 years experience in Human Resources management and currently serves as Employee Relations Director and Deputy Director of Human Resources at George Mason University in Fairfax, Virginia. Prior to joining Mason in December of 2003, she held human resources positions of increasing scope and responsibility in the private sector and worked as a principal in her own HR consulting firm, Donini Associates.

Ms. Donini holds a BA in Psychology from the College of New Rochelle, New York, completed extensive graduate coursework in Counseling at Manhattan College, and is currently finishing a Master of Arts in Interdisciplinary Studies (MAIS) at George Mason University, with a concentration in Workplace Conflict Analysis and Resolution.

Jae Fratzl, MA, ATR, is a Registered Art Therapist with the American Art Therapy Association and a Professional Member of the Canadian Art Therapy Association. She runs her own counseling practice. One aspect of the practice provides support for employees through employee assistance programs. She works with adults with mental health and addiction issues, illness, aging, and concerns related to sexual and physical abuse, as well as youth with learning disabilities. She also consults and publishes in the area of workplace bullying.

Tricia Bertram Gallant, PhD, directs the Academic Integrity Office at the University of California, San Diego (UC San Diego) and is a longstanding board member with the International Center for Academic Integrity. She has taught leadership and higher education courses at both the undergraduate and graduate levels. Bertram Gallant has published numerous articles in journals such as the *Review of Higher Education, Journal of Higher Education,* and the *Canadian Journal of Higher Education.* She is the author of *Academic Integrity in the Twenty-First Century: A Teaching and Learning Imperative* (Wiley's Jossey-Bass, 2008), co-author (with Stephen Davis & Patrick Drinan) of *Cheating in School: What We Know and What We Can Do* (Wiley-Blackwell, 2009), and editor of *Creating the Ethical Academy: A Systems Approach to Understanding Misconduct & Empowering Change in Higher Education* (Routledge, 2011).

Linda H. Harber is Associate Vice President for Human Resources and Payroll at George Mason University. Ms. Harber joined Mason in September 2003 after 25 years at Virginia Commonwealth University (VCU). She earned her bachelor's degree from Indiana University and her Master's degree from the University of Kansas.

She has served as Southern Region chair and on both the regional and national boards of directors for the College & University Professional Association for Human Resources (CUPA-HR). Additionally, she has done HR consulting at public universities and presented at both national and regional conferences over the past 20 years. Linda's areas of interest include bullying, generational differences, work/life initiatives, and employee reward and recognition.

Loraleigh Keashly is Interim Chair and Associate Professor in the Dept. of Communication, Wayne State University, Detroit. She is also the Academic Director for the MA program in Dispute Resolution. Dr. Keashly's research and consulting has focused on conflict and conflict resolution at the interpersonal, group, and inter-group levels. Her current research focus is the nature and personal and organizational effects of emotionally abusive and bullying behaviors in the workplace. She has a particular interest in the role of organizational structure and culture in the facilitation or prevention and management of emotionally abusive behavior among employees. In the past three years, her work has begun to focus on academic environments and bullying. Her work has appeared in *Work & Stress, Journal of Emotional Abuse, Violence and Victims, Employee Rights and Employment Policy Journal, the Journal of Management and Organizations, Administrative Theory and Praxis, Journal of the International Ombudsman Association, the International Journal of Adolescent Mental Health and the Journal of Healthcare Management*. Book chapters related to emotional abuse and bullying in the workplace have appeared in *Bullying and Emotional Abuse in the Workplace: International Perspectives in Research and Practice* (Taylor & Francis), *Counterproductive Work Behavior: Investigations of Actors and Targets* (American Psychological Association), *The Handbook of Workplace Violence* (Sage Publications), *The Destructive Side of Organizational Communication: Processes, Consequences and Constructive Ways of Organizing* (Routledge LEA), *Insidious Workplace Behavior* (Lawrence Erlbaum), *Bullying and Harassment in the Workplace: Developments in Research, Theory and Practice* 2nd Ed. (Taylor Francis), and *Gender and Dysfunctional Behavior in Organizations* (Edward Elgar). She has been called in as expert witness on workplace bullying. Dr. Keashly also has experience as a consultant and trainer in conflict analysis and resolution.

Carrie Klein is a graduate student pursuing a Masters of Interdisciplinary Studies degree with a Higher Education Administration focus from George Mason University, where she works in the student affairs division. Her undergraduate degree in anthropology, earned at the University of Arizona, has been useful in her work and research interests around individuals at the intersection of higher education's organizational sub-cultures. Upon completion of her degree in 2013, Klein will continue to a PhD program in Higher Education Administration.

Jaime Lester is currently an Associate Professor of Higher Education, George Mason University. Lester holds a PhD and MEd in higher education from the Rossier School of Education at the University of Southern California. Lester also holds a dual BA from the University of Michigan in English and Women's Studies. Dr. Lester received the Barbara Townsend Emerging Scholar Award from the

Council for the Study of Community Colleges in 2009. She was also the George Mason University Rising Star Nominee for the Virginia State council awards in 2011. The overarching goal of her research program is to examine the relationship between workplace practices and identity to promote the equitable and effective leadership of higher education institutions. Dr. Lester's approach is to apply organizational and feminist theories to examine the situations where inequity is most evident—at the intersection between individual identity and organizational norms. To investigate these situations is to locate opportunities for organizational change. This approach is influenced by her belief that in order to promote more equitable workplace practices and structures in complex, diverse, and fragmented cultures of colleges and universities today, we must understand how individuals interpret and adopt organizational norms as part of their identity.

Dr. Lester has published articles in the *Community College Journal of Research and Practice, Community College Review, Journal of Higher Education, Liberal Education, National Women's Studies Association Journal*, and *NEA: Thought & Action* among others. She also has four books on gendered perspectives in community colleges, family-friendly policies in higher education, and ways to restructure higher education to promote collaboration. Her most recent book on non-positional leadership and change in higher education was published by Stanford University Press, and she is finishing a research project on ways to establish a culture of work-life integration.

Ruth McKay is an Associate Professor at Carleton University in the Sprott School of Business in the area of management and strategy. She teaches courses in organizational theory, international management, leadership, strategy, and change management. Her research interests include workplace bullying, the natural environment, ethics, and international management. In examining workplace bullying she is particularly interested in the influence of organizational structure on employee success in addressing interpersonal conflict. Ruth also consults in the area of workplace bullying.

Joel H. Neuman is associate professor of management and organizational behavior and the founding director of the Center for Applied Management in the School of Business at the State University of New York at New Paltz. His research and consulting activities focus on workplace aggression and violence, workplace bullying, and related forms of counterproductive work behavior. His research in these areas has appeared in publications such as the *Journal of Applied Behavioral Science, Journal of Management, Journal of Vocational Behavior, Public Administration Quarterly, Employee Rights and Employment Policy Journal, Aggressive Behavior, Journal of Healthcare Management*, and the *Journal of Management & Organization*. Book chapters related to workplace violence, aggression, and bullying have appeared in *Antisocial Behavior in Organizations, Bullying and Emotional Abuse in the Workplace,*

The Dark Side of Organizational Behavior, Counterproductive Work Behavior, the Destructive Side of Organizational Communication, Insidious Workplace Behavior, and the forthcoming *Handbook of Unethical Work Behavior, Gender and the Dysfunctional Workplace,* and *Work and Quality of Life: Ethical Practices in Organizations.*

Interviews with Dr. Neuman have appeared in *The New York Times, Washington Post, USA Today, Boston Globe, New York Post, San Francisco Chronicle, Fortune Magazine, Essence Magazine,* and the *Chronicle of Higher Education.* In recognition of his seminal research on workplace aggression, Dr. Neuman was among the first recipients of the Chancellor's Award for Excellence in Research from the Research Foundation of the State University of New York. He currently serves on the Advisory Board of the New Workplace Institute at Suffolk University Law School, a not-for-profit research and education center promoting healthy, productive, and socially responsible workplaces.

Shernita Rochelle Parker, JD, has worked at George Mason University in Fairfax, Virginia, since 2003. She currently works in the area of Employee Relations, but held an administrative leadership position in one of the university's colleges for seven years. She has been working in higher education for nearly 15 years—including *William and Mary Law School, Georgetown University Law Center,* and *American University.* She received her Juris Doctor from The University of Maine School of Law. Her areas of interest include workplace bullying, civility in the workplace, conflict resolution, and employee coaching.

Margaret W. Sallee is Assistant Professor of Higher Education at the University at Buffalo (State University of New York). She earned her PhD in Urban Education with a Graduate Certificate in Gender Studies from the University of Southern California. Her research uses a critical lens to examine the intersection of individual experiences and organizational culture to interrogate the ways that gender and other social identities operate on college campuses. At the individual level, she considers how men and women have different experiences, both within the professoriate and in graduate school. At the organizational level, she considers how the practices of various departments and the university as a whole produce a culture that privileges one gender over others. Her most recent project focuses on the experiences of faculty fathers and the ways that universities facilitate and impede their involvement in the home. She is the co-editor, along with Jaime Lester, of *Establishing the Family-Friendly Campus: Models for Effective Practice.*

Soko S. Starobin is Assistant Professor in the School of Education at Iowa State University. Starobin began her higher education in Architecture at Toyota National College of Technology in Japan. As a transfer student, she continued her education and obtained a doctorate in Higher Education from the University of North Texas. Starobin joined the Office of Community College Research and

Policy (OCCRP) in 2004 and was appointed as Assistant Professor at Iowa State University in 2008. She is currently serving as the Director at OCCRP.

Her research agenda focuses on gender issues in science, technology, engineering, and mathematics (STEM) fields among community college students. She served as the lead-guest editor of the Special Issue on Community Colleges for the *Journal of Women and Minorities in Science and Engineering* (volume 16, issue 1, 2010). Her research in STEM fields among community colleges and her early career accomplishments have been recognized as the recipient of the Barbara K. Townsend Emerging Scholar Award from CSCC in spring 2010.

Kerri Stone is an Associate Professor who teaches Employment Discrimination, Employment Law, Labor Law, and Contracts at the FIU College of Law. After receiving a BA in English and Comparative Literature from Columbia University, *magna cum laude*, Professor Stone received her Juris Doctorate from NYU School of Law, where she was named a Robert McKay Scholar and served as the Developments Editor of the *NYU Journal of International Law and Politics*.

She has served as a law clerk to the Honorable Michael H. Dolinger in the Southern District of New York, the Honorable Julio M. Fuentes and the Honorable Maryanne Trump Barry, both of whom sit on the United States Court of Appeals for the Third Circuit in Newark, New Jersey. Professor Stone was then associated with the law firm of Proskauer Rose in New York, New York, at which time she was appointed to the Federal Legislation Committee of the Association of the Bar of the City of New York. She served as an adjunct professor at Montclair State University's School of Business in Upper Montclair, New Jersey. Professor Stone then became an Honorable Abraham L. Freedman Teaching Fellow and Lecturer in Law at Temple University's Beasley School of Law.

Her research focuses on examining anti-discrimination jurisprudence, and her work has appeared or will appear in the *Hastings Law Journal*, the *NYU Annual Survey of American Law*, the *Yale Journal of Law and Feminism*, the *Akron Law Review*, the *Loyola Law Review*, the *Kansas Law Review*, the *NYU Journal of Legislation and Public Policy*, the *Columbia Journal of Gender & Law,* and the *NYU Journal of International Law and Politics*, among other journals. She is an officer of and advisor to the Rosemary Barkett Appellate Inn of Court, and she was recently appointed as a Research Fellow of NYU's Center for Labor and Employment Law and as a Contributing Editor for Jotwell's Labor & Employment Law Section.

Susan Taylor After a career in nonprofit management, Susan Taylor transferred her organizational leadership skills to higher education. She began a career in university advancement at Minnesota State University, Mankato, where she served as a co-chair of the Workplace Bullying Survey Task Force. She earned her

PhD in Educational Policy and Administration at the University of Minnesota. Dr. Taylor's dissertation research focused on the relationship of tenure with faculty experiences and responses to workplace bullying. She has delivered workshops on workplace bullying for higher education institutions as well as public, nonprofit, service, and professional organizations.

INDEX